Archery

at the Dark of the Moon

ARCHERY
AT THE DARK
OF THE MOON

Poetic Problems
in
Homer's *Odyssey*

NORMAN AUSTIN

UNIVERSITY OF CALIFORNIA PRESS

BERKELEY • LOS ANGELES • LONDON

UNIVERSITY OF CALIFORNIA PRESS
BERKELEY AND LOS ANGELES, CALIFORNIA
UNIVERSITY OF CALIFORNIA PRESS, LTD
LONDON, ENGLAND

FIRST PAPERBACK PRINTING 1982
ISBN 0-520-04790-7

LIBRARY OF CONGRESS CATALOG CARD NUMBER: 73-94442

PRINTED IN THE UNITED STATES OF AMERICA

1 2 3 4 5 6 7 8 9

Contents

Abbreviations

PERIODICALS

AJA	American Journal of Archaeology
AJP	American Journal of Philology
CJ	Classical Journal
CP	Classical Philology
CQ	Classical Quarterly
CR	Classical Review
CW	Classical World
HSCP	Harvard Studies in Classical Philology
JHS	Journal of Hellenic Studies
MH	Museum Helveticum
RE	Paulys Realencyclopädie der classischen Altertumswissenschaft
RÉG	Revue des études grecques
RhM	Rheinisches Museum
TAPA	Transactions of the American Philological Association
YClS	Yale Classical Studies

BOOKS

HHI	*History and the Homeric Iliad* by Denys Page
HO	*The Homeric Odyssey* by Denys Page
HU	*Homerische Untersuchungen* by Ulrich von Wilamowitz-Moellendorff
SH	*The Songs of Homer* by G. S. Kirk
ST	*The Singer of Tales* by Albert B. Lord

Preface

"Big book big evil," sighed Callimachus, a sigh in which I concur as I ready for the press this study of Homer and his *Odyssey* which has engaged much of my attention since 1968. Were it not for encouragement and aid from many sources this book would have been consigned to the winds, or worse, long ago. The Senior Fellows of the Center for Hellenic Studies in Washington, D.C., by granting me a Fellowship in 1968-69, provided me with the haven where I could first begin serious scholarly work on the ideas that had been germinating for some time in my mind. To them I owe great thanks, especially to Professor Bernard Knox, who as director of the Center did his utmost to ensure that it would be, in fact, a haven for research and contemplation. To the University of California, and my colleagues there, I am grateful for sabbatical leaves and financial support which also have made it possible for me to continue my Homeric studies. To Mr. Robert Zachary, editor of the University of California Press, to other persons in the Press, and to the readers to whom the Press submitted my manuscript, I also owe thanks for their encouragement, and patience, as this work neared completion.

Along the road there have been many other allies. I think here of the late Anne and Adam Parry, who were solicitous of my work and always ready with friendly and wise criticisms. Only after their death did I realize to what extent I had been writing this book with them in mind as my readers. Their studies on Homer and their conversations seemed full of perceptive understanding, and as I began to formulate my own ideas on Homer, I looked to them both as friends and as critics with observations of value. It is a great regret to me that I could not draw on their advice as my manuscript came to completion. Professor F. M. Combellack is another Homeric scholar to whom I owe much. At times, over the years, he has frowned at the tack my craft was taking, but he has nevertheless been always liberal in his support. Though assuredly Professor Combellack would disagree with many of the arguments and interpretations in this study, it would satisfy me to win his respect, even in disagreement. Other colleagues will trace in the following pages echoes of conversations we have had over the years. Professor Jaan Puhvel has always been ready to loan me some Indo-European ballast when my craft threatened to capsize. I am grateful to him, as I am also to Professors Bond Johnson, Ralph Johnson, Steven Lattimore, and Wesley Smith, whose help I have drawn on freely, though they themselves may not remember or know when such help was offered. Numerous other friends have led me to understand Homer better simply through the quality of their friendship or through their understanding of the creative process. To name these here would be impossible, but it is an appropriate time to acknowledge their subliminal influence on this work. The two friends to whom I dedicate this book have followed, and shared in, the development of my ideas on Homer for a longer continuous period than any others. It is a pleasure to dedicate to them this study as a token of those many hours we spent exploring ancient poetry together. To all these friends and colleagues, and those many others unnamed, I owe more than acknowledgment can reveal.

Most of all I owe thanks to the divine poet himself, as they used to call him before the Age of Enlightenment. In my nursery days, when my nurse's gaze was averted, he used to flash before me mythopoeic fragments which my tender eyes could but dimly perceive. In later years he began to speak distinctly, first through the professor with whom I began my study of Homer and Greek at the University of Toronto and then more distinctly still through my dissertation director at the University of California. After that I began to hear his voice more frequently — in a poet's line, a scholar's paragraph, a friend's conversation. There came times, finally, when the poet would dispense altogether with any other medium. On the coast at Malibu, perhaps, as the sun was slipping beneath the western horizon, and the ocean was suckling pacifically our mother Earth, then for a moment or two I would hear him speak in his own voice alone.

Infelicities of thought and expression abound in these pages. For all such, blame my disorderly Muse alone (bless her heart), who would carelessly hand me the wide-angle lens when I called for the close-up, and vice versa, and gave me for my birthday an old secondhand camera with a wheezing diaphragm when I specially pointed out in the shop window the sleek Glaucopti-con II with the interchangeable lenses which was my heart's desire.

N.A.

Los Angeles
1974

Introduction

Surface and depth, around these terms revolves the major task of Homeric literary criticism. In antiquity, despite whatever minor flaws might be discerned in the Homeric poems, it was orthodox and sufficient to say Homer was best. Whoever has even a minimal acquaintance with Homeric scholarship of the last hundred years will know how unorthodox such an opinion has become in modern times. Perhaps only another member of the poets' guild, untutored in the problems of Greek metrics, linguistics, and Bronze Age archaeology, would venture so rash a judgment today. Best, yes, Homer's scholarly docents will say, best at painting surfaces, best for singing a fluent yarn, but where's the metaphysical thought, where's the depth we expect, say, in our psychological novels? The young admirer of Homer will find, to his confusion, poets almost unanimously acclaiming Homer as their master, while the docents point to the many unsightly loose threads and fissures in that antique tapestry. Whom is the young admirer to believe, the poets, known to be unreliable in their hectic enthusiasm and union loyalties, or the more sober scholars who, shunning an enthusiast as they would a plague, turn upon the poet relentless engines of demolition?

The theory of evolution came opportunely to provide a foundation for the modern inclination to separate the Homeric poems from what we associate with serious thought or the highest creative process. In its modern way the theory was an affirmation of an opinion as old as Plato, that the rhythmic enthusiasm of poetry was a way of looking at phenomena that had been made obsolete by scientific thought. It was in the nineteenth century that the pickaxes of higher criticism appeared to demolish the Homeric gold mine. The poems were strip-mined away, hexameter by hexameter, thousands of hexameters thrown on the slag heap, or if suffered to remain in the poems, then compelled to cower beneath the frown of a scholar's lemniscate. Individual hexameters were dissected, their parts reallocated and tacked to the *disiecta membra* of other hexameters. Whole scenes were excised or lifted out, deposited indifferently from one book to another.

By a curious sleight of hand this ravaging of the poems was in ostensible pursuit of the real Homer. While the right hand was busy with demolition, the left was busy with assertions that indeed there was, or rather had been, a Homer – who had been, as the poets said, the best – but he had existed in some Elysian landscape of prehistory, not, alas, in our temporal field. The Homer whose works we possess, and sometimes read, so the axiom ran, is but the *eidolon* that the gods fashioned to pass for the real Homer, whom they had meanwhile spirited away to Egypt – or somewhere, at least, out of our reach.

We today are perhaps in a better position to understand the motives underlying the legerdemain of Homeric scholarship. It being a tenet of the evolutionary theory that Homo sapiens is the pinnacle of achievement, and that at the pinnacle of the species stands modern European man, it was incumbent upon so eminent a creature to outline the steps by which he had mounted from the darkness of prehistory to enlightenment. To say, then, that Homer was the best would be counter to every evolutionary impulse. To assert that the best comes first is to posit a sense of time and temporal development which it was almost impossible to accept, since in such a time value the latest is axiomatically the best. Homer's hexameters reflect at times quite brilliant light from out of the Dark Ages, so the scholars agreed, flashes of what the human spirit could be, Homo laboring to become sapiens, but these flashes are engulfed in great clouds of primitive superstitions. Homer was not, to be sure, a person, a conscious, thinking, ordering individual, a Plato, say, or a Hegel. Rather, the name was a convenient label for that curious *Volkssammlung* that has come down to us, and those momentary flashes in its hexameters were the random inspirations from diverse places and persons and times. They are in no way to be construed as the orderly synthesis of experience by a single controlling intelligence, which did not evolve into existence until a later time. Brought within such bounds, Homer could continue to be read for his mellifluousness, for his charm, as one would enjoy a fairy tale, but his true purpose was to stand out as a paradigm of the primitive, of how not to be a poet now.

Anthropologists may have abandoned the simplistic dichotomy between the primitive and the sophisticated, but in contemporary Homeric scholarship the assumption, however modified the language in which it is uttered, still forms the ground of orthodoxy. Scholars may preface their analysis of Homer with deep bows for Homer's genius, but we find, once we are finished with the bows, the same old insistence on the primitive versifier working towards poetry. A generation ago the theory of oral composition emerged, which seemed at first a threat to the established Analytical position. It soon became evident, however, that the theory was the new way to be an Analyst, and nowadays the most ardent Analyst relies on it as his very cornerstone. The old way of being an Analyst was to argue that Homeric times were too primitive to produce anything but an assemblage of folk lays, superficial in concept, crude in execution and value. The new mode was to ascribe the assemblage to a single composer, but one limited to simple paratactic thoughts and endless repetitions of those simple thoughts, all strung together in simple paratactic metrical units devised through the centuries for the very purpose of being strung together in crude assemblages. Marcel Jousse, whose book, *Le style oral rythmique et mnémotechnique chez les verbo-moteurs,* published in 1924, had a decisive influence on Milman Parry as he began to formulate his theory of metrical parataxis, teaches us the rules of the game. From Jousse we learn that the modern soul creates *poésie,* but the primitive has only mnemotechniques and verbomotor skills. It's the same old argument. Homer, ignorant of Newton's and Kant's imperatives, having never seen Copernicus' model of our stellar cage, could have no *poésie*. If his verbomotor skills occasionally produce something that corresponds to our *poésie,* well, we can take pleasure in the accident, but most forbear from the intentional fallacy of supposing that Homer did it on purpose. This new Homer was at the mercy of an elementary vocabulary and equally elementary rules of syntactic and metrical combination. He had "phrases ready-made," writes the eminent modern Homerist Denys Page, "instantly adaptable to the limited range of ideas which the subject matter of the Greek epic may require him to express." Still the same old Homer, his preconscious verbomotor skills are his great and only gift – the quintessential Homer, his formulas, are to be discarded. Neither Homer nor his audience paid them much mind, seeing them for what they were, the mnemotechnical glue to keep the assemblage rolling. If modern studies proclaim unity in the Homeric poems, the unity they laud barely reaches the grammar school level of conception and execution. Homer's hexameters, though acknowledged to be forceful paratactic strides, still receive the scholars' lemniscate of disapproval, now not because they are the spurious artifacts of the *eidolon* but because they are from the master himself, whose compositions turn out to be as makeshift as we had thought only those of the *eidolon* could be. In those primitive and childlike times, makeshift formula-shuffling passed for *poésie.*

The problem the critics see is a real one, and one complex to resolve. It is true, possibly, that Homer was ignorant of logic, of Newton's theory of light, that he had not seen through Galileo's telescope or Pasteur's microscope. That, for want of better instruments, he was content to rely on his eyes (if he had them) which see, perforce, only deceptive surfaces. Must we then conclude that Homer's limited instruments prevent his penetrating anywhere to the depths? Must it be true that in Homer there are eyes but no soul, formulas but no *poésie?*

The relation of surface and depth does not reveal itself by frontal attack – the problem demands an oblique approach, a certain dexterity in parallax. Much of the art of our century, whether musical, visual, plastic, or verbal, seems to insist that there is only the surface, yet what art critic would boldly claim there is no depth in Matisse, Picasso, Duchamp, to mention but three artists whose vision has shaped our century's way of seeing the world? In the verbal art, how does one show depths in a limpid line or prove the delicate and subliminal webbing that binds one line to the rest of the fabric? Is there more depth in T. S. Eliot because he writes of angst and uses abstract words or polysyllables? The modern poet has the advantage that subliminal webs are assumed in his poetry, and the more subliminal the webs a critic discerns the greater the praise for the critic's insight. When a critic traces such webs in antique poetry he is, more often than not, called to task for subjective intrusion into criticism.

The interpreter's rule of thumb goes like this. Take a line, *Nel mezzo del cammin di nostra vita.* We parse its aesthetic syntax thus: *cammin* = metaphor, that is, complexity wending its way to the surface, ergo *poésie,* borrowing simplicity as its vehicle. We add to the balance our knowledge that Dante was a lettered gentleman with access, therefore, to the esoteric lettered lore of astronomy, geometry, and theology. All of which reassures us that when Dante writes *cammin,* he does not mean a road really, but the idea of a road.

Now we parse an ancient line; ἦμος δ᾽ ἠριγένεια φάνη ῥοδοδάκτυλος Ἠώς. Eos with her rose fingers = personification, that is, simplicity struggling towards maturity but falling faint on her surface. The composer of the line, presumed to be unlettered, with access to no knowledge but that of the five senses of his body, can only synthesize his immediate sense impressions at the low psychic level of personification. In the one poet the simplest metaphor is the sign of sophistication condescending into simplicity, in the other it is the sign of simplicity flailing a pathway towards thought. The attentive reader will find this thumbprint on almost any page he cares to select from modern Homeric criticism, though the print may be more intricate than my schematic diagram.

Though convinced of the error of supposing Homer to be in any way, whether stylistically or ideologically, a primitive recorder of sense impressions, I can claim no resolution of a genuine and complex problem, one that takes us to the inner core of human language and psychology. What I have attempted to do in this study is to make soundings at various points, the relation between surface and depth hovering always in the background, in an attempt to steer towards an understanding of Homer's poetics which is freer of the condescension prevalent in Homeric scholarship.

In the first two chapters I attempt to discern beneath the paratactic structures of Homeric thought and style a more elaborate, and a more elaborately executed, concept of synthesis. In the first chapter my aim is to suggest that the meaning of the Homeric formulas will always evade us if we read them as metrical fillers. They are not, surely, the poor poet's technique for carrying forward an enchanting tale; it may be more correct to reverse the order and say that the tales are inventions for carrying the formulas. They are the fundamental elements to which Homer comes back again and again, as a musical composer may return again and again to his fundamental scale or to his themes. Homer's formulas and their rhythms are the content as much as the composer's musical themes are his content. If Homer's style is paratactic (as I suspect much musical composition to be), his combination and repetition of formulas goes beyond parataxis to create for us a world rich in resonance and diversity.

In the second chapter I suggest that we cannot understand Homer's structures of the human and cosmic universes if our method is simply to check Homer's vocabulary against terms in our language which convey to us important or abstract concepts. If Homer's *psyche,* for example, is not Plato's soul, that is no argument for Homer's inability to conceive of a unified human intelligence. The grid of one linguistic structure cannot be placed so easily over another linguistic structure, though such has been the method of measuring Homer's intelligence quotient. That Homer knows nothing of the ego, superego, and

id, which occupy so much of our attention, is not in itself proof
that Homer was ignorant of psychological motive and complexity of motive. If we are to understand Homer's universe we need
to move away from mere vocabulary tallies to perceive inter-
related structures underlying linguistic usage.

Chapters 3 and 4 are concerned specifically with the events
of Odysseus' journey through the *Odyssey,* a journey I interpret
as the poem's means for outlining the hero's search for, and
progressive discovery of, structure. Any interpretation of the
symbolism of Odysseus' journey is beset with hazards, and I
hope to have avoided the worst excesses of psychological
interpretation by keeping my analysis as close as possible to the
structural elements in the various episodes, and to the relationship of these elements to each other. In chapter 3 I concentrate
on the episodes prior to Odysseus' arrival in Ithaka, to see in
them paradigms of order which are meteorological, political,
theological, and psychological. Chapter 4 then focuses on the
events in Ithaka, where the paradigms of the previous adventures guide Odysseus as he reweaves the torn fabric of his
community. The order he re-creates, or which is re-created
around him, is, as the previous paradigms lead us to expect, one
that synthesizes all elements, again the meteorological, political,
and psychological. Scholars, because of an inclination to fasten
on certain events in the plot — such as the recognition scenes, or
the slaughter of the suitors — overlook what is really the
important event of the last books of the *Odyssey* — the
reweaving of psychological harmony in Odysseus' household,
the synthesis of mind with mind. What I suggest, most inade-
quately, is that this event passes by scholarly attention because
it is the re-creation of a rhythm — a rhythm between Odysseus
and Eumaios, between Odysseus and Telemachos, between
Odysseus and Eurykleia, and finally between Odysseus and
Penelope. "Would you seek to make a rhythm of my pain?"
Creon asks Haimon in Sophocles' *Antigone,* and the lexicon
informs us that Creon's verb *rhythmizo* is a Greek way of saying
"to define." So it is. And so it is in the *Odyssey,* as Odysseus
and his family learn to put their pain into rhythm and through

rhythm to discover the order that will contain the pain. Odysseus, at one time at war with the elements of time and space and mind, becomes at last one with his gods, his society, his family, and himself. Odysseus' reweaving of himself into the temporal rhythm is the event to engage our attention as it engages Homer's art.

The fifth chapter is a summation, a brief reminder of where we are to train our sextants if we would discover the origin of that rhythm Odysseus learns to imitate, and so to become. It relates back to the second chapter where I discuss the implications in Homer of the temporal word *hora,* a term virtually ignored in studies of Homer's cosmology, though it is a word of prime importance in the *Odyssey. Hora* is "season," as the lexicon translates it, but "season" has a special meaning for the *Odyssey. Hora* is the flowing together of many separate rhythms into a single rhythm, and it is the discovery of this principle which enables Odysseus to return to his place at the only possible and right moment. The poem is, as I interpret it, the progressive revelation of the meaning of *hora.*

Two scholars, Milman Parry and Professor Bruno Snell, have represented for me the most lucid exponents of the prevalent modern opinion in Homeric criticism. Parry, by asserting the paratactic and almost mechanical construction of the formulas, and Snell, by unveiling the parataxis of Homeric vision, both corroborate the orthodox axiom that Homer is pre-literate, which, whatever it means in other disciplines, in classical studies still means pre-poetic and pre-philosophic. Since my disagreement with the axiom is fundamental, argument with the work of these scholars is unavoidable. My very disagreement, however, is testimony to the strong and persistent influence their work has had on my understanding of Homer. Their perception of certain structures in Homer, and the clarity and elegance of their exposition, have been models for my own thought for several years. In questioning the conclusions which they based on their perceptions, and in attempting to widen the scope of their investigation, my study is, I trust, a continuation rather than a refutation of their work. Both scholars have for long been my pedagogues, walking me day after day to Homer's academy and then testing my knowledge as they walked me back home again.

If this study fails to prove depth of field in the *Odyssey*, then let it be a plea for Homeric criticism to reorient itself and so frame its questions as not to beg always the worst of answers. In our age of electricity and spaceships it is easy to smile in condescension on ancient poets who knew more of feet than of jet propulsion. But it is time now, surely, to put aside the bulldozers and pneumatic drills with which we have been excavating the Homeric fountainhead, and to let more sensitive instruments reveal to us what Homer still has to teach of the rhythms of life and art.

I

The Homeric Formula

"The Greek Epic is (to use a convenient term) oral poetry. Its language differs from that of all other Greek poetry inasmuch as its units are not words, selected by the poet, combined by him into phrases, and adjusted by him to his metre: its units are *formulas*, phrases ready-made, extending in length from a word or two to several complete lines, already adapted to the metre, and either already adapted or instantly adaptable to the limited range of ideas which the subject-matter of the Greek epic may require him to express. The oral poet composes while he recites; he must therefore be able to rely on his memory. He makes his lines out of formulas which he knows by heart, and which he has learnt to use in this way as one learns to use an ordinary language. Whatever he needs to say next is immediately supplied, not by words which he must combine and versify, but by phrases already complete and metrical."[1]

So Denys Page stated in 1959 what has become since Milman Parry the orthodox opinion on the composition of the Homeric poems. Parry asserted that the oral poet "cannot think without hurry about his next word."[2] It was that thesis, defended by Albert Lord and generally diffused in the scholarly world, which led F. M. Combellack to lament, also in 1959, that Ruskin's famous remark on the pathos of the epithet phrase φυσίζοος αἰα in Helen's words at *Iliad* 3.243 is "the classic example of the kind of Homeric criticism which Parry has made impossible."[3] No matter that φυσίζοος αἰα occurs nowhere else in the *Iliad;* nor that the only other use of φυσίζοος in the poem occurs in the phrase γῆ φυσίζοος at 21.63, where exactly the same contrast holds between the life-giving earth and the dead

11

men beneath it. Paucity of occurrence is to be explained as the result of cataclysmic extinction of epic hexameters; the formulas in Homer's 27,000 hexameters are, Page reminds us, "only a fraction of the whole."[4] Contemporary orthodoxy now absolves Homer of all responsibility for his individual words as cleanly as Page absolves Homeric man of responsibility for his actions.[5] Homeric man, so Page argues, is at the mercy of his gods; Homer, so modern theorists argue, is at the mercy of his formulas. To find irony or pathos in a Homeric epithet is to fall victim to what Lord calls a new kind of " 'pathetic fallacy' in that it attributes to an innocent epithet a pathos felt only by the critic, but not acknowledged or perhaps even dreamed of by either the poet or his audience."[6] Hard words for the gentiles who have walked amid the vain deceits of literary criticism; hardest of all for the critic of the *Odyssey* who once had reveled, in all ignorance, in the poem's many ironies. Now he learns that the poem is all formula, and therefore he must repress his pathetic smile when Penelope replies to the stranger's promises of Odysseus' return with the quite formulaic lines (19.309-310): "Ah, would that that would happen. Then would you receive love and many gifts from me." To renounce the fallacious pleasure derived from such lines as these is indeed an auto-da-fé.

We might do well to set beside Page's statement of contemporary orthodoxy a scene from Homer himself. In the *Odyssey,* when Odysseus arrives in disguise at Eumaios' hut, Eumaios welcomes him and begins to talk of his master's wealth and generosity, but without naming him. Odysseus then asks who his master is, and Eumaios replies with a long speech of twenty-six lines, in which the name Odysseus appears only after twenty-two lines of evasion (14.122-147). Eumaios, when he finally names Odysseus, follows the name with an immediate apology and, in effect, a retraction of the name (vv. 145-147): "Him I dread to name even when he is not present, for he loved me exceedingly. But I call him ἠθεῖον – Honorable – even when he is absent." Eumaios may not address himself to the problem of the formula but his speech is illuminating for the relationship between Homeric man and his language. Eumaios goes to great lengths to avoid a single word, *Odysseus,* because the mere articulation of the name invites perilous conse-quences.[7] Odysseus' name is an important word in the poem, to be sure, and Eumaios' evasion may be of a different order than the poet's use of epithets. When a humble character in the poem, however, shows a reverence for the word, and treats language with finesse, should we rashly deny the same finesse to the poem's creator? Eumaios' careful use of Homeric language may restrain us from premature auto-da-fé.

It is scholarly consensus that the Parry theory is conclusively proven. Page gave it an authoritative imprimatur and relied on its distinction between traditional and nontraditional epithets as a serious basis for arguing that Ajax figured in the original Mycenean *Iliad;* for this argument he received Sterling Dow's cautious approval.[8] And yet in the few years since Page used the theory to infer historical facts, and Combellack feared that it spelled the demise of old-fashioned literary criticism, study after study of the Homeric formula has appeared, many begin-ning to suggest that Ruskin's appreciation of Homer may not be invalid after all.

"In the diction of bardic poetry," Parry wrote in his first French thesis, "the formula can be defined as an expression regularly used, under the same metrical conditions, to express an essential idea. What is essential in an idea is what remains after all stylistic superfluity has been taken from it. Thus the essential idea of the words ἦμος δ' ἠριγένεια φάνη ῥοδοδάκτυλος Ἠώς is 'when day broke'; that of βῆ δ' ἴμεν is 'he went'; that of τὸν δ' αὖτε προσέειπε is 'said to him'; and, as we shall have occasion to see in detail further on, that of πολύτλας δῖος Ὀδυσσεύς is 'Odysseus.' "[9] The definition is familiar, simple, and unequivocal — and Parry tabulated suffi-cient data to make the definition seem unassailable. Yet what a thorn that simple statement has become in Homeric studies. The formula is emerging as one of the central problems of Homeric poets, leading to a bibliography as voluminous as the bibliographies on every other aspect of the Homeric Question.

Where scholars could bypass the Homeric Question, on the assumption that Parry had laid it to rest, now they find themselves confronting the Parry Question before anything else. There is still a consensus that the Homeric poems are oral and that there are such things in Homer as formulas and formulaic systems, but beyond that consensus evaporates. No two scholars, it seems, can agree on the definition of the minimum requirements for a formula. Is it to be one word or two, half a verse or a full verse, two syllables, four syllables or more, two repetitions or ten repetitions, or even a *hapax legomenon*? A diversity of definitions exists to match the possible permutations. There is almost universal agreement that Homer is a formulaic poet matched by an almost equally universal disagreement on the basic definition of formula. The scientists, from whose vocabulary we have borrowed the concept of formula, might be astonished to find Homeric scholars exercising idiosyncracy at the level of the primary axiom and yet reaching unanimity at the level of general theory.[10]

The variety of definitions of oral formula which now prevails is symptomatic of a general dissatisfaction with Parry's theory as he left it to us. Attempts proceed apace either to modify it by various restrictions or to extend it almost indefinitely to make epic poetry approach as closely as possible 100 percent formulaic structure. In view of the lack of agreement on basic definitions and principles, it is worthwhile to go back to Parry's theory to separate distinctly what Parry actually proved from the deductions he made from his proven facts.

Concentrating particularly on "name-epithet" (name plus epithet) phrases, Parry demonstrated that there was a set of such phrases for each name, with often several phrases of varying metrical length for each grammatical case. With few exceptions there seemed to be only one such phrase of a particular metrical length for each grammatical case. Whenever a poet needed to name a person or an object, he had at his disposal a variety of metrical formulas with which to do so; he had merely to select the convenient one from his repertoire. The system of formulas seemed to be elaborate and complete and yet marked by economy in that formulas did not duplicate each other's duties. One formulaic phrase and one only of a particular metrical length for each grammatical case seemed to be a phenomenon sufficiently regular to be called a law of Homeric composition.

The phenomenon was as Parry recorded it. It was his great contribution to demonstrate the existence of a system marked by consistency, regularity, and economy. Whatever disagreement there may be about the definition of formula, there can be no doubt that Parry discovered a coherent pattern behind the Homeric repetitions. Parry's system functions, however, in the personal name-epithet formulas and in the verbal phrases that may combine with such formulas to give complete lines. On the basis of the name-epithet formulas, Parry was led to posit a totally formulaic system for the Homeric poems. At first, as A. Hoekstra notes, Parry recognized that from name-epithet formulas to a totally formulaic system was a large leap, but by the time of the publication of his second French thesis he had made the leap and since then the hypothesis has been assumed into the corpus of Parry's theorems.[11] If the Homeric poems were entirely formulaic in the way Parry argued, we should find the same economy and consistency operating for all other nouns in the poem. There should be a system as elaborate and complete for *ship, shield, cow,* or *sea* as for *Odysseus* or *Achilleus,* but since the system has been assumed proven there have been few attempts to continue Parry's work in this direction.[12]

Parry was led also to the postulate that has most influenced subsequent Homeric scholarship, that the epithet is of metrical utility only. Parry, perceiving a complex system, could explain its presence and operation only by assuming it to be a vast interlocking mnemonic device to aid generations of oral singers in the telling of their tales. Homer needed his ready ways of saying "Achilleus," "Odysseus," "Agamemnon," which could conveniently fill certain parts of the hexameter. Though allowing a distinction between certain "specialized" epithets and ornamental (or "fixed") epithets, and admitting that the poet could at times modify a formula for the occasion or create some new formulas by analogy, Parry was emphatic that sense and meaning could have only the slightest importance in the epithet or in the details of the periphrasis. Epithets were generic or ornamental; they added a pleasing tone to heroic poetry but could not be classified by particulars of character, sense, or context. Regarding it as impossible that an oral poet could be preoccupied with the sense of the epithet during oral delivery, he concluded that the poet must be guided primarily by "considerations of versification and in no way by sense."[13] Epithets within regularly repeated phrases are, for Parry, devices for the rapid construction and oral delivery of hexameter verse. The epithet's purpose is "to help the poet fit a noun into a line of six feet; once the noun has been fitted in and the line is complete, the epithet has no further function."[14]

There is much in Homer to support the thesis that epithets are ornaments serving metrical rather than semantic purposes. We can observe metrical pressure producing such variants as Ὀδυσσεύς or Ὀδυσεύς, Ἀχιλλεύς or Ἀχιλεύς, or producing two epithet formulas of the same metrical length for the same grammatical case, with one having an initial vowel, the other a consonant, or one beginning with a single consonant and the other with a double. More telling still is the ubiquity of a word like δῖος which forms with trisyllabic names like *Odysseus* a convenient formula after the diaeresis. Then there are those myriad lines such as "swift-footed Achilleus spoke," where the epithet seems to owe its presence more to metrical convenience than to contextual appropriateness. Finally, in the formulaic system, Odysseus may be πολύμητις when his name appears in the nominative case, but when his name is in the oblique cases he is given other epithets, a fact which strongly suggests that the choice of epithet is dictated by the metrical quantity of the name rather than by immediate context. The most vexing part of Parry's theory has been his insistence that words are metrical fillers in Homer, and scholars have responded either by accepting the idea entirely, however reluctantly, or by wresting as many words as possible from the category Parry called "ornamental" to the category he called "particularized."

From the formulaic system Parry was led to other postulates which were more in the nature of his personal interpretation of the evidence, although they have been generally accepted along with the system he had documented. The variety and complexity of the system suggested that Homer was a "traditional" poet – Parry used the term not in the sense that any poet within a particular linguistic and poetic tradition is traditional, but rather to signify a specific kind of oral tradition. No single man, he thought, could have perfected the system he discovered in Homer; he concluded that the Homeric vocabulary must be the perfected repertoire of generations of oral poets. The "traditional" epithet or phrase must be part of the common metrical idiom. Although an individual poet within an oral culture could invent a certain number of new formulas, his originality lay rather in his judicious use of the metrical formulas the communal repository made available to him. Here we might interject that mastery of the name-epithet formulas in Homer would be no stupendous labor for one individual. It would be within the powers of a sufficiently motivated student of beginning Greek.

Subsequent studies of oral cultures make Parry's assumption more dubious. Oral cultures possess a vast quantity of traditional verse, in proverbs, folk songs, and the like, but there is little to show that poets in such societies share a body of already existing metrical formulas to which they are restricted. Yugoslav oral poetry, by Lord's own admission, does not support Parry's supposition of a formulaic system common to all poets. Pope, remarking on this, notes that the thrift Parry assumed can be observed "provided one confines one's attention to a single singer!"[15] Each singer has his own system of formulas.

Yugoslav poetry apart, Parry's theory of the traditional formula assumes memorization, not of fixed texts to be sure, but of vast quantities of epithets and fixed metrical units from the common stock. We must assume in oral poets an admirable unanimity in restricting themselves to formulas already created and in constant use by all their competitors. Some time after a formula such as "Achilleus swift of foot" was created, poets must have voluntarily abandoned any other metrical equivalent in order to perpetuate the new coinage through the centuries. Such compliance would be a remarkable psychological phenomenon. It suggests a rigidity at variance even with our own etiolated oral tradition, in which many of the most durable proverbs and popular songs have many variants of metrical equivalence. It would be more natural to suppose that the greater the formulaic economy the greater the likelihood of a single poet working with his own set of formulas.[16]

The rigidity Parry had to assume to account for the preservation of the formulas and the memorization necessary to ensure that preservation were antithetical to the Unitarian point of view. It is true that Homer could now be a single man, but a man not overly preoccupied with the exact meaning of his formulas, who relied instead on the hoard that others had bequeathed to him. He was a compiler of hexameter fragments centuries old, who could say, even allowing him a degree of creativity, pretty much what the fragments permitted him to say. He said "Achilleus swift of foot" because that is what the oral fragment permitted him to say. Parry's theory suggested that the compiler(s) of the *Iliad* and the *Odyssey* was/were greater than the separatists had supposed, but its effect was to make explicable how one man – call him a poet – could make all those un-Vergilian repetitions that separatists had attributed to the *Bearbeiter*.

It is not facetious irony to say "call him a poet." Page understands the implications of Parry's theory when he decides that the true poets were the Mycenaeans who invented the vast formulaic system which was intricate, apt, and economical, and that our Homer is the Ionian (or Ionians, as Page prefers to call him) who inherited the system without the imagination.[17] It is at this point that we see the enormous influence of M. Jousse on Homeric scholarship. Just three years before the publication of Parry's first French thesis, Jousse had distinguished between "oral style" and our literary poetry, going so far as to exclude from discussion of oral style any terms like "poetry" or "verse" as being misleading vehicles of aesthetic bias.[18] When Croiset expresses some surprise that the pre-Socratics should have written in verse — "dans la langage de la sensibilité et de l'imagination" — Jousse reproves him for confusing "le style oral rythmé avec notre poésie."[19] The rhythmic schemes and mnemonic devices develop, argues Jousse, into the language of sensibility and imagination in literate cultures, but it is an error to consider them as such in oral cultures.[20] It was Jousse's distinction between literary aesthetics and oral utility which determined Parry's interpretation of the formulaic system in Homer, and through Parry became the cornerstone of Homeric studies. Parry permitted himself some aesthetic license in his Berkeley Master's thesis, and occasional lapses into aesthetics in some of his later papers, but in his French theses he maintained a rigorous distinction between aesthetics and utility. His adamant insistence on pure utility and convenience in Homeric language we find first in Jousse, from whom Parry learned that *poésie* — the language of sensibility and imagination — comes into existence only in a literate culture. Homer was oral, Parry concluded, therefore his rhythmic schemes (as Jousse would call them) could not be *poésie*. Parry could not quite exclude the terms "poet," "poem," or "poetry," but he is careful not to impute *poésie* to Homer. Lord later admitted that creativity (seen more in the use of formulas than in the creation of new ones) is more extensive than Parry had at first assumed.[21] He calls the Homeric poems "the product of a great oral poet in a rich oral tradition," echoing the conclusion of Parry's Master's thesis, that "the genius of the artist has blended with that of his race so inextricably that the two are hard to distinguish." [22] Jousse's dichotomy, however, between oral style and *poésie* remained a cardinal tenet through Parry's studies and through Lord's, as it persists in Combellack's warnings against reading beauty in Homeric language where none was intended. Indeed, it is impossible to read a study of Homer since Parry in which Jousse's dichotomy between the deliberate aesthetics of literary *poésie* and the accidental aesthetics of the oral style is not the primary axiom, accepted as principle even when attacked in particulars.[23]

We can now see the fallacy in Jousse's dichotomy between aesthetics and utility. Even the most mundane formulas of oral lore seek aesthetic form. The thesaurus of proverbs in George Herbert's *Outlandish Proverbs* or Cervantes' *Don Quixote* reveals the large role that wit, paradox, style, and imagery play in proverbial formulas. If Jousse's argument falters even on the simplest homespun saws, how much more fallacious to level indiscriminately to the same plane multiplication tables, proverbs, the Lord's Prayer, and ἦμος δ᾽ ἠριγένεια φάνη ῥοδοδάκτυλος Ἠώς as merely the information retrieval systems of oral Mnemosyne. Aesthetics is itself a major mnemonic device, as Jousse failed to understand.

Parry saw a system of mnemonic techniques in Homer and could not interpret it in any way except in Jousse's terms as a utilitarian system. Here too was a fallacy. Every language is a system. Homer, familiar with the supple rhythms of inflected Greek, would be dismayed to find a grammar that absolutely forbids rearranging the terms of the formula *bard sings tale*. It is an inviolable formula. But I, nurtured within its restrictions, can write: The Serbo-Croatian bard, whether Christian or Moslem, as the field work of Parry and Lord has shown, sings — or rather, since sings suggests something lyric or operatic, chants to the accompaniment of the gusle — a tale of bygone heroes. In so writing I have honored the formula; its inviolability is intact, though I have woven it into a web of other equally inviolable syntactic formulas. To discover a system is but the first step in understanding its usage. Homeric scholarship since Parry has often seemed satisfied to have discovered that Milton and Milton's chambermaid both shared the same traditional stock of linguistic structures.

Another important assumption that Parry based on the formulaic system is that poetry characterized by such a system must be orally *composed* and delivered. The poet has available an enormous reservoir of formulas and formula patterns, memorized if you will or at least retained in the memory, but there is no fixed text, either in his mind or on paper. Parry's insistence on extemporaneous delivery is linked to his assertion of the essentially ornamental nature of the epithets. No poet, composing as he sang, could reflect on the significance or appropriateness of his formulas; he must rely on the available supply. Parry allows that occasionally an oral poet may strike out on his own to find a new formula, but he takes Calhoun to task for supposing that an oral poet could be expected to meditate on the appropriateness of epithets within formulaic repetitions at the moment of delivery.[24]

The formulaic system might lend support to the idea of such improvised oral poetry, almost mindlessly improvised we might say, but since Parry evidence suggests other hypotheses. In societies where oral poetry flourishes, memorization is assiduously practised by poet and nonpoet. The Incas, for example, had specially appointed poets and chroniclers whose task was, first, to incorporate traditions and laws in poetic form, that is, in a form that could be easily memorized by the populace, and then to commit their own poems to memory, preserving absolute accuracy by the use of various mnemonic devices and by incessant repetition. The *Rig Veda,* whatever its date of composition, was preserved orally with verbatim fidelity for centuries before it was first written down. It is only reasonable to assume that in an oral culture memory will be directed to encompassing traditions, genealogies, histories, proverbs, and catalogues of information, rather than disjointed formulas. When memory is the only means of preserving information there is a premium not just on memory, but on accurate memory. If rhapsodes, children even, in the classical period were expected to memorize the Homeric poems, could not the creator of the poems have done likewise? There is, of course, a difference between memorizing information imposed from without, as we might memorize the multiplication tables or a poem by Keats, and memorizing from within, when the process of creation, with constant meditation on alterations, additions, and revisions, lays its own mnemonic patterns in the brain. Then one remembers without being aware of having memorized. So it must be with a singer like Zogíc who sang for Lord in 1951, with almost verbatim recall, a song he had sung seventeen years before.[25] That is not extemporaneous composition. Lord's singers, in fact, although they claimed the ability to sing extemporaneously on any assigned subject, did rather poorly in extemporaneous compositions if they were not permitted at least a day of reflection.[26]

Even granting all of Parry's assumptions, his theory has still shed no light on what remains one of the great mysteries of the Homeric Question — the transmission of the poems. As we possess them the poems are not oral but written. Parry and Lord recorded and transcribed modern oral poems, but we have no evidence to show whether or how a transcription was made for the Homeric poems. Lord's accounts of their recording of modern poetry show the painstaking effort required to transcribe an oral poem from dictation and even the difficulty that the oral singer experiences when called on to sing to a microphone.[27] The difficulties must have been vastly greater, almost insurmountable one would think, when writing and writing materials were more primitive than modern pen, paper, and tape recorder. There seems to be a tacit assumption that Homer, the best of oral poets, came at the end of the oral tradition while his scribe, the best of scribes, simultaneously emerged at the very birth of writing and thus the one ancient art was successfully transmitted into the new. Transubstantiation derives its authority more from its nature as miracle than from logical argument.[28]

The transubstantiation of oral poetry into written poetry was not Parry's chief concern, but it is a problem central to his theory which insisted on an orally composed, an extemporaneously composed, poetry in which the poet had little time for reflection on individual words or even lines. Of one thing, however, we can be sure: the Homeric poems are documents entirely different not only in length but also in nature from the Yugoslav poems that Parry and Lord collected, just as they are different from Hesiodic poetry. The transcription of the Homeric poems was a labor to stagger the imagination. If the poems are from oral tradition, either they were memorized, to a large extent at least, so that poet and scribe could collaborate in their recording, or the scribe's mechanical ability compelled the poet to dictate so slowly that he had ample time to gather his formulas, shape his lines, reflect on his formulas, and perhaps even have his earlier versions read back to him. In short, our Homer would have behaved exactly as an Apollonios or a Vergil composing in his study, for surely that is how we imagine Vergil composing — creating his verses in his mind and reciting them to his *librarius*. In either case it seems less extemporaneous composition than Parry envisioned, and if not extemporaneous composition, what of the formulas as metrical necessities?

Parry's theses, then, demonstrated a system with an enviable precision, but we must distinguish between the system and the inferences Parry drew from it. The system itself is far from proven, being an inference from a small core of Homeric vocabulary, but grant that the system is as complete as Parry and his successors argue, however, and we are no closer to resolving the fundamental problems of the Homeric Question. The system can tell us nothing of the transmission of the poems. It is not an instrument that can distinguish between a traditional and nontraditional formula. For such a distinction we must prove that oral singers invariably prefer traditional coinage to contemporary mint; better still, we must unearth a storehouse of Mycenaean hexameters on clay tablets, where Achilleus is swift-footed and Odysseus much-enduring. Parry's system is silent, too, on the question of single or multiple authorship. Again we need contemporary documents as a control, collections from eighth- or seventh-century Greece like Parry's and Lord's records from Serbo-Croatian bards. Until we know who Homer is, in all his consistencies and inconsistencies, how can we distinguish in Homer between the Homeric and the un-Homeric, or between oral and imitation of oral? After Parry we are still left to ponder why the impulse of oral composition towards thrift and economy should produce poems some 15,000 lines in length, in a meter more complex than that of any indubitably oral poems, and with a vocabulary richer than that of most *poésie,* whether oral or literary. Products of oral cultures, whether sagas, epics, folk songs or proverbs, have a simplicity quite at odds with the complexities of Homeric meter, vocabulary, and dialect.

Lord has called for more direct analysis of the poems.[29] His criticism of the subjective speculation is justified: many scholars have accepted Parry's theory, or criticized it, but few have attempted to subject the Homeric poems to the same kind of systematic analysis Parry undertook. Several critical studies have extended our knowledge of the formulaic system in Homer beyond Parry's original research, but the problems are forbidding, probably beyond the compass of an individual or even a generation. In the rest of this chapter I attempt to accept Lord's challenge and build in a small way on the foundation Parry erected.

A major problem of Parry's theory lies in the question of the utility, range, and necessity of the formulaic system. Parry's original thesis shows the debt it owes to the scanning of concordances. More recent studies have begun to turn to context, with gratifying results, but still the concordance is preferred to the poem. Even in these studies the usual assumption has been Parry's, that metrical convenience is the norm in formulaic usage, with significant deviation occurring only on isolated occasions. In order to test Parry's inferences I have taken the same phenomenon he analyzed, the name-epithet formulas, and investigated it from different perspectives. Constructing other systems for Parry's data can reveal the lacunae in his schemata, and it is just those lacunae that give us confidence that there is more than metrical convenience at work in Homer's selection of formulas. We can see that the name-epithet formulas are not as essential as Parry believed, nor as useful, and that their selection is governed by various contextual forces. A heretic, perceiving the incompleteness of the name-epithet system and the contextual restrictions on it, might be tempted to argue that epithet formulas represent a movement away from thrift.

The *Odyssey* is a good testing ground for the oral theory, since the *Iliad* represents a narrower world of experience and formula usage may therefore have a greater uniformity to reflect that world. The *Odyssey* includes a variety of classes, social institutions, kinship relations, and modes of behavior. The epithet usage reflects this variety, sometimes in striking ways. The formulaic system exists but operates effectively for certain characters and certain grammatical cases only, for others infrequently or not at all. There are metrical formulas but we find them restricted to certain situations; for other situations the poet must resort to other expressions. Parry recognized the complexity of the formulaic system, but his system ignored context and therefore failed to note how often it dictates one formula instead of another.

To provide a basis for analysis I include here tables of epithet usage peculiar to the *Odyssey*. The tables illustrate the usage for the name *Odysseus* in all its cases and variants, the usage for the names *Penelope* and *Telemachos,* and then for all the names the usage both with and without epithets. By epithet I mean an attributive word or phrase directly joined to the name, eschewing attributive or predicative epithets not directly attached, though some might consider such usage as formulas or formulaic. I have tried to collate the information in Henry Dunbar's *Concordance,* H. Ebeling's *Lexicon Homericum,* and Augustus Gehring's *Index Homericus.* For those whose concern may be the position of the formula in the verse, I have included the position with each name-epithet formula, using the system given by Eugene G. O'Neill, Jr., in "The Localization of Metrical Word-types in the Greek Hexameter: Homer, Hesiod, and the Alexandrians," namely:

1	1½	2	3	3½	4	5	5½	6	7	7½	8	9	9½	10	11	12
—	∪	∪	—	∪	∪	—	∪	∪	—	∪	∪	—	∪	∪	—	—

| | 2 | | 4 | | 6 | | 8 | | 10 | |

Though I have tried to exercise care in my compilation, these tables undoubtedly contain some errors (few I trust). They are also incomplete because, ultimately, no formulas can be isolated — what I have tabulated as a name without epithet may, in fact, be an element in some other kind of formula. Nevertheless, despite such flaws, I trust that the tables will provide data of interest and reliability.

EPITHETS FOR ODYSSEUS

I. Nominative: Total (Ὀδυσσεύς and Ὀδυσεύς) 317

   A. Ὀδυσσεύς: Total 250

This form occurs in the *Odyssey* 250 times, 150 times with epithet, 100 times without epithet. The commonest epithets are δῖος, πολύτλας δῖος, πολύμητις; very rare are ἐσθλός and πτολίπορθος. The occurrences and usages are as follows:

δῖος Ὀδυσσεύς	$(- \cup\cup - \frac{12}{})$	x 40
πολύτλας δῖος Ὀ.	$(\cup --- \cup\cup - \frac{12}{})$	x 37
πολύμητις Ὀ.	$(\cup\cup - \cup\cup - \frac{12}{})$	x 66
πτολίπορθος Ὀ.	$(\cup\cup - \cup\cup - \frac{12}{})$	x 3
ἐσθλὸς Ὀ.	$(- \cup\cup - \frac{12}{})$	x 3
Ὀ. δῖος	$(\cup --- \overset{5\frac{1}{2}}{\cup})$	x 1

Included in this group are three instances in which another epithet occurs in the verse but is separated from the name-epithet phrase:

διογενὴς ὦρτο πτολίπορθος Ὀ.	x 1
διογενὴς μετέφη πολύμητις Ὀ.	x 1
υἱὸς Λαέρταο πολύτλας δῖος Ὀ.	x 1

Of the 100 instances of name without epithet, 88 occur at position 12, the remainder at position 4. Included in this group are lines such as these, where there is an epithet or epithet phrase in the verse:

ἦ σύ γ᾽ Ὀδυσσεύς ἐσσι πολύτροπος	(10.330)
οὐ σύ γ᾽ Ὀδυσσεύς ἐσσι πατὴρ ἐμός	(16.194)
ἦ μάλ᾽ Ὀδυσσεύς ἐσσι φίλον τέκος	(19.474)

These 3 examples are a minor, but instructive, illustration of the force of context on formula. Each is certainly a formulaic line in the *Odyssey* but the formula of the second half of the line depends on the speaker (Kirke, Telemachos, Eurykleia).

The nominative form Ὀδυσσεύς is more commonly found with an epithet than without, in the ratio of 1.5 to 1, but the proportion taken in isolation is a highly misleading figure. Mere tabulation of figures shows us little. When we examine the uses of the epithets more closely we begin to wonder how large is the influence of metrical convenience. There are, first, two formulas for the shape $-\cup\cup--$ at the end of the verse, one beginning with a consonant, the other with a vowel. Only one of these formulas, however, is in general use, namely δῖος Ὀδυσσεύς. Its counterpart, ἐσθλὸς Ὀδυσσεύς, occurs only three times and is spoken by Telemachos in this form:

τείρεσθ᾽, εἰ μή πού τι		x 1
	πατὴρ ἐμὸς ἐσθλὸς Ὀ.	
λίσσομαι εἰ ποτέ τοί τι		x 2

The same is true for the two formulas of the shape $\cup\cup-\cup\cup--$; πτολίπορθος Ὀ., which could replace πολύμητις Ὀ. after a preceding short vowel, is limited to only three instances, and certainly in one of these instances seems particularly apt: at 22.283 Odysseus, as he is striking Eurydamas, is no longer the enduring Odysseus, but Odysseus the destroyer of citadels, here the suitors' citadel. These two expressions then, ἐσθλὸς Ὀ. and πτολίπορθος Ὀ., though metrically convenient for completing the verse, the one after the bucolic diaeresis and the other after the masculine caesura of the fourth foot, offer no real help to the poet in composition.

The more common epithets might seem to offer greater scope to the poet. Certainly δῖος Ὀ. is the closest thing to a set formula among these expressions; it occurs frequently and lends itself to a variety of larger metrical units. Its most frequent use is with aorist verb forms (ἐβήσετο, ἐδύσετο, ἵστατο, and the like) or with imperfects with similar scansion in the final syllables (ἐδείπνεε, προσεφώνεε, ὑπολείπετο, etc.). Some half of its occurrences are with such aorist or imperfect middle or passive forms.

The longer expression, πολύτλας δῖος 'Οδυσσεύς, also seems to be a true formula in that it can fit neatly into a variety of lines. Its primary use is with aorist and imperfect verb forms, but this time in the active voice (ἄκουσε, νόησε, ἦσθε, γήθησε, γήθησεν δέ, προσέειπε, etc.).

The epithet formula that occurs most frequently in the *Odyssey* also offers the most surprises. It has a convenient shape, πολύμητις 'Οδυσσεύς (∪∪ – ∪∪ – –), occurs 66 times, yet combines with other words to form essentially only four different lines:

i. τὸν ⎱
      ⎰ δ᾽ ἀπαμειβόμενος προσέφη πολύμητις 'Ο.   x 44
      τὴν ⎱

ii. 'Αργεῖοι, μετὰ δέ σφω ἔβη πολύμητις 'Ο.   x 1

iii. αὐτὰρ ὁ γυμνώθη ῥακέων πολύμητις 'Ο.   x 1

iv. ὣς ἄρ᾽ ἔφαν μνηστῆρες· ἀτὰρ πολύμητις 'Ο.   x 1

The remaining 19 instances are all variants of (*i*) with the verb replaced once by μετέφη, with another participle substituted for ἀπαμειβόμενος, or with the name of the person addressed in the accusative case. Of these 19, more than a third (i.e., 7) are the formulaic line:

τὸν ⎱
     ⎰ δ᾽ ἄρ᾽ ὑπόδρα ἰδὼν προσέφη πολύμητις 'Ο.
τὴν ⎱

For those who believe that formulas are essential for oral composition it should seem a curious fact that the poet of the *Odyssey* has created or borrowed this epithet formula, used it frequently, but, with three exceptions, had it yield what is essentially the same general idea in one verse structure. In 63 out of 66 instances the poet uses the formula in a line expressing the idea "Odysseus spoke." As a formula it is placed under rigid limitations, restricted as it is to introducing a speech.

Some scholars, resorting to the lost hexameter theory, have classified as formulas those phrases that may recur only two or three times within one poem, or even within the whole Homeric corpus. The usage of πολύμητις ’Ο. casts doubt on the viability of the theory, for it shows that though an expression may recur with the greatest frequency it yet remains localized only to certain contexts. Within the *Odyssey* the formula is not a necessary one, nor even particularly useful, for *oral composition*. It is not a formula floating in free suspension in the repertory, but a formula devised for one particular situation, and its frequency depends on the recurrence of that kind of situation.

Parry recognized clearly enough that the frequency of many formulas is in direct proportion to the frequency of certain ideas and situations and that the abundance of nominative formulas depends on the frequent occurrence of lines introducing a speech. What his tables obscure, however, is that the purpose of many nominative formulas is solely, or almost exclusively, to introduce speeches. Were Odysseus not such a speechmaker the *polymetis* formula would virtually drop from the tables. His tables also are not constructed to reveal the variety of expressions in Homer for what Parry called "the same essential idea." προσέφη πολύμητις ’Οδυσσεύς is by no means the only expression for "Odysseus spoke." In 11 out of its 37 occurrences, πολύτλας δῖος ’Οδυσσεύς gives a whole line formula to express the same general idea:

i.	τὸν δ’ αὖτε προσέειπε πολύτλας δῖος ’Ο.	x 6
ii.	τὴν δ’ ἠμείβετ’ ἔπειτα πολύτλας δῖος ’Ο.	x 3
iii.	τοῖς δ’ ἄρα μύθων ἦρχε πολύτλας δῖος ’Ο.	x 2

The poet thus has two sets of formulas for saying "Odysseus spoke," and there is no metrical reason for preferring one over the other. That the two formulaic systems exist for the same general idea suggests that there is some conscious attempt at variety within formulaic situations. We note also that in eight instances of πολύτλας δῖος 'Ο. the verb is γήθησε, yet for those eight instances there are three different arrangements for that verb + the name-epithet formula, an illustration of the limitation on formulas and also of the apparent attempt at variety.

To summarize the uses of the nominative formulas with 'Οδυσσεύς: of the 150 instances of name-epithet, 74 are restricted to a whole line formula introducing a speech (63 with *polymetis,* 11 with *polytlas dios*); half, that is, are used to convey one single idea, with minor modifications. If we add to those the 6 instances of *esthlos* and *ptoliporthos,* we have 80 epithet formulas placed under special restrictions, in contrast with 69 formulas sufficiently versatile to lend themselves to a variety of contexts. Against all these epithet formulas, there are 100 instances where 'Οδυσσεύς occurs without attached epithet. We might conclude that the most adaptable and versatile formula for the nominative case is simply the name 'Οδυσσεύς.

B. 'Οδυσεύς: Total 67

    1. With epithet: Total 9

'Ο. Ἰθακήσιος	$(\cup\cup - \cup\cup - \cup\overset{8}{\cup})$	x 2
διογενὴς 'Ο.	$(- \cup\cup - \cup\cup \underline{5})$	x 3
	$(- \cup\cup - \cup\cup \underline{7})$	x 2
'Ο. Λαερτιάδης	$(\cup\cup - - - \cup\cup \underline{7})$	x 1
('Ο. γε ἐμὸς πάϊς)		(x 1)

    2. Without epithet: Total 58

$(\cup\cup \underline{3})$	x 36
$(\cup\cup \underline{5})$	x 14
$(\cup\cup \underline{7})$	x 8

In position 7 the name occurs always with another name following.

Clearly, with this nominative, when the ratio of epithet formula to name alone is 9 to 58, the epithet cannot be considered a necessary or convenient adjunct. Of the epithet formulas here, the one used by Laertes at 24.328, Ὀ. γε ἐμὸς πάϊς, certainly contains no ornamental element, and we can say of the rest that they are at least appropriate to context. Only Ithakans speak of Odysseus *Ithakesios* when they talk of his return (Leiokritos, Eurymachos). Odysseus introduces himself to the Phaiakians quite properly with name and patronymic, *Odysseus Laertiades*. *Diogenes* is used by the poet twice, once by Telemachos in speaking to Eurykleia, and by Eurykleia in her reply to Telemachos. At least Homer avoids the infelicity of putting such an epithet in the mouth of the suitors.

The two forms of Odysseus in the nominative give an even distribution of 159 instances with epithet, 158 without, a distribution that suggested to Parry that metrics decided in favor of one or the other form — but the solution is not so simple. It is, in fact, a very complicated matter to take into consideration simultaneously the various factors in the system for the nominative for the single name of Odysseus. If it were possible, however, to consider the total interplay within the system — the use of two nominative forms which multiplies the positions available for the name, the frequent repetition of but a few epithet lines, the number of epithet phrases which by anyone's analysis must be excluded from the ornamental category — then we could scarcely avoid the conclusion that it is not the name-epithet formula but the name alone that is the most versatile element in this particular system.

II. Vocative: Total (Ὀδυσσεῦ and Ὀδυσεῦ) 35

   A. Ὀδυσσεῦ: Total 24

      1. With epithet: Total 21

διογενὲς Λαερτιάδη	}	x 15
	πολυμήχαν' Ὀδυσσεῦ	
ὄλβιε Λαέρταο παῖ	}	x 1
φαίδιμ' Ὀδυσσεῦ	$(- \cup\cup - ^{\underline{12}})$	x 5

Here the epithet formula is mostly restricted to a single verse which occurs 14 times, and one further time with a slight modification. The formula is used by Kirke (x 4), Kalypso (x 1), Athena (x 3), figures in the underworld (x 6), and Eumaios (x 1).

    2. Without epithet: Total 3

$$(\cup - \underline{12}) \quad \text{x 2}$$
$$(\cup - \underline{4}) \quad \text{x 1}$$

B. Ὀδυσεῦ: Total 11

    1. With epithet: Total 1

πολύαιν᾽ Ὀδυσεῦ μεγακῦδος Ἀχαιῶν   (said by the Sirens)

    2. Without epithet: Total 10

$$(\cup\cup \underline{5}) \quad \text{x 8}$$
$$(\cup\cup \underline{3}) \quad \text{x 2}$$

III. Genitive: Total (Ὀδυσσῆος and Ὀδυσῆος) 130

  A. Ὀδυσσῆος: Total 71

    1. With epithet: Total 37

Ὀδυσσῆος θείοιο $(\cup ----- \overset{12}{\cup})$ x 24

  of these:

$$\begin{cases} φίλος υἱὸς \text{ (-ον) } \text{Ὀ. } θείοιο & \text{x 7} \\ κατὰ (πρὸς) δώματ᾽ \text{ Ὀ. } θείοιο & \text{x 9} \end{cases}$$

Ὀδυσσῆος ταλασίφρονος $(\cup --- \cup\cup - \overset{8}{\cup\cup})$ x 12

Ὀδυσσῆος μεγαθύμου (Ὀ. μ. φαίδιμον υἱόν)   x 1

Here we note that despite its potential usefulness as a replacement for Ὀ. ταλασίφρονος before a consonant, Ὀ. μεγαθύμου is used only once. It could also have potential use as a substitute for Ὀ. θείοιο and is thus a metrically useful formula which is not exploited at all.

    2. Without epithet: Total 34

$$(\cup -- \underline{5}) \quad \text{x 16}$$
$$(\cup -- \underline{9}) \quad \text{x 18}$$

In this group I have included the following, which are not name-epithet formulas although perhaps others would call them formulaic:

ὡς τότ᾽ Ὀδυσσῆος περικήδετο κυδαλίμοιο	x 1
ὃν καὶ Ὀδυσσῆος φθῖσαι γόνον ἀντιθείοιο	x 1
ἀλλά μ᾽ Ὀδυσσῆος πόθος αἴνυται οἰχομένοιο	x 1
δμωαὶ Ὀδυσσῆος δὴν οἰχομένοιο ἄνακτος	x 1
μνάσκετ᾽ ⎫	x 1
⎬ Ὀδυσσῆος δὴν οἰχομένοιο δάμαρτα	
μνώμεθ᾽ ⎭	x 1

These expressions include phrases that function as name-epithet formulas, but there is no question of ornament here. Also, the only phrase that is repeated is Ὀ. δὴν οἰχομένοιο (x 3); for the rest it would be hard to determine what is formula and what is not. In addition, under genitive name without epithet I have included Ὀδυσσῆος φίλος υἱός (x 9) which, as a name-epithet formula, belongs with the epithets of Telemachos rather than of Odysseus; but in any case we cannot talk of ornament. For the *Odyssey,* the periphrasis "son of Odysseus" is surely as important as the simple name "Telemachos."

B. Ὀδυσῆος: Total 59

   1. With epithet: Total 25

Λαερτιάδεω Ὀδυσῆος	$(- - \cup\cup - \cup\cup - \overset{12}{\cup})$	x 12

     of these:

⎧ ὦ γύναι αἰδοίη Λ. Ὀ.		x 5	⎫
⎪ ἐλθών ⎫		x 1	⎪
⎨ ⎬ ἐς μέγαρον Λ. Ὀ.			⎬
⎪ ἐλθόντ᾽ ⎭		x 1	⎪
⎩ δεύτερον		x 1	⎭

Two whole line structures account for 75 percent of the uses of this epithet. The formula is used also for the comrades of Odysseus (x 1), his heart (x 2), and his knees (x 1). Altogether, it occurs in only five different verses.

'Οδυσῆος ἀμύμονος   (∪∪ – ∪∪ – ∪$\overset{8}{∪}$)   x 8

Half of the occurrences of this epithet are in the whole line
formula within the vow: ἱστίη τ᾽ 'Οδυσῆος ἀμύμονος "ἥν
ἀφικάνω (x 4).

ἀντιθέου 'Οδυσῆος   (– ∪∪ – ∪∪ – $\overset{12}{∪}$)   x 1

                                      (– ∪∪ – ∪∪ – $\overset{5½}{∪}$)   x 1

θείου 'Οδυσῆος   (– – ∪∪ – $\overset{12}{∪}$)   x 2

('Οδυσῆος ἐγὼ θείοιο λαθοίμην)   x 1

2. Without epithet: Total 34

                                      (∪∪ – $\overset{12}{∪}$)   x 19

                                      (∪∪ – $\overset{5½}{∪}$)   x 13

                                      (∪∪ – $\overset{9½}{∪}$)   x 1

                                      (∪∪ – $\overset{3½}{∪}$)   x 1

IV. Dative: Total ('Οδυσσῆι and 'Οδυσῆι) 32

    A. 'Οδυσσῆι: Total 8

        1. With epithet: Total 4

        'Οδυσσῆι μεγαλήτορι   (∪ – – – ∪∪ – $\overset{8}{∪∪}$)   x 3

        'Οδυσσῆι πτολιπόρθῳ   (∪ – – – ∪∪ – $\underline{12}$)   x 1

        2. Without epithet: Total 4

                                      (∪ – – $\underline{5}$)   x 4

    B. 'Οδυσῆι: Total 24

        1. With epithet: Total 8

        ἀντιθέῳ 'Οδυσῆι   (– ∪∪ – ∪∪ – $\underline{6}$)   x 3

                                      (– ∪∪ – ∪∪ – $\underline{12}$)   x 2

        'Οδυσῆι δαΐφρονι   (∪∪ – ∪∪ – ∪$\overset{8}{∪}$)   x 3

        2. Without epithet: Total 16

                                      (∪∪ – $\overset{5½}{∪}$)   x 5

                                      (∪∪ – $\underline{12}$)   x 6

$$(\cup\cup - \overset{9\frac{1}{2}}{\cup})\quad \text{x 3}$$
$$(\cup\cup - \overset{3\frac{1}{2}}{\cup})\quad \text{x 2}$$

V. Accusative: Total ('Οδυσσῆα, 'Οδυσῆα, 'Οδυσσῆ', 'Οδυσῆ')
77

A. 'Οδυσσῆα: Total 15

   1. With epithet: Total 7

'Οδυσσῆα μεγαλήτορα $(\cup - - - \cup\cup - \overset{8}{\cup\cup})$ x 3

'Οδυσσῆα πτολιπόρθιον $(\cup - - - \cup\cup - \overset{8}{\cup\cup})$ x 2

'Οδυσσῆα πτολίπορθον $(\cup - - - \cup\cup - \underline{12})$ x 2

   'Ο. μεγαλήτορα and πτολιπόρθιον fall in the identical
position in the verse, so we must assume other than metrical
reasons for the distinction between them.

   2. Without epithet: Total 8

$$(\cup - - \underline{9})\quad \text{x 2}$$
$$(\cup - - \underline{5})\quad \text{x 6}$$

B. 'Οδυσῆα: Total 54

   1. With epithet: Total 18

'Οδυσῆα πόλύφρονα $(\cup\cup - \cup\cup - \overset{8}{\cup\cup})$ x 5

This formula occurs always in the whole verse: νοστήσειν
(-ῆσαι) 'Ο. πολύφρονα ὅνδε δόμονδε.

   'Ο. δαΐφρονα ποικιλομήτην   x 4

   'Ο. ἄνακτα δαΐφρονα ποικιλομήτην   x 1

ἀγακλυτὸν ἀμφ' 'Οδυσῆα $(\cup - \cup\cup - \cup\cup - \underline{12})$ x 1

κλυτὸν ἀμφ' 'Οδυσῆα $(\cup\cup - \cup\cup - \overset{12}{\cup})$ x 1

Λαερτιάδην 'Οδυσῆα $(- - \cup\cup - \cup\cup - \overset{12}{\cup})$

   as ἄγχι παρισταμένη Λαερτ. 'Ο.   x 2

'Οδυσῆα φίλον πόσιν $(\cup\cup - \cup\cup - \overset{8}{\cup\cup})$

   as κλαῖεν ἔπειτ' 'Ο. φίλον πόσιν, ὄφρα οἱ ὕπνον   x 4

2. Without epithet: Total 36

$$(\cup\cup - \overset{5\frac{1}{2}}{\cup})\qquad \text{x } 29$$
$$(\cup\cup - \overset{12}{\cup})\qquad \text{x } 4$$
$$(\cup\cup - \overset{3\frac{1}{2}}{\cup})\qquad \text{x } 3$$

With this form of the accusative the epithet formulas are far outnumbered by the occurrence of the name alone. We should also note that there are seven epithet formulas, yet these give only nine different whole verses (with slight modification in one repetition). All the epithet formulas, except 'Ο. δαΐφρονα ποικιλομήτην, give only one verse, or one verse repeated several times.

C. 'Οδυσσῆ': Total 1

No epithet

D. 'Οδυσῆ': Total 7

No epithet

$$(\cup\cup \,\underline{3})\qquad \text{x } 5$$
$$(\cup\cup \,\underline{5})\qquad \text{x } 1$$
$$(\cup\cup \,\underline{9})\qquad \text{x } 1$$

Totals for Odysseus

All occurrences of the name *Odysseus* in the *Odyssey*: 591

Grammatical Case	With Epithet	Without Epithet
Nominative	159	158
Vocative	22	13
Genitive	62	68
Dative	12	20
Accusative	25	52
Total	280 (47%)	311 (53%)

Parry himself seemed to argue, and certainly some Parryites have assumed, that formulas had an essential function as building blocks in the oral composition of hexameters. The statistics for name-epithet formulas belie this assumption, however, at least in its simple form. The incidence of epithet formulas roughly approximates that of the name alone, but we must discount this parity in several ways. First, we should have to consider the number of formulas which occur in whole verses repeated verbatim or with trifling variants, for example, πολύμητις (x 63) in sentences expressing "Odysseus spoke," πολύφρονα occurring only in the sentence νοστήσειν 'Ο. πολύφρονα ὄνδε δόμονδε (x 5), and many other similar exact repetitions. Frequency of occurrence is due largely to repetition of identical sentences, a phenomenon Parry's tables are not designed to reveal.

Then, the formula system is most fully developed and exploited for the nominative case. There we see the true economy and extension Parry observed. There are few formulas, they are highly localized, and they are repeated frequently, combining with other phrases in a great variety of ways. We see a preponderance of formulas in the vocative also, but it is questionable whether we can, without more ado, label all repeated epithets there as ornamental. To address a character by name alone is an abrupt practice which Homer generally avoids; whether we call the vocative epithet an ornament or a title, surely it is an essential part of the address. In the other oblique cases the formulaic system functions far less noticeably. The name alone occurs much more frequently than the epithet formulas and there is, furthermore, a great variety of epithet formulas, each used only a few times. In the oblique cases in particular, the repetition of formulas reflects the repetition of identical sentences.

Finally, we find that the epithet system is strongly oriented towards the end of the verse. The majority of formulas occupy two positions: (1) after the bucolic diaeresis (x 48); (2) after the feminine caesura (x 64). The occurrence of formulas in other positions is markedly less frequent. We should also note that the figures for the two positions of highest frequency represent only a few formulas in the nominative and vocative cases. By contrast, for the name alone, although the incidence is still high at the end of the verse, the most favored positions are near the beginning. There seems to be a balance between the two phenomena: the formulas cluster at the end but the name alone predominates near the beginning, where the system seems to be tenuous.

Parry excluded the occurrence of name without epithet from his tables, but exclusion is not so easily done if we are to construct an accurate and complete system for the name *Odysseus.* For those who extend the definition of formula to include participles, or monosyllabic relative pronouns, the word *Odysseus* is as much a formula as any other word, and must be if we insist on the formulaic system not as a partial but a total order. Then for the name Odysseus in the nominative we would have a total of 12 formulas: 10 epithet formulas and the 2 formulas Ὀδυσσεύς and Ὀδυσεύς. We should notice that of the 10 epithet formulas 7 are used once, twice, or three times at most, in this respect resembling Vergil's *magnanimum Aenean* (x 2) or *bonus Aeneas* (x 2) in the *Aeneid,* leaving 3 epithet formulas used with frequency, and half of their occurrences (including virtually all the occurrences of one formula) are to introduce a speech. Only 2 epithet formulas are useful in a variety of situations, and they occur approximately 40 times each. A poet who wished to introduce the word *Odysseus* in the nominative into a line has the "choice" (hypothetically granted him) of 10 formulas. What choice does he make? Our poet in some 12,000 lines uses most of the formulas scarcely at all, and no epithet formula more than 40 times, except in the repeated line "polymetis Odysseus spoke," but the name without epithet he uses 158 times − and the nominative case is where the epithet system is most exploited. If metrics explains all, the conclusion is inescapable: metrical compulsion is towards the formula of name without epithet. Occasionally (relatively) in his 12,000 lines the poet falls back on one or two convenient epithet formulas when the name alone, for some reason, involves him in some difficulties.

If we omit the simple name from the formulaic system, we should then have to assert that the epithet formula is metrically useful only half the time. Even this admission grants the epithet formula too much, when half of the occurrences are to express one essential idea. In any case, as long as we exclude the simple name, we must argue that the system operates intermittently, sometimes necessary, sometimes not, and we are left to wonder what higher principle governs this fluctuation in the system's operation.

Here it perhaps needs emphasis that the system indeed exists in Homer, but not in Vergil. Vergil may use *pius Aeneas* 17 times, *pater Aeneas* 16 times, and several other epithet phrases for Aeneas, but Parry has adequately demonstrated that despite epithet frequency the *Aeneid* shows nothing of an interlocking system for formulas.[30] The *Odyssey* has its epithet formulas for Odysseus which, with rare exceptions, do not overlap in metrical shape or grammatical case. Homer does not search for the novel epithet for every mention of Odysseus; he has a limited stock, whether his own or from the tradition, and to that he must turn. The important corollary to Parry's work is that the poet turns to his formulaic stock with relative infrequency.

That relative infrequency suggests that context may play its part after all, not in demanding a new epithet for every occasion, but at least in the choice to use or not to use the epithet formula. Since the epithet formulas are considerably less common than the occurrences of the simple name, we could follow Parry's reasoning to argue that they are, in fact, specialized instances, not the norm. Can that most formulaic epithet, *polymetis,* be entirely ornamental when its association is with Odysseus as speaker? It might be better to translate the formula in that context as "thinking hard, Odysseus spoke," or "while his mind ranged far, Odysseus spoke." Such translations would remind us that when Odysseus speaks he is usually pleading a case, marshalling his most persuasive arguments.[31] We note also that Telemachos, when about to speak, is always *pepnumenos,* and Penelope *periphron* in like circumstances. Three members of the family and each has one epithet formula emphasizing intelligence which introduces their speeches — there is more than meter at work here. True formulaic economy should also demand that Achilleus, whose name is the metrical equivalent of Odysseus, should be *polymetis;* but in the *Iliad* when he is about to speak he is always πόδας ὠκὺς Ἀχιλλεύς. Again there is something besides meter to explain why Odysseus is always an intelligent speaker and Achilleus a swift-footed one. If the epithets were virtually devoid of meaning we might expect a poet to suffer an occasional lapse and sing προσέφη πολύμητις Ἀχιλλεύς, but any such lapses have been erased from our texts.[32]

To argue the validity of every formula in its context would be an endless labor, and an unprofitable one, since it would be an essentially negative proposition to demonstrate that formulas were not inappropriate. A more oblique, but perhaps more persuasive, course would be to determine whether there are any recognizable patterns of epithet usage. We could construct a catalogue of the epithet formulas used for Odysseus in the *Odyssey,* to determine distinctions between one character and another in formula usage or between the characters and the poet speaking through his own persona.

In the following table I have attempted such a list as a basis for further discussion. The list is as complete as possible, but excludes the frequent use of simple pronouns. Nor does it include the various titles given to Odysseus, particularly ξεῖνος, πτωχός, and γερόν, words used to describe or address Odysseus when his identity is unknown. These are the epithets and epithet formulas used by characters in the *Odyssey* to address, mention, or describe Odysseus (each expression is used once unless otherwise noted):

By members of his family

Penelope:

Ὀ. θείοιο   x 2

Ὀ. ἀντιθέοιο

πολύμητις . . . 'Ο.

'Ο. ταλασίφρονος

κεῖνον δύστηνον

φίλου . . . πατρός ⎫
                    ⎬   (when speaking to Telemachos)
σοῦ πατρός   ⎭

σοῖο ἄνακτος   ⎫
                    ⎬   (when speaking to Eurykleia)
'Ο. . . . φίλον   ⎭

ἐμὸς (-ον) πόσις (-ιν)   x 3

πόσιος φίλοιο

δαιμόνι'

ἀνδρὸς, ⎫
          ⎬ τοῦ κλέος εὑρὺ καθ' Ἑλλάδα καὶ μέσον Ἄργος   x 2
ἐσθλὸν, ⎭

πόσιν ἐσθλὸν . . . θυμολέοντα
                                                                x 2
παντοίης ἀρετῆσι κεκασμένον

δῖος 'Ο. (κοῦροι ἐμοὶ μνηστῆρες, ἐπεὶ θάνε δῖος 'Ο.)

Odysseus, speaking of himself in the third person:

δῖος 'Ο.   x 2

πολύμητις 'Ο.

'Ο. πτολιπόρθιον

'Ο. θείοιο   x 2

'Ο. ἀμύμονος   x 5

πολυτλήμων ⎫   (as predicates, when Odysseus speaks
πολύστονος ⎬   in the first person)

'Ο. ἄνακτος

'Ο. δὴν οἰχομένοιο ἄνακτος

Λαερτιάδεω 'Ο.   x 5

υἱὸν Λαερτιάδεω

διωγενὲς Λαερτιάδη πολυμήχαν' 'Ο.

Telemachos:

πατὴρ ἐμός   x 2

πατὴρ ἐμὸς ἐσθλὸς Ὀ.   x 3

Ὀ. . . . πατὴρ ἐμός

πατέρ' ἐσθλόν

ὦ πατέρ   x 4

πατὲρ φίλε   x 2

πατρός   x 4

τοῦ πατρός   x 2

πατρὸς ἐμοῦ

πατρὸς ἐμοῖο

πατρὸς ἀποιχομένοιο

πατρὸς δὴν οἰχομένοιο   x 2

πατρὸς οἰχομένοιο

πατρί τ' ἐμῷ

πατέρ' ἀντίθεον

θείοιο

Ὀ. ταλασίφρονος   (to Penelope)

δίου Ὀ. ταλασίφρονος   (to Nestor)

διωγενὴς Ὀ.   (to Eurykleia)

κρατερόφρονος ἀνδρός   (quoting Menelaos)

δῖος Ὀ.   x 2

⎰ ἐπεὶ θάνε δῖος Ὀ.   (1.396)
⎱ οὕς μοι λήΐσσατο δῖος Ὀ.   (1.398)

The name *Odysseus* (with no epithet)   x 11
(1.354; 2.59; 15.157, 267, 522; 16.34, 119 bis; 17.131, 136; 20.265).

Laertes:

σὸν ξεῖνον δύστηνον,

δύσμορον

Antikleia:

τέκνον ἐμόν   x 2

φαίδιμ' 'Ο.

περὶ πάντων κάμμορε

By the gods

Zeus:

'Ο. θείοιο

'Ο. ταλασίφρονος

δῖος 'Ο.

Athena:

δῖος 'Ο.

'Ο. δαίφρονι

'Ο. πολύφρονα

'Ο. ταλασίφρονος

'Ο. θείοιο

πατρὸς φίλου ⎫

⎬   (to Telemachos)

πατρός ⎭

πολυμήχανός (ἐστιν)

σχέτλιε, ποικιλομῆτα, δόλων ἆτ'

διογενὲς Λαερτιάδη πολυμήχαν' 'Ο.   x 3

Hermes:

ἄνδρα . . . ὀϊζυρώτατον ἄλλων

ὦ δύστηνε

Sirens:

πολύαιν' 'Ο. μέγα κῦδος 'Αχαιῶν

Helios:

(ἐτάρους) Λαερτιάδεω 'Ο.

Kalypso:

    διογενὲς Λαερτιάδη πολυμήχαν' 'Ο.

Kirke:

    σύ γ' 'Ο. ἐσσι πολύτροπος

    διογενὲς Λαερτιάδη πολυμήχαν' 'Ο.   x 4

By friends

Nestor:

    δῖος 'Ο.   x 2

    'Ο. . . . κυδαλίμοιο

    'Ο. ἄνακτα δαίφρονα ποικιλομήτην

    πατέρ' ἐσθλόν   (to Telemachos)

Menelaos:

    δῖος 'Ο.

    'Ο. ταλασίφρονος

    φίλου ἀνέρος (υἱός)

    υἱὸς Λαέρτεω

    καρτερὸς ἀνήρ

    κρατερόφρονος ἀνδρός

Helen:

    'Ο. μεγαλήτορος

    'Ο. ταλασίφρονος

    καρτερὸς ἀνήρ

Eurykleia:

    διογενὴς 'Ο.   (quoting Telemachos' words)

    τέκνον

    θεουδέα θυμὸν ἔχοντα

    φίλον τέκος

    τέκνον ἐμόν

Eumaios:
  ἄναξ εὔθυμος
  Ὀ. . . . . οἰχομένοιο
  οἰχομένοιο ἄνακτος
  ἐμοῖο ἄνακτος
  ἀντιθέῳ Ὀ.
  ἠθεῖον
  παῖδος οἰχομένοιο   (sc. son of Laertes)
  παῖδος κυδαλίμοιο   (sc. son of Antikleia)
  διογενὲς Λαερτιάδη πολυμήχαν' Ὀ.

Halitherses:
  ἀνδρὸς ἀριστῆος
  πολύμητις Ὀ.

Mentor:
  Ὀ. θείοιο

Aigyptios:
  δῖος Ὀ.

Philoitios:
  Ὀ. ἀμύμονος
  οἰχομένοιο ἄνακτος
  τὸν δύστηνον

Theoklymenos:
  Ὀ. ἀμύμονος
  Λαερτιάδεω Ὀ.
  ἀντιθέου Ὀ.

Odysseus' sailors:
  διογενές
  δαιμόνι'
  φαίδιμ' Ὀ.

ὁ θρασὺς Ὀ.

διοτρεφές   x 2

Heroes in the underworld:

Elpenor:

διογενὲς Λαερτιάδη πολυμήχαν᾽ Ὀ.

ὦ δύστηνε

φαίδιμ᾽ Ὀ.

Agamemnon:

διογενὲς Λαερτιάδη πολυμήχαν᾽ Ὀ.

ὄλβιε Λαέρταο πάϊ πολυμήχαν᾽ Ὀ.

Ὀ. πτολίπορθον

Achilleus:

διογενὲς Λαερτιάδη πολυμήχαν᾽ Ὀ.

φαίδιμ᾽ Ὀ.

Herakles:

διογενὲς Λαερτιάδη πολυμήχαν᾽ Ὀ.

Amphimedon (speaking to Agamemnon in Book 24):

Ὀ. δὴν οἰχομένοιο

Ὀ. θείοιο

πολύτλας δῖος Ὀ.

δῖος Ὀ.   (quoting Penelope)

By enemies

Antinoos:

δῖος Ὀ.   (quoting Penelope's line κοῦροι ἐμοὶ μνηστῆρες,
                                        ἐπεὶ θάνε δῖος Ὀ.)

Λαερτιάδεω Ὀ.   x 2

ἀγαυοῦ πατρός   (to Telemachos, when he feigns
                                 cooperation, 2.308)

Eurymachos:

πτολίπορθος Ὀ.   (to Penelope)

ἀντιθέου Ὀ.   (in embarrassment, 21.254)

ἀμύμονος ἀνδρὸς (ἄκοιτιν)   (in embarrassment, 21.325)

Ὀ. Ἰθακήσιος   (to Odysseus after Odysseus has
                                 killed Antinoos)

Amphinomos:

δμώων . . . Ὀ. θείοιο

Agelaos:

δμώων . . . Ὀ. θείοιο

Ὀ. πολύφρονα

Melanthios:

Ὀ. θείοιο

Ktesippos:

δμώων . . . Ὀ. θείοιο

Eupeithes:

ἀνὴρ ὅδε

Leiokritos:

Ὀ. Ἰθακήσιος

This list reveals the remarkable paucity of name-epithet
formulas uttered by characters in the poem. The characters use
such formulas about 90 times, that is, in less than one-third of
the total instances. This figure is striking when we consider that
Odysseus is the topic of almost every conversation in the poem.
People are always talking about him or to him, but their
preference is for other circumlocutions, commonly those that
express his relationship to them as father, husband, child, or

master. Telemachos' practice is illustrative: he names Odysseus 11 times without epithet; he once uses an epithet formula that does not include the name, κρατερόφρονος ἀνδρός, a loan from Menelaos who had used the expression earlier; some 27 times he uses a formula based on some form of *pater*; finally, he uses a name-epithet formula for his father only 6 times. If we consider all the ways in which he refers to his father, excluding pronouns, we find a ratio of name-epithet formulas to all other expressions, including the name alone, of 6 to 39. Since name-epithet formulas and the name alone occur in almost equal numbers in the poem, the difference between the usage in the whole poem and the usage in Telemachos' case is surely significant.

Telemachos' practice finds its counterpart in that of other members of Odysseus' family or household. Penelope uses name-epithet formulas for Odysseus only five times. Her preference is for a simple pronoun (τόν, κεῖνος), for some oblique circumlocution such as κεῖνον δύστηνον, or for some formulaic term that includes *posis*. So too for Eumaios and Eurykleia. They usually use the name alone, but prefer even to that some periphrasis based on ἄναξ, or an endearment like *tekos* or *teknon*. Book 19 provides a good illustration of the disparity in formulaic practice between the poem itself and the characters. Book 19 is not necessarily a random choice, but it is useful as a test since it has several characters, including Odysseus, who speak about Odysseus, and often in some extended way. The table below will show that the majority of the name-epithet formulas are used by the poet himself. Only Odysseus shows any inclination to follow in the poet's path; in his case all but one of his name-epithet formulas occur not when he is speaking about Odysseus, but when he is addressing Penelope as the wife of Odysseus, son of Laertes.

The totals are revealing. In the poem as a whole, name-epithet formulas for Odysseus and the name alone occur with approximately equal frequency (47 to 53%), but in this book where most of the references to Odysseus are made by the characters instead of the poet himself, that parity disappears,

Expressions for Odysseus in *Odyssey* 19

Speaker	Name-epithet formulas	Name alone	Other expressions (excluding pronouns)
Poet	16	14	2
Odysseus	6 (δῖος ᾽Ο. x 1) (Λαερτιάδεω ᾽Ο. x 5)	14	2
Penelope	1 (δῖος ᾽Ο.)	8	6
Telemachos	0	0	2 (πατέρ, πατρός)
Eurykleia	0	2	3
Autolykos	0	1	0
Totals	23	39	15

and the incidence of name alone far predominates (now 37 to 63%). A glance at the table merely gives dramatic confirmation of this same fact. In Book 19, in the poet's own narrative, the ratio of name-epithet formulas to name alone is still approximately 1 to 1, but the ratio for all the other speakers combined comes closer to 1 to 4 (i.e., 7 to 25). If we consider all the expressions used for Odysseus in the book, we have a ratio of name-epithet formulas to other expressions (name alone and other periphrases, excluding simple pronouns) of 1 to 5 (i.e., 7 to 38). The conclusion is inescapable. Name-epithet formulas for Odysseus in the *Odyssey* are to a significant degree the property of the poet, not of his characters.

The use of epithets by the characters is admittedly slight, yet it is sufficient to make certain assumptions tenable. As we have seen, the members of Odysseus' family and household adopt expressions denoting their relationship to Odysseus. They are sparing in their use of name-epithet formulas. As if to establish the characters as discrete identities in the poem, the poet puts in their mouths expressions that are individual and even unique. Penelope, for example, twice uses a long periphrasis for Odysseus which is never used by any other character or by the poet:[33]

$$\pi\acute{o}\sigma\iota\nu\ \grave{\epsilon}\sigma\theta\lambda\grave{o}\nu\ \dots\ \theta\nu\mu o\lambda\acute{\epsilon}o\nu\tau a,$$

παντοίη; ἀρετῆσι κεκασμένον ἐν Δαναοῖσιν,

ἐσθλόν, τοῦ κλέος εὐρὺ καθ᾽ Ἑλλάδα καὶ μέσον Ἄργος.

(4.814-816)

Eurykleia, too, has a unique expression which echoes a part of Penelope's expression: σε ... θεουδέα θυμὸν ἔχοντα (19.363-364). Telemachos uses certain epithets occasionally, such as *dios, diogenes, dios talasiphron,* and once he quotes Menelaos' formula *kraterophronos andros,* but he never uses those distinctive epithets of Odysseus, *polymetis, polytlas, polymechanos.* It is interesting that the character whose epithet and epithet formula usage approximates the poet's is Odysseus himself. He uses the greatest variety of epithet formulas, and with the greatest frequency. This is not surprising since he substitutes for the poet through much of the poem, appropriating the narrator's role in Ithaka as in Scheria.

That wife and son should refer to Odysseus with their own sets of expressions is perfectly normal and may put no demands on the poet's formulaic repertory. But the individuality is maintained for others like Eurykleia and Eumaios no less than for the immediate family. Eurykleia only once uses a name-epithet formula (*diogenes O.*), and that only after Telemachos has used it in speaking to her. Eumaios once uses the formula ἀντιθέῳ Ὀ., and once the formal address διογενὲς Λαερτιάδη, πολυμήχαν᾽ Ὀ., in the thick of the fray when Odysseus has just shown himself truly *polymechanos.* But normally they have other expressions which even reveal a distinction in rank between them. Both are coevals, and slaves in the household, but Eurykleia is the old nurse and Eumaios the swineherd. Thus for Eurykleia Odysseus is "child," "my child," or "dear child"

as well as master, but for Eumaios he can only be "master," or
else son of Laertes, or son of Antikleia. Eumaios, on the
occasion mentioned at the beginning of this chapter, resists
naming Odysseus as a consistent and studied policy. At first he
refers to Odysseus by pronoun only (14.61, 70, 90, 96). In
answer to Odysseus' direct question he continues evasively with
another five pronouns (vv. 122, 133, 135, 137) and then finally
names his master (v. 144):

$$\text{ἀλλά μ' Ὀδυσσῆος πόθος αἴνυται οἰχομένοιο.}$$

Eumaios recognizes the potency of the word, and his recognition is paralleled in the practice of Odysseus' closest relatives
who avoid the poet's formulaic expressions for Odysseus.[34]

The suitors have less chance to address Odysseus (as
Odysseus), or to talk about him, but even for them there seems
a consistent pattern. They never use those epithets that indicate
Odysseus' intelligence or endurance, *polymetis, polytlas, talasiphron,* and the like. How could they and still remain in the
man's house importuning his wife? Only a man like Halitherses
is permitted such expressions; in the assembly in Book 2 he uses
the formula *polymetis Odysseus,* appropriately enough since he
is recalling his former prophecy that Odysseus would return.
The suitors do not even use the simple *dios Odysseus,* except
when repeating Penelope verbatim. The one epithet formula
they use with any frequency is 'O. θείοιο, but it is a verbatim
repetition of a line, used once each by Amphinomos, Agelaos,
and Ktesippos and once, with a variation, by Melanthios. In
each case the speaker acts in a proprietary fashion towards
Odysseus' palace; the epithet is a small but telling indication of
their simulated respect for Odysseus. Their other uses of the
complimentary epithets seem equally appropriate in their
context. Antinoos calls Odysseus the "illustrious father" of
Telemachos when he promises to obtain a ship for Telemachos
(2.308). Eurymachos, unable to handle the bow, groans at the
disgrace of being inferior to *godlike* Odysseus (21.254); a short
while later he expresses the same fear when Penelope suggests
that the stranger be given a chance at the bow. He is dismayed

at the prospect of the gossips who will say that inferior men are courting the wife of a man who is *amumon,* though they cannot use the man's bow, but then a beggar comes along and strings it easily (21.325-328). In his case the epithets express his reluctant admission of Odysseus' superiority. Once Agelaos uses the epithet *polyphron* in a line that is a repetition of one used three times previously: νοστήσειν Ὀδυσῆα πολύφρονα ὅνδε δόμονδε (20.329). At that moment Ageloas is attempting a conciliatory role between the suitors and Telemachos; the epithet appropriately indicates his momentary espousal of Telemachos' rights. Insofar as the epithets are part of the vocabulary of the characters in the poem, we can conclude that they belong more to Odysseus' partisans than to his enemies. Menelaos, Nestor, and the gods (except Poseidon) can use a variety of complimentary epithets, but the suitors do so only in obvious irony or embarrassment.

One epithet formula is interesting in its usage: πολυμήχαν' Ὀδυσσεῦ. This address is repeated 14 times, but only twice by an ordinary mortal. It is the flattering and astonished exclamation with which denizens of the other world greet Odysseus when he crosses the threshold that divides their temenos from the mortal world. Kirke uses it four times after Odysseus has successfully negated her magic. Then in the underworld the heroes address him thus one after another — Teiresias, Agamemnon, Achilleus, Herakles. In the second Nekyia Agamemnon, hearing of Odysseus' success in the world above, modifies the formula to address Odysseus in his absence: ὄλβιε Λαέρταο πάϊ, πολυμήχαν' Ὀδυσσεῦ. Most of the occurrences of *polymechanos,* then, occur in the underworld and on Kirke's island where Odysseus rests before and after his visit to the underworld. The other characters to use the formula are Kalypso, on the occasion when she tries to hold Odysseus within her world, and Athena on three occasions after Odysseus has returned from the mythical world to his own island. When Odysseus uses the formula once in a false tale to Eumaios we may attribute that either to his braggadocio or to the license he has as surrogate poet. When Eumaios in the battle scene in the palace uses the title that is otherwise restricted to deities and heroes in the underworld, he too may be permitted the license, since Odysseus has just metamorphosed from a beggar willing to tolerate the vilest abuse to an avenging hero. *Polymechanos* is no faded metaphor but one that proclaims that Odysseus is about to contrive, or has just contrived, some new stratagem bordering on the magical.

So far we have studied the epithets and their usage for but one character, albeit the character whose exploits constitute most of the poem. The same kind of analysis for Penelope and Telemachos is instructive as corroborating the evidence given by the epithets of Odysseus. Below are tables listing, as for Odysseus, the epithet formulas by grammatical case, first for Penelope and then for Telemachos.

EPITHETS FOR PENELOPE

I. Nominative:

περίφρων Πηνελόπεια	$(\cup---\cup\cup-\overset{12}{\cup})$	x 40
ἐχέφρων Πηνελόπεια	$(\cup---\cup\cup-\overset{12}{\cup})$	x 3
Without epithet		x 9

II. Vocative:

περίφρον Πηνελόπεια	$(\cup---\cup\cup-\overset{12}{\cup})$	x 4
Without epithet		x 2

III. Genitive:

Without epithet		x 3

IV. Dative:

περίφρονι Πηνελοπείῃ	$(\cup-\cup\cup-\cup\cup-\underset{}{\overset{12}{\_}})$	x 6
ἐχέφρονι Πηνελοπείῃ	$(\cup-\cup\cup-\cup\cup-\underset{}{\overset{12}{\_}})$	x 4
Without epithet		x 4

V. Accusative:

ἐχέφρονα Πηνελόπειαν	$(\cup-\cup\cup-\cup\cup-\overset{12}{\cup})$	x 1
Without epithet		x 7

Other expressions for Penelope:

ὦ γύναι αἰδοίη Λαερτιάδεω Ὀδυσῆος	x 5
Ἰκαρίου κούρη τηλεκλειτοῖο	x 1
κούρη (-ῃ) Ἰκαρίοιο (-ίου)	x 3

Of the epithet formulas for Penelope the following are the main uses:

1. Twenty-five instances of the 43 nominative formulas occur in the whole line repetitions introducing a speech:

τὸν (τὴν) δ᾽ ἠμείβετ᾽ ἔπειτα περίφρων Πηνελόπεια	x 4
τὸν (τὴν) δ᾽ αὖτε προσέειπε περίφρων Πηνελόπεια	x 18
τοῖσι δὲ μύθων ἦρχε περίφρων Πηνελόπεια	x 3

Of the 9 instances of the nominative without epithet, 3 are in lines expressing the idea "Penelope spoke."

2. Four instances of the nominative formula, 4 of the vocative, and 3 of the dative are used in a whole line identifying Penelope:

κούρη Ἰκαρίοιο περίφρων Πηνελόπεια   x 11 (all cases)

3. There are three different whole line constructions to express simply "Penelope" (one is only 5 feet):

(ὦ) γύναι αἰδοίη Λαερτιάδεω Ὀδυσῆος

κούρη Ἰκαρίοιο περίφρων Πηνελόπεια

(– –) Ἰκαρίου κούρη τηλεκλειτοῖο

TOTALS FOR PENELOPE

Total occurrences of name Penelope in the *Odyssey*	83
Total occurrences of name without epithet	25
Total occurrences of name with epithet	58

EPITHETS FOR TELEMACHOS

I. Nominative:

A. With epithet: Total 60

Τηλέμαχος θεοειδής	$(- \cup\cup - \cup\cup - \overset{12}{-})$	x 5
ἱερὴ ἲς Τηλεμάχοιο	$(\cup\cup - - - \cup\cup - \overset{12}{\cup})$	x 7
Τηλέμαχος θ᾽ ἥρως	$(- \cup\cup - - \overset{5}{-})$	x 2
Τηλέμαχος πεπνυμένος	$(- \cup\cup - - - \overset{8}{\cup\cup})$	x 46

B. Without epithet: Total 68

$(- \cup\cup \overset{3}{-})$	x 29
$(- \cup\cup \overset{5}{-})$	x 33
$(- \cup\cup \overset{7}{-})$	x 6

Of the epithet formulas, 51 occur in whole line sentences introducing speeches by Telemachos:

τὸν (τὴν) δ᾽ αὖ ⎫		ἀντίον ηὔδα	x 43
⎬ Τηλέμαχος πεπνυμένος		ἦρχ᾽ ἀγορεύειν	x 1
τοῖσι δὲ ⎭		ἤρχετο μύθων	x 2

τοῖσι δὲ καὶ ⎫		
⎬ μετέειφ᾽ ἱερὴ ἲς Τηλεμάχοιο	x 5
τοῖσι δ᾽ αὖτις ⎭		

Thus 85 percent of the nominative epithet formulas for Telemachos enable the poet to express some variation of one general idea, "Telemachos spoke." We might also note that the introductions to speeches thus account for all the uses of two of the nominative epithet formulas, except for two instances of ἱερὴ ἲς T. in combinations with other verbs.

II. Genitive:

A. With epithet: Total 4

μεγαθύμου Τηλεμάχοιο	x 1
Τηλεμάχου μεγαθύμου	x 1

Τηλεμάχοιο δαΐφρονος   x 1

Τηλεμάχου . . . μεγαλήτορος   x 1

B. Without epithet: Total 14

Τηλεμάχοιο $(- \cup\cup - \overset{12}{\cup})$ x 2

                                          $(- \cup\cup - \overset{3\frac{1}{2}}{\cup})$ x 1

                                          $(- \cup\cup - \overset{5\frac{1}{2}}{\cup})$ x 1

                                          $(- \cup\cup - \overset{9\frac{1}{2}}{\cup})$ x 1

Τηλεμάχου $(- \cup\cup \;\underline{3})$ x 7

                                          $(- \cup\cup \;\underline{5})$ x 2

III. Dative:

A. With epithet: None

B. Without epithet: Total 22

Τηλεμάχῳ $(- \cup\cup \;\underline{3})$ x 12

                                          $(- \cup\cup \;\underline{5})$ x 5

                                          $(- \cup\cup \;\underline{7})$ x 4

                                          $(- \cup\cup \;\underline{9})$ x 1

IV. Accusative:

A. With epithet: Total 2

Τηλέμαχον $\left\{ \begin{array}{l} \theta\epsilon o\epsilon i\kappa\epsilon\lambda ον \qquad\qquad\qquad\qquad\qquad\quad x\;1 \\ \\ \theta\epsilon o\epsilon i\delta\epsilon\alpha \qquad\qquad\qquad\qquad\qquad\quad\; x\;1 \end{array} \right.$ $(- \cup\cup - \cup\cup - \cup\overset{8}{\cup})$

B. Without epithet: Total 36

Τηλέμαχον $(- \cup\cup \;\underline{3})$ x 14

                                          $(- \cup\cup \;\underline{5})$ x 20

                                          $(- \cup\cup \;\underline{7})$ x 1

                                          $(- \cup\cup \;\underline{9})$ x 1

V. Vocative:

A. With epithet: Total 6

Τηλέμαχ᾽ ὑψαγόρη	$(- \cup\cup - \cup\cup \underline{5})$	x 3
Τηλέμαχε γλυκερὸν φάος	$(- \cup\cup - \cup\cup - \cup\overset{8}{\cup})$	x 2
Τηλέμαχ᾽ ἥρως	$(- \cup\cup - \underline{12})$	x 1

B. Without epithet: Total 24

Τηλέμαχ᾽	$(- \cup\overset{2}{\cup})$	x 22
Τηλέμαχε	$(- \cup\cup \underline{3})$	x 2

TOTALS FOR TELEMACHOS

Name Telemachos, all occurrences	236
Name with epithet, all occurrences	72
Name without epithet, all occurrences	164

Other formulas for Telemachos not included in the above categories:

Τηλέμαχος (-ον) φίλος υἱὸς Ὀδυσσῆος θείοιο	x 5 (includes accus.)
Τηλέμαχον . . . τεὸν φίλον υἱόν	x 1
Τηλέμαχον . . . ὃν φίλον υἱόν	x 6 (includes nom.)
Ὀδυσσῆος φίλος υἱός	x 9

Expressions clearly dependent on context (i.e., Telemachos must be understood as subject):

υἱὸς ἀμύμων	x 1
φαίδιμος υἱός	x 4
ἰσόθεος φώς	x 2 (once with Telemachos at beginning of verse)

At some points the epithet usage for Penelope and Telemachos exemplifies even better the kind of principles shown in the epithets of Odysseus. Penelope is severely limited in her epithets, but a system does exist for her name; there is a name-epithet formula for all the cases except the genitive. The system, however, is scarcely exploited. Her name occurs with an epithet about twice as often as without (58 to 25), but the ratio is the result of repetition of whole lines. The nominative with *periphron* allows the poet to say 25 times, in only three different whole line formulas, "Penelope spoke." In addition, the epithet *periphron* gives the poet a whole line formula simply to say "Penelope" 11 times, in nominative, vocative, and dative. In percentages, four whole lines, repeated with but minor variations, account for 86 percent (36 out of 42) of all the instances of the phrase *periphron Penelopeia*. The system barely functions in the accusative where the name occurs only once with epithet against seven times without epithet. In the dative it is slightly more serviceable; the epithet is used with 10 of the 14 occurrences of the name. It is curious that Penelope's name, though a poet's delight since it falls neatly after the diaeresis, occurs far more frequently with epithet than do the names Odysseus or Telemachos. In comparison, the ratio of name-epithet formula to name alone for Penelope is 58 to 25 (70 to 30%); for Odysseus, 280 to 308 (47 to 53%); for Telemachos, 70 to 164 (30 to 70%).

For Telemachos the *Odyssey* also shows an adequate system, a set of metrical shapes to cover the different cases, but it is a system even less exploited than that for Penelope. The commonest name-epithet formula, *Telemachos pepnumenos,* is used in only one way, to introduce a speech by Telemachos. The epithet has no other function; its frequency in the poem is an emphatic reminder that Telemachos makes many speeches. Of the seven instances of the formula ἱερὴ ἲς Τελεμάχοιο, five are also used to introduce speeches by Telemachos. The poet has, then, two epithet formulas to express the idea "Telemachos spoke," and these two epithet formulas serve virtually no other function. The lines expressing the idea "Telemachos spoke" account for 85% of the instances of the nominative name-epithet formula and 71% of the total instances of such formulas for Telemachos in the poem.

The versatile epithet formulas are Τ. θεοειδής and Ὀδυσσῆος φίλος υἱός. But Τ. θεοειδής occurs only five times, two instances being repetitions of the same whole line (1.113, 17.328). Ὀδυσσῆος φίλος υἱός is the most versatile phrase, occurring nine times, each time with a different verb. There are formulas to refer to Telemachos which fit after the diaeresis, but these are limited to a context that makes the identity of the subject clear:

σὸς φίλος υἱός	x 1
ὃν φίλον υἱόν	x 2
οἱ φίλος υἱός	x 1
μιν φίλος υἱός	x 2
φαίδιμος υἱός	x 4 (Ὀ. καὶ φαίδιμος υἱός, x 3)
υἱὸς ἀμύμων	x 1
ἰσόθεος φώς	x 2

In the oblique cases of the name Telemachos the epithets play so small a part that it is questionable whether we can consider them part of a genuine formulaic system. The dative is illustrative: the name occurs 22 times in the dative, but there are no dative epithets at all. This seems an extraordinary hiatus if we posit the necessity of an epithet system for composition. In the accusative the situation is almost as striking: the name appears 38 times but only twice with an epithet. In the vocative the ratio of name to name-epithet formula is 4 to 1; in the genitive the same ratio is 14 to 4. We should note that for the genitive there are four name-epithet formulas, each used only once, so there are in reality no epithet repetitions at all in the genitive. Parry's theory cannot explain why epithet formulas can be so numerous in the nominative and yet so evidently unnecessary in the oblique cases.

In the case of Odysseus the epithets are, as I have shown, part of the poet's narrative and only rarely part of the vocabulary of the characters in the poem. The epithets, when they occur in the characters' speeches, are always specialized. The dichotomy in epithet usage between speech and poetic narrative applies as much to the name of Telemachos as to that of Odysseus, as the following table shows.

Epithets and phrases used in speeches to or about Telemachos

I. Vocative:

Τηλέμαχ᾽	x 7
Τηλέμαχ᾽ ἥρως	x 1 (by Menelaos, 4.312)
Τηλέμαχ᾽ ὑψαγορή	x 3 (by Antinoos)
φίλε τέκνον	x 3 (by Eurykleia, Nestor, Theoklymenos)
ὦ φίλ᾽	x 6 (Nestor, Medon, Theoklymenos, Odysseus, Eumaios)
τέκνον	x 5 (by Nestor, Eumaios, Odysseus, Eurykleia)
φίλον τέκος	x 2 (by Menelaos, Eumaios)
τέκνα φίλ(α)	x 2 (by Nestor, Menelaos)
τέκνον φίλε	x 1 (by Helen)
Τηλέμαχε γλυκερὸν φάος	x 2 (by Eumaios, Penelope)
τέκνον ἐμόν	x 2 (by Eurykleia, Penelope)

II. Nominative:

ἄναξ ἐμός	x 1 (by Eumaios)
Τ. θεοειδής	x 2 (by Eumaios)
φίλος πάϊς	x 1 (by Eumaios)
Ὀδυσσῆος φίλος υἱός	x 3 (by Nestor, Eumaios)
φίλου ἀνέρος υἰὼς	x 1
σὸς παῖς	x 1 (by Athena as Penelope's sister)
παῖς ἀγαπητός	x 1 (by Penelope)
πατρὸς πάϊς οἰχομένοιο	x 1 (by Peisistratos)

III. Genitive:

μεγαθύμου Τηλεμάχοιο	x 1 (by Athena)
Τηλεμάχοιο δαΐφρονος	x 1 (by Penelope)
Τηλεμάχου μεγαθύμου	x 1 (by Nestor)

IV. Accusative:

φίλος υἱὸς Ὀδυσσῆος θείοιο	x 1 (by Amphimedon's ghost to Agamemnon)
παῖδ᾽ ἀγαπητόν	x 2 (by Penelope, Athena)

And a few additional phrases such as:

τέον φίλον υἱόν

Τηλέμαχον κεχολωμένον   x 1 ⎫
⎬ (by Eurymachos)
Τηλέμαχον μάλα περ πολύμυθον x 1 ⎭
ἐόντα

Most of the expressions used for Telemachos by other characters appear so seldom that it is hard to differentiate in detail. A few facts, however, are salient. The poet's two commonest phrases, ἱερὴ ἲς T. and T. πεπνυμένος, never occur in characters' speeches. The commonest expressions in speeches are τέκνον and its variants. It is interesting that Menelaos addresses Telemachos as ἥρως; certainly we should be surprised to find members of his family addressing Telemachos thus, but at Sparta Telemachos is in the heroic world and recognized as a hero himself. It is interesting, too, as a subtle indication of character, that it is always Antinoos who uses the angry form of address: Τηλέμαχ᾽ ὑψαγόρη, μένος ἄσχετε. Small as the sample is, it is enough to indicate that the ways in which people refer to Telemachos are dependent on the exigencies of the moment and the relationship of the speaker to Telemachos.

The conclusion, then, is that without speeches the formulaic system for Telemachos' name would disappear almost completely, since we have only isolated instances of various epithets for situations other than speech making. The system would also be so reduced for Odysseus' name that we should hesitate to call it a system at all. Here we may note again the variety within regularly recurring formulaic situations. How many ways are there to say, in six dactyls, "X spoke"? A remarkable number, in fact, for so formulaic a poetry. The poet can, for example, introduce Odysseus as speaker in the following ways:

1. τὸν δ᾽ ἀπαμειβόμενος προσέφη πολύμητις Ὀδυσσεύς
2. τὸν δ᾽ αὖτε προσέειπε πολύτλας δῖος Ὀ.
3. τὴν δ᾽ ἠμείβετ᾽ ἔπειτα πολύτλας δῖος Ὀ.
4. τοῖς δ᾽ ἄρα μύθων ἦρχε πολύτλας δῖος Ὀ.
5. δή ῥα τότ᾽ ἀμφιπόλοισι μετηύδα δῖος Ὀ.
6. δὴ τότ᾽ ἄρ᾽ Ἀλκίνοον προσεφώνεε δῖος Ὀ.
7. τὸν δ᾽ αὖ διογενὴς Ὀδυσεὺς ἠμείβετο μύθῳ
8. αὐτὸς διογενὴς μετέφη πολύμητις Ὀ.
9. τοῖς δ᾽ Ὀδυσεὺς μετέειπε συβώτεω πειρητίζων
10. ἔνθ᾽ Ὀδυσεὺς δμώεσσι καὶ υἱεῖ μῦθον ἔειπεν
11. αὐτίκα μειλίχιον καὶ κερδαλέον φάτο μῦθον
12. καὶ τότε δή μιν ἔπεσσι προσηύδων μειλιχίοισι
13. εὐχόμενος δ᾽ ἄρα εἶπεν ἔπος τ᾽ ἔφατ᾽ ἔκ τ᾽ ὀνόμαζε
14. αἶψα δὲ Φαιήκεσσι φιληρέτμοισι μετηύδα
15. ἀντίον ἧς ἀλόχου καί μιν πρὸς μῦθον ἔειπε

These are the basic structures, which can be further modified as, for example, (1) is modified by the substitution of various particles for ἀπαμειβόμενος:

τὸν δ᾽ ἄρ᾽ ὑπόδρας ἰδών

καί μιν φωνήσας

τὸν δ᾽ ⎰ ἀναχωρήσας
⎱ ἐπιμειδήσας

τοῖς δὲ δολοφρονέων

This catalogue, it should be emphasized, covers the introductions of only one speaker in the *Odyssey*. Most items can be

adapted for other speakers and there are many other intro-
ductory lines which are used of other speakers in the *Odyssey*
but never of Odysseus. It is no exaggeration to say that there
are some fifty ways for the poet to say "X began to speak."
Prodigality on such a scale is not the mark of a poet for whom
metrical convenience is the primary consideration. Did the
nineteenth-century novelist have any greater variety of formulas
for beginning speeches? Were his connectives — "he said," "he
remarked," "he laughed," "he retorted," "he interrupted" —
richer than Homer's connectives, or any less formulaic?

Metrics alone cannot give the answer to the problem of
repetitions in Homer. Metrics plays its part, and an important
part, as it must in any highly structured poetry, as do the many
other subtle patterns of euphony. There are many creative
principles jointly operative in Homer, but it is doubtful whether
meter is more significant than it is in Vergil. It should be a
truism that a poet with his eye fixed chiefly on metrical
economy could never have produced either the *Iliad* or the
Odyssey. The vast vocabulary, the richness and variety of
expressions, the conjunction of rhythm, sound, and sense, are
not the work of a mnemonic efficiency expert.

Perhaps Parry's use of the word *formula* has sown confusion
by creating categories alien to poetry. The word is one
borrowed from science and lends an aura of scientific authority
to poetic analysis.[35] Undoubtedly Parry's early death contrib-
uted to the stabilization of the system he had sometimes very
confidently, sometimes rather hesitantly formulated. Perhaps
the reason for such ready acceptance of his theory is also to be
found in the peculiarly modern compulsion for analytic
systems. The twentieth century venerates a formula. Parry's
system, itself an elaborate formula, came as a revelation. As a
system it promised incontrovertible proofs on various aspects of
the Homeric Question. Systems, we had thought, were answers.

It is now becoming questionable whether systems can in
themselves provide the answers. Parry's system cannot solve any
of the problems of authorship, provenance, method of composition, or transcription. It would be a mistake to suppose that

statistics could lead to the author, when the very opposite is the case. Statistics are valid only when accompanied by an array of other kinds of data. Statistical studies of Milton's poetry cannot tell us when he went blind, but if we knew from other sources the exact progression of his blindness, then the computer can perhaps reveal a parallel progression in his poetry. Where the elementary data are missing — the identity of the poet, for example, and his/her/their dates — statistics is a sandy soil indeed.

It now transpires, through the modern controversy on the Homeric formula, that Parry was analyzing only a certain aspect of Homeric language, the recurrent metrical-lexical patterns. He devalued to as close to zero as possible the language of the poetry and then assumed that the abstractions thus produced were what Homer was trying to express in a more cumbersome hexametric way, thus denying to Homer his unique imagination, everything, in fact, that makes the *Iliad* and the *Odyssey* what they are as poems. "Wily Odysseus" is quite obviously not an equivalent for "godlike Odysseus" or "Odysseus son of Laertes," or we should, by the law of averages, find Telemachos or the suitors sooner or later saying πολύμητις Ὀδυσσεύς — but Homer prevents them from that mistake. Even in our prosaic and egalitarian society a man has a variety of names and titles, each with its proper function and occasion. To forget a man's name may be a faux pas, but to use one of his variant names in the wrong way is an intentional insult. Parry was reluctant to admit such distinctions, so elementary and obvious in our culture, in a poetry preeminently sensitive to rank and occasion and, above all, to the sound and meaning of language.

Parry, confronted with so elaborate a system in Homer, could only conclude that the system explained all, whereas it is really only tangential unless used in conjunction with other data. Even with perfect unanimity on primary definitions, we should still have no valid grounds for distinguishing between ornamental and particularized epithets. Is a word repeated only two or three times less ornamental than one repeated fifty times? The word repeated only twice, and even the *hapax,* are all just as much part of the system as the word repeated fifty times, and the system cannot inform us as to the reasons for the choice between one word and another, between name alone and name-epithet formulas. The system can only describe the phenomena, not account for them.

Parry could legitimately devalue semantic meaning for the purpose of demonstrating the system. It is one thing to say, for the purpose of statistical analysis, that the essential idea of πόδας ὠκὺς Ἀχιλλεύς is "Achilleus," but it is quite another thing to suggest that the poetic content of both is identical. Science is not as servile a handmaiden to literature as that. Science cannot tell us which element in that formula is the essential poetic idea, even if it is a formula repeated many times in certain regular ways. From the scientific point of view it is as arbitrary to decide that the essential idea of the formula is "Achilleus" as to say it is "swift," "swift-footed," or "swift-footed Achilleus." To reduce everything to essential ideas, or to talk of formulas as metrical variations of essential ideas, reveals our modern bias. It is we who strive for formulas, but formulas expressed as scientific abstractions. Our language is rapidly becoming for us a mere utilitarian mechanism to be streamlined and processed as much as possible. Our ideal, it seems, is for language to approximate the system of mathematical symbols.[36]

Everything about Homeric language, its complexity of word and rhythm, its vivid detail, its cadences, shows a language in love with particularity and nuance. Orators are essential on the Homeric battlefield, just as singers are necessary for the *euphrosyne* of Homeric banquets. The Greek army's best orators, Nestor and Odysseus, are highly honored first for their practical advice but also because they can transmute the chaos of action into the order of language. The Trojan War is a trifle in itself; it derives its value only through recognition and definition in the language of poetry. The heroes, even at the moment of action, project themselves into the realm of poetry, thus validating their ephemeral actions by visualizing them as the themes of song. It would be a grievous irony to deny semantic meaning in the one genre of literature that the Greeks themselves characterized and defined as "word." Other genres they defined in terms of action — drama, komoedia, choros, lyrikos, historia, mimos — but Homer was and remains simply Epos.

In its preference for the graphic, the particular, and the concrete, Homeric language reveals a trait shared in common with the language of many so-called primitive peoples. Language alone does not produce its Homer, but it can do much of the work for him. One has but to read, for example, a book like Nilsson's *Primitive Time Reckoning* to feel oneself immediately in the Homeric world.[37] Abstractions for time in our language — mere formulas, one might say — appear in primitive language clothed in metaphor, metaphor woven into the very fabric of the people's lives. Such language is poetic in itself because it is a language that recreates the visual and the sensual.

In such languages the detail is significant, and therefore necessary. The language is still directly a *mimesis* of visible phenomena or of social organization, but more than that it is still perceived as *mimesis.* A language that is felt as a concrete representation of reality will be traditional, "formulaic" in Parry's sense, because it is repetitive. It is likely that repetition is not so much dependent on meter as that meter is invented to preserve repetition. Where words are mere tools repetition loses its value, but where words are *mimesis,* there repetition is valued in itself. Planned obsolescence must apply to language too in a culture that believes obsolescence is the mother of invention.

In our culture there are certain spheres, of course, that are so important that the words appropriate to them assume an extraordinary reality. Prayer books and missals are filled with formulas which are formulas because they are considered to correspond with, and preserve, the highest reality. Formulaic expressions for the three Persons of the Trinity in Christian theology are not interchangeable because the Persons they represent are distinct. Only an alien to the tradition could suppose that Father, Son, and Holy Ghost could be addressed in identical language and identical situations. Prayers, oaths, treaties, curses, and legal codes are expressions rigidified into formula. Men have gone to war over the wording of this kind of formula, and men fight over only those words that they believe exert a control over that which they signify.

The study of Homer must hold something of the same reverence for language as Homer had, as Homer's Eumaios had. Modern studies, however theoretical and abstract, must first feel the quality of Homeric language. When Homer tells us "Dawn, morning Goddess, stretched her fingers across the sky, in a radiant glow," he is not trying to say something as feeble as "at dawn." Our phrase "at dawn" is more truly the formula since it is entirely devoid of descriptive content. It is not so much interested in the phenomenon as in an abstract point on a temporal continuum. Homer has, in fact, his corresponding shorthand phrases: ἄμ᾽ ἠοῖ, ἅμα δ᾽ ἠοῖ φαινομένηφιν, ἠῶθεν, expressions which, we might note, except for the single occurrence of ἄμ᾽ ἠοῖ, are all used by characters in the poem when nothing more is intended than the point on the continuum. By contrast, ἦμος δ᾽ ἠριγένεια φάνη ῥοδοδάκτυλος Ἠώς is not a generalized formula. It is an event, an epiphany of a goddess. If for us the epiphany dulls into formula through repetition, should we impute our sensibilities to Homer? Should we not rather suppose that Homer wished to re-create that epiphany with each occurrence of the phrase, so that we should feel the slow diffusion of light in the first half of the verse, and Dawn suddenly bursting forth, like a rose in bloom, at the end of the verse?

As if to remind us that he is not writing railroad schedules Homer lavishes poetic resources on that glorious miracle that occurs every day at daybreak. There are a variety of ways of expressing Dawn's appearance: the full verse with the familiar rosy epithet, or shorter variations when the epithet is *euthronos* or *chrysothronos*. In addition, there are in the *Odyssey* even more expansive descriptions of dawn or of the rising sun, each a unique event. On the day when Hermes visits Kalypso to send Odysseus on his homeward way, Dawn rises from the couch of

Tithonos to bring light to gods and men (5.1-2). Odysseus' arrival in Ithaka is marked by the appearance of the morning star which heralds the light of early-born Dawn (13.93-94). For Telemachos' first morning abroad, Helios rises to spread his light for men and gods (3.1-3). Helios rises from deep and gentle Ocean to spread new light across the land on the day when Odysseus kills a boar and proves his name (19.433-434). One magnificent description establishes in the most emphatic way that Eos is a goddess, not an event, and the morning light her personal visitation. On the final morning in the poem, when the suitors are dead and Odysseus reunited with Penelope, Athena herself urges early-rising Dawn of the golden throne up from Ocean to bear light to mortals (23.347-348). The Indians, Lucian tells us, would greet the sun each day by facing the east in silence and performing a dance miming the movement of the sun god (*Saltatio* 17). Homer's sensuous and dramatic descriptions of dawn have more in common with the Indian's mimetic dance than with modern chronometric formulas.

It is fallacious to assume that Parry's system has rendered obsolete such comments as Ruskin's on the ironic pathos of the Homeric phrase "life-giving earth" at *Iliad* 3.243. In fact, the phrase is a *hapax* in the *Iliad,* though it is repeated again in the *Odyssey,* where it is likewise used in reference to Kastor and Pollux. But even if there were ten repetitions, Parry's analysis can neither commend nor prohibit Ruskin's interpretation. If Homer can evoke Dawn in so many poetic ways, or control his language so that the suitors never say πολύμητις Ὀδυσσεύς, it is by no means implausible that he should be able to draw a contrast between the dead brothers of Helen and the life-giving earth which held them. To condemn, or support, Ruskin we should have to resort to old-fashioned subjective criticism, that is, to a personal sense of Homeric language and the patterns of his thought. We could then say in support of Ruskin that the contrast between the dead heroes and the life-giving earth is a theme that runs, subliminally and explicitly, through both the *Iliad* and the *Odyssey.* The ephemeral nature of living creatures against the eternal stability of the gods, the sea, and the earth is one of the axioms of Homeric consciousness. "The wind drives one season's leaves to the ground," says Glaukos, "but when the new spring comes around, the forest swells again with fresh foliage. So it is with men" (*Il.* 6.145-149). We might add that the only other use of *physizoos* in the *Iliad* occurs in a quite different formula, attached to *ge* instead of *aia,* placed in a different position in the line, and yet the theme is the same: the contrast between the earth and the dead. The sight of Lykaon, who has escaped from slavery in Lemnos, is for Achilleus like the vision of a man returned from the dead. Achilleus, about to strike, muses "Now I shall see whether he will return even from there where the *physizoos* Earth will hold him, she who holds even the strong man" (*Il.* 21.61-63). Odysseus adds his gloss on the theme when he draws an image, in the *Odyssey,* of all living creatures as the helpless offspring of earth: "Of all her litter, crawling in dependence about her body, Earth nurses none more frail than man" (*Ody.* 18.130-137). Homer nods, perhaps, but even over his best lines?[38]

It may seem otiose to belabor the significance of language in Homer when several modern studies of the formula have already begun to assert that significance. Whallon, for example, has argued for epithets as being true to character and, more often than Parry would allow, to context also.[39] He has shown, too, that although the Iliadic σάκος and ἀσπίς are synonyms, their use cannot be explained by any law of economy but by a poetic policy of distinguishing Achilleus and Ajax, who carry the σακος, from their opponents, Hektor and Aineias, who invariably carry the ἀσπίς.[40] Hainsworth has gathered formidable tabulations on the quantity of unique expressions in Homer, on the modifications, in displacement or separation, in even the most stable formulaic systems. He has gone far in proving that the formulaic poet must be actively thinking at all times if he is to compose in a medium that has varying degrees of formulaic rigidity, where the name-epithet is but one type of formula, bound by rules not necessarily applicable to other types of formulas.[41]

Such studies as these, however, represent the hermetic tradition. The orthodox tradition appears in Lord when he criticizes Anne Amory for supposing that an oral poet could reflect on symbolic associations of horn or ivory (or ad hoc associations, at least) while singing of the Gates of Horns and Ivory.[42] It appears also in Page whose statements, based on Parry's theories, are misleading where not actually erroneous. When he writes of the words for "sea," that "the traditional formula-system accounts for more than nine-tenths of the composition," he means the repeated noun-epithet formulas account for nine-tenths of the 143 instances of the noun-epithet phrases for the sea.[43] But there are altogether 384 occurrences of nouns for the sea in Homer; Page should more correctly state that repeated noun-epithet formulas account for 33.3 percent of all the occurrences of the words for "sea." Even with this adjustment, Page's statement ignores all subtleties in favor of a persuasive simplicity. We could not guess from Page that there are no epithets at all for θάλασσα in the nominative, accusative, or dative cases; that there are no formulas for θάλασσα (nom.), but only repetitions of whole lines or else unique sentences; that three lines repeated account for 9 of the 14 instances of θάλασσαν; that each of the four instances of θαλάσση is unique; that none of the formulas with θαλάσσης — including noun-epithet phrases and other kinds of phrases — are synonyms; that, finally, of the 88 instances of θαλάσσης there are only 12 noun-epithet repetitions, based on three epithets, and of those three epithet formulas two are metrically equivalent. Page might argue that θάλασσα cannot be taken in isolation, since four different nouns with their epithets constitute the formulaic system by which Homer can express the idea "sea." This is true, but what then of economy if the epic requires four nouns for the simple concept "sea"? We fall back on much-enduring *Tyche*, "mere chance," as Page calls her, "which has suppressed such convenient formulas as πολιὸν κατὰ πόντον, πόντον ἐπ᾽ εὐρύν, and hundreds of others."[44] Mere chance, which has taken from us an epithet system based on the single noun θάλασσα and substituted a system based on four nouns, has been a formidable opponent of formulaic economy.

Other studies have been more sympathetic than Page's to Homeric artistry but they too are based on Parry's distinction between ornamental and vital epithets.[45] M. Edwards has analyzed various aspects of Homeric language and style with considerable care, yet he too adheres to the belief in the epithet as ornamental or metrical filler. He finds, for example, the adjective *ambrosial* describing night at *Iliad* 18.268 to be "meaningless," even though its presence there is a distinct deviation from the customary formula.[46] Like Combellack, Edwards has been led by Parry's hypotheses to hold all epithets suspect, whether in formula or out of formula. In fact, the epithets for night follow a recognizable convention, and even in formulaic repetition retain their significance no less than the epithets for Odysseus in the *Odyssey*. *Ambrosial* is not a decorative word in Homer, least of all when it defines night in the *Iliad*. Night there means the end of a day's fighting. It is relief from weary battle, but, more important for the Homeric hero, it means survival through another day.[47] In the *Iliad,* perils threaten by day; night is a time for thanksgiving. Relief is exactly the emotional tone of Poulydamas' speech at *Iliad* 18.254-283. Achilleus has entered the battle again, it has been a day of bitter fighting, but now, says Poulydamas, "night has fallen thank God [sc. *ambrosial*], and put a stop to Achilleus' fury. Let us seize the opportunity and make our escape back behind the city walls." Poulydamas' whole speech specifically informs us why that night was ambrosial for the Trojans. In a parallel situation at *Iliad* 14.79, Agamemnon uses the epithet *abrote* of the night when he urges much the same advice to the Greeks as Poulydamas gives the Trojans, but Agamemnon's stress is on the darkness of night, under cover of which the Greeks can sail away unnoticed.

For Poulydamas night is relief, ambrosial. But the night that encloses one in death is never ambrosial; it is always black night: κελαινή (*Il.* 5.310), ἐρεβεννή (*Il.* 5.659), μέλαινα (*Il.* 14.439). When Odysseus and Diomedes go out to reconnoiter they slip through the dark night (μέλαιναν). When dim figures loom up in the darkness, when the night is so black that the Greeks cannot discern Athena's bird of omen, night is ὀρφναίην (*Il.* 10.83, 276, 386). Since the epithets of night are emotional, qualitative words they are susceptible to no hard and fast definition. They reflect the speaker's attitude towards night at that moment. In *Iliad* 10, in which the word *night* occurs more often than in any other book (16 times), there seems also a conscious attempt at variation of the epithets. Menelaos, meeting Agamemnon at night, asks him whether he intends to send a scout out in the ambrosial night (i.e., when men should be taking their rest, v. 41). Agamemnon then goes to Nestor, who calls out "Who's stumbling around in the darkness?" (ὀρφναίην, v. 83). Nestor goes to Odysseus, who hears his voice and calls out to know who is wandering about in the ambrosial night; again, that is, when men should be at rest (v. 142). Menelaos and Odysseus in calling night *ambrosial* express what is the normal attribute of night. It is what night should be, but this night turns out to be far from ambrosial for the Greeks. Once the leaders have assembled and Agamemnon has revealed his anxiety night is never called *ambrosial* again in Book 10; from that point it always pitch black. The word *night* occurs nine times after the leaders have gathered but its epithet, when there is one, is either ὀρφναίην or μέλαιναν.

We might single out the use of *erebenne* at *Iliad* 8.488 as one clear example of the judicious use of epithet. At that point there is a description of nightfall which makes a strong emphasis on the contrast between the light of day and the darkness of night: "The fiery globe of Sun plunged into Ocean, drawing black night [*nykta melainan*] across the ploughlands. Reluctant were the Trojans to see the light set, but the darkness of night which descended [*nyx erebenne*] was a joy to the Greeks, a prayer fulfilled" (vv. 485-488). Here the darkness of night spells frustration for the Trojans, but relief for the Greeks. The rest of the book shows that we are experiencing night from the Trojan side rather than from the Greek. Hektor advises enormous fires to be built against the black night, the light of which would reach the sky, so that the Greeks might not take advantage of darkness to escape on their ships. Let the whole city, he adds, be ablaze with fire and watchmen stationed at the towers. Thus the Trojans illuminated the city and ringed it with fires across the plain so that, like the moon set in a sky brilliant with stars, it casts its glow over every dale and headlong crag (8.497-565).[48] In Book 18, when Poulydamas calls the night ambrosial, a blessing, the situation is reversed. Night is welcome since the Trojans are the pursued, but in Book 8 the Trojans are the pursuers and night is hindrance to their advance. Hektor then calls upon the Trojans to let their city be, like the moon, a substitute for the light of day.[49]

Even for objects, then, the epithets are never simply formulas; they are connotative words which carry a certain emotional force. Scholiasts ancient and modern have been vexed over Penelope's stout hand (χειρὶ παχείῃ) at *Odyssey* 21.6.[50] But here is an epithet that illustrates particularly well the emotional quality in a word. The norm in Homer for the word *hand* is noun without epithet. There are some 60 instances in the two poems of χειρί without epithet, as against 5 instances of χειρὶ παχείῃ in the *Odyssey* and 13 in the *Iliad*. The epithet formula is specialized and, therefore, should hardly be classed as ornamental by anyone's standards, but the influence of Parry's studies has been to make all words in Homer suspect. Hefty hands are not, we must insist, the normal attribute of either epic heroes or heroines. The epithet is applied only once to Penelope's hand and that on the occasion when she grasps the key to the storeroom. The epithet, though focusing on externals, on the size of the hand, calls attention to a certain kind of action. Its connotation is not so much size as vigor, or vigor translated into physical size and shape. When a fallen hero braces himself on the ground with tremendous effort (*Il.* 5.309), when he takes up a spear, a sword, a shield (*Il.* 10.31, 14.385, 20.261), when Athena fells the god of war with a boulder "black, jagged and enormous" (*Il.* 21.403), or sends Aphrodite reeling to the ground with a blow on her breast (*Il.* 21.424), it is a grim energy that παχείῃ is describing.

It requires resolute energy for Penelope to seize the key at *Odyssey* 21.6, for when she does so she makes irrevocable her decision to end twenty years of waiting for her absent husband. The moment is charged with significance for her and the key to the palace storeroom is full of symbolic meaning. In opening the door of the room she will be quite literally surrendering her rights to it, and likewise her rights as the wife of Odysseus, lord of Ithaka. Her entrance into the storeroom is fraught with emotional tension. It is no wonder that Penelope's gesture in raising the key should be marked by a special epithet. The epithet describes her mental effort — it is a determined hand. A translation of the word simply as "large" would be a misunderstanding of the quality of Homeric language.

It may be well to conclude a study of epithet usage in Homer by examining another epithet, *pepnumenos,* one which is important for the *Odyssey* and at the same time as formulaic as any word in Homer. The etymology of *pepnumenos* is still uncertain, but the word is generally translated as "prudent, sensible, intelligent."[51] Here again, usage may further define its meaning and connotation. As an epithet of Telemachos in the *Odyssey* it is used only in lines introducing a speech by him. Such a fixed convention suggests certain possibilities. Like other words signifying intelligence, *polymetis* for example, it is closely associated with speech. This association is confirmed by other uses of the word in the two poems. In the *Iliad* the nominative occurs seven times, always in a whole line formula of this sort:

τοῖσι δὲ Πουλυδάμας πεπνυμένος ἦρχ᾽ ἀγορεύειν

(*Il.* 18.249; cf. 3.203; 7.347; [11.821]; 13.254, 266; 23.586). A variant, with the neuter plural form, occurs in 7.278, when the herald Idaios is introduced:

κῆρυξ Ἰδαῖος πεπνυμένα μήδεα εἰδώς

At 9.58 Nestor uses the neuter plural in an address to Diomedes:

ὁπλότατος γενεῆφιν· ἀτὰρ πεπνυμένα βάζεις

A variant phrase is used three times of heralds:

Οὐκαλέγων τε καὶ Ἀντήνωρ		(3.148)
Ταλθύβιός τε και Ἰδαῖος	πεπνυμένω ἄμφω	(7.276)
Αἴας καὶ κήρυκε δύω		(9.689)

Is it accident that forms of the participle are used seven times to introduce a herald or a counsellor (Idaios, Antenor, Poulydamas, Talthybios, Oukalegon)? Its other subjects are young men (Antilochos, Eurypylos, Meriones) or Diomedes, whom Nestor praises specifically as a young man and as an adviser: "You are very young, but you have spoken in a way worthy of a mature counsellor" (9.58).

The epithet's close association with heralds is dramatically emphasized at 7.276-278. The two heralds advance between the armies, *pepnumenos* both, and Idaios begins to speak, knowing *pepnumena medea*. The *Odyssey* provides further confirmation of the association of the word with heralds and advisers. The phrase *pepnumena eidos* is four times used of the herald Medon, *pepnumena medea eidos* is used once of the herald Peisenor (Medon: 4.696, 711; 22.361; 24.442; Peisenor: 2.38). When Athena and Telemachos arrive at Pylos, Athena encourages Telemachos to approach Nestor boldly (3.20):

ψεῦδος δ᾽ οὐκ ἐρέει. μάλα γὰρ πεπνυμένος ἐστί.

Surely it is not intelligence alone which is meant here, but the character of advisers: true advisers will not deceive. Nestor repeats this line when suggesting Menelaos as a still better adviser for Telemachos (3.328). Later, at Menelaos' palace, Peisistratos, about to make a delicate request that Menelaos and his party should leave off their lamentation, compliments Menelaos on his judgment by repeating, and even exaggerating, Nestor's words (4.190-191):

Ἀτρεΐδη – περὶ μέν σε βροτῶν πεπνυμένον εἶναι
Νέστωρ φάσχ᾽ ὁ γέρων κτλ.

Peisistratos conveys his request with such tact that Menelaos responds with effusive compliments on Peisistratos' judgment, thus continuing the cycle of the epithet first used by Athena (4.204-206):

> ὦ φίλ᾽ ἐπεὶ τόσα εἶπες ὅσ᾽ ἂν πεπνυμένος ἀνήρ
>
> εἴποι καὶ ῥέξειε, καὶ ὃς προγενέστερος εἴη
>
> τοίου γὰρ καὶ πατρός, ὃ καὶ πεπνυμένα βάζεις.

"Young as you are, you speak as a true diplomat, just like your father."

The relationship of the epithet to speech is stressed in the line expressing Penelope's reaction to Telemachos' advice (1.361; 21.355):

> παῖδος γὰρ μῦθον πεπνυμένον ἔνθετο θυμῷ.

When on the shore of Pylos Peisistratos welcomes Athena and Telemachos with a particularly diplomatic speech which reverences simultaneously guests, gods, and the dignity of age, the poet remarks (3.52):

> χαῖρε δ᾽ Ἀθηναίη πεπνυμένῳ ἀνδρὶ δικαίῳ.

When Odysseus professes himself astonished at the skills of the Phaiakians, Alkinoos replies that the stranger certainly seems *pepnumenos* − diplomatic − and immediately suggests that the twelve princes of the realm show their generous appreciation for Odysseus' unsolicited testimonial on their prowess (8.387-397). Later in the palace at Ithaka, Odysseus uses the same phrase to thank Amphinomos for his short but gracious wish for Odysseus' prosperity, and in gratitude for Amphinomos' sentiments advises him to quit the palace (18.125f.):

> Ἀμφίνομ᾽, ἦ μάλα μοι δοκέεις πεπνυμένος εἶναι.
>
> τοίου γὰρ καὶ πατρός, ἐπεὶ κλέος ἐσθλὸν ἄκουον.

Conspicuous indeed are the rewards for rhetoric throughout the *Odyssey* but never, perhaps, as conspicuous as those the wanderer receives at Penelope's hands. The more he talks to her the higher he rises in her estimation and in the social status she accords him. Penelope makes the stranger her confidant, acquiesces in his advice, reveals her dream to him, and finally insists that he be permitted to enter the bride contest. After Odysseus has complimented her in many ways, has promised that her husband is about to return, has declined her offer of comfortable clothes and bed, and has asked for a wise old woman to give him his bath, Penelope replies with a veritable paean to his judgment (19.350-352):

ξεῖνε φίλ'. οὐ γάρ πώ τις ἀνὴρ πεπνυμένος ὧδε

ξείνων τηλεδαπῶν φιλίων ἐμὸν ἵκετο δῶμα,

ὡς σὺ μάλ' εὐφραδέως πεπνυμένα πάντ' ἀγορεύεις.

In her words, tumbling fast one after the other, *pepnumenos* is a gloss on *phile* – explaining why Penelope has taken the liberty to address the stranger thus – and the whole of verse 352 is a gloss on *pepnumenos* in verse 350. A man who is *pepnumenos* she may call *philos,* so the logic of her syntax runs, and certainly Odysseus' conversation is entirely *pepnumena,* therefore she took the liberty.

Why, then, if *pepnumenos* is an attribute of speakers, heralds, and advisers, is it used also of young men? The answer may lie, in part at least, in the idea common to many societies that the young man's role is to offer respectful suggestions to his elders while patiently awaiting his maturity when he can engage as a full peer in the male community's work. Without experience as warrior or as leader, he cannot yet be distinguished by the heroic attributes, but rather by the attributes that suggest potential. In the Homeric world, if a young man is noted as gifted with words, a true diplomat, his elders are intimating that here is a man of promise. The ideal young man is one who speaks well but knows when to defer to his elders; this is the man whom the elders will welcome, in due course, into full participation in the community life.

Such is the kind of character we find in Telemachos. As the young son of Odysseus and Penelope, he must possess an epithet embodying his heredity, but inexperience prevents epithets of action. He cannot be wily or clever, as Odysseus is, and still remain the immature boy in need of guidance. But he can reveal a glimmer of the character of Odysseus as speaker; *pepnumenos* is a happy epithet to suggest the Odyssean potential in the boy.[52] Telemachos' speeches, always complimentary to his hosts, persuasive, modest, and candid only in appearance, are subtle imitations of the father's more practised rhetoric. When Telemachos is able to decline both Menelaos' offer of extended hospitality and his promised gift of horses and chariot while at the same time gracefully flattering Menelaos and deprecating Ithaka, Menelaos is filled with amusement and admiration: "There's no mistaking from your conversation, dear child, whose blood runs in your veins" (4.611).

Telemachos is *pepnumenos,* on one hand because the epithet, slightly less active, less defined than Odysseus' epithets, yet comments on the family likeness. On the other hand the parallel between Telemachos and heralds also makes it an appropriate epithet. In Homer the gods motivate action on earth, but there is also a parallel psychological motivation on earth. In the *Iliad* gods motivate heroes, and heroes in their turn motivate other heroes in council, and council motivates assembly, in an ever-widening circle of motivation. It is a kind of psychic energy emanating from one source and gradually diffusing through the army. The human councils and assemblies thus perform the same function as the assemblies of the gods on Olympos. Both create plans, that is, mental and verbal conceptions of actions, and then translate the conceptions into dynamic form.

The *Odyssey* dramatically represents this parallel process. The Telemachy, reduced in scale to adapt to the capabilities, age, and character of its central figure, is a parallel of the action in Books 5 to 13. Athena in Book 1 first motivates Zeus, and when his approval makes action permissible she goes to motivate Telemachos. Once Telemachos' action is well under way, Athena returns to Olympos where she motivates Hermes to go out on his parallel mission. The human leaves his home to search for Odysseus in the world of men; the god leaves his home to find Odysseus in the world beyond the human world. Both are messengers, each from his respective world, and both are *psychopompoi*. Hermes negotiates the transfer of the physical man back into life while Telemachos duplicates Hermes' role in the human, psychological realm. He is the agent who resurrects the memory of Odysseus, first in himself and then in Odysseus' friends. When Telemachos calls an assembly in Ithaka the morning after Athena's first appearance, Aigyptios at once recalls Odysseus (2.26-27). Shortly thereafter, in response to an omen, Halitherses too remembers Odysseus, as he remembers his former prophecy that *polymetis* Odysseus would return in the twentieth year of his absence (2.161-176).

The note struck in Book 2 is repeated in Books 3 and 4. The presence of Telemachos, whose person in its form, gestures, and speech is itself a physical imitation of Odysseus, unlooses wherever he goes a flood of memories of his father. And memory in Homer is more than recall; it is an act of creation. Thus Telemachos is as much retrieving Odysseus and assuring his safe conduct home as is Hermes. The Telemacheia is the longest, most fully developed Embassy Scene in Homer. It is appropriate that the epithets for Telemachos should be those otherwise principally attributed to ambassadors.

Parry's great contribution was to provide a way out of the impasse of the Homeric Question by demonstrating the existence of a system where once was thought to be chaos. We can continue to build on Parry's foundation, but only after disabusing ourselves of the idea of a distinction between specialized and ornamental epithets, or between significant and insignificant repetitions. All repetitions are formulas by Parry's definition. His schemata can reveal the pattern behind the repetitions but cannot of themselves distinguish between one kind of repetition meant to exert full semantic weight and another meant merely to complete a hexameter verse. With Parry's schemata in mind, if we turn back to context we find the patterns to be richer, more varied and intricate than his original schemata could suggest. Far from eliminating literary criticism from Homeric studies, Parry has, in fact, opened up possibilities that Analytic studies had made seem highly suspect. A grammar of Homeric poetics can be written, but not if we suppose that Homer is, either wholly or substantially, a victim of his metrical formulas.

II

Unity in Multiplicity:
Homeric Modes of Thought

> Knowing, as it is found at the start, mind in its immediate
> and primitive stage, is without the essential nature of mind, is
> sense-consciousness. . . . The task of conducting the individual
> mind from its unscientific standpoint to that of science had to be
> taken in its general sense; we had to contemplate the formative
> development of the universal individual, of self-conscious spirit.

> — G. W. F. Hegel, *The Phenomenology of Mind*

Hegel had a venerable tradition behind him, going back to
Plato and indeed to the pre-Socratics, for his distinction
between naive sense-perception and self-conscious knowledge,
but his projection of that logical distinction into a historical
process had a strong influence on subsequent thought. Hegel
gave support to the antiromantic concept of a dichotomy
between the Ignoble Savage, all sense-consciousness, and Civilized Man, all self-conscious spirit. Primitive and civilized were
the two extremities of a scale by which man was measured
according to deficiency or proficiency in Western conceptual
systems. Hegel's insistence that the logical processes that
constituted his phenomenology of mind were duplicated in the
history of human culture straightened the vagrant path of
history into a broad upward highway leading to the apex of
Western philosophical thought. Scientific principles discovered,
forgotten, and rediscovered two millenia later have no place in
his linear progress. Nor is there recognition that purely abstract

This chapter appeared in *Arion*, n.s. 1/2 (1973/1974): 219-274.

thought has never been the possession of any but the smallest minority of the population at any time in any culture — it has, in fact, always aroused venomous hostility, whether in the time of Socrates, Galileo, or Einstein. Modern structural anthropology is only now learning to uncover the workings of the human mind which Hegel's confusion between logical and historical development had done much to conceal.

Hegel's influence is clearly discernible in the work of Prof. Bruno Snell whose book, *Die Entdeckung des Geistes,* has had a wide reception as much among educated readers as among classical scholars. Snell, continuing the kind of philosophical anthropology Hegel initiated, undertook to demonstrate the evolution in Greek literature from primitive sense-consciousness to self-conscious knowledge; to document, in short, the development of that *Geist* Hegel had broadly adumbrated.[1] In such an evolution Homer, prior in time, is the primitive sense-consciousness whose words for the mind denote physical organs, or functions of those organs, rather than the intellectual concepts they came to signify in later Greek.

Snell builds his interpretation of the Homeric *Weltanschauung* by examining first the words describing vision in Homer. There are words for many different kinds of vision, aspects and qualities of vision, but no single word "to refer to the function of sight as such."[2] The situation is analogous, Snell finds, in the vocabulary pertaining to the parts of the body. Once again, there are words in Homer for individual organs and the discrete parts of the body but no words for the living body as a whole. Snell sees in Geometric art, which represents the human body as a set of articulated muscles and joints, a corroboration of his view that Homer has no conception of the body as an organic unity. Snell argues for the comparable situation in Homer's concept of soul or mind (*Seele* and *Geist*). In Homer, the functions of our abstract construct, soul, are distributed among the various "organs" of emotional and intellectual activity. Homer has words for various kinds of mental activity, words like *thymos, noos, psyche,* but he had no single word to embrace all the mental functions under one head

(Snell's case appears stronger in German than in English since there is no entirely satisfactory equivalent in English for Hegel's or Snell's all-inclusive *Geist*). Although Snell avoids the distinction between *abstract* and *concrete* as being subject to question, he makes a similar distinction: between particular and general, between articulation and synthesis. Homer, Snell believes, knows the parts but not the whole; modes of vision but not vision; parts of the body but not body; parts of the soul but not soul.

Snell's premises invite immediate questions. If it is true that *soma* is used in Homer only of the corpse but never of the living body, we may wonder why Homer should have had the generic term for the dead body but not for the living. We may also question whether the modern child's drawing of a human figure as one small circle balanced on a larger one, with sticklike protuberances for limbs (as illustrated in Snell's first chapter), represents unity of the body more truly than the Geometric representation of musculature and joints. The child's drawing sees only external shape, and rather poorly at that, but the Geometric picture sees the internal structure that molds external shape. The child sees only surface; the Geometric artist sees inner construction.[3]

These questions aside, we may grant that Homer and Socrates could not have participated in a dialogue on *psyche,* any more than Homer could discuss spectrometry with a modern physicist. It is well to have Snell's demonstration that Homer and Plato, in using such words as *noos* or *psyche,* are not talking of identical substances. We may grant too, and with pleasure, that Homer is sense-conscious (though Snell surely underestimates the degree of self-consciousness in Homer). That the Homeric soul is different from the Platonic soul, that it is somewhat shallower, less resonant perhaps, less stable than its nineteenth-century Judaeo-Christian equivalent, is a fact of cultural history we can face without dismay. The nineteenth-century European soul, after all, suffered a quick extinction in twentieth-century literature, shattered into a thousand shards in Proust's and Joyce's ephemerides of human nature. "The threadbare glomerate of compulsions" is how Djuna Barnes has an Irish Catholic character define the soul in her novel *Nightwood* in 1937. But to define, as Snell does, Homer's mental orientation as one that sees the phenomena without grasping the principles underlying the phenomena leads to implications that are serious for Homeric criticism. If Homer discerns only multiplicity but never unity even in physical phenomena, can there be in Homer the conception of something as abstract as *poiesis?*[4]

Snell's view, quite unrelated as it is to Parry's formulaic studies, yet provides a certain kind of confirmation of Parry's theory. As Parry believed that Homer composed by parataxis – free-floating formula attached to formula, stitched together rather than woven – so Snell suggests that Homer thinks in parataxis – parts attached to parts rather than organically related. Snell's view reinforces in the intellectual sphere Parry's conclusions in the technical sphere of poetic composition. For both, Homer is Paratactic Man.[5]

Modern studies in structural anthropology and in the symbolic nature of language have made the dichotomy between primitive and civilized seem overly simplistic. There is no culture so primitive that it has not its own, often highly intricate and inclusive, generic categories. Even if Hegel's historical evolution is a fact, and Homer primarily sense-conscious, to treat Homer as merely the primitive on that evolutionary ladder is to ignore the intellectual concepts by which Homer organizes sense data into coherent systems. Homer's picture of the world, as Snell sees it, is vivid but chaotic, the Homeric mind a passive receptor of external impressions, incapable of imposing any structure on those impressions. That view is inevitable if Homer is graded according to his understanding of the Platonic conception of body and soul.

Snell attempts to penetrate Homeric thought by looking at Homeric vocabulary without preconceptions derived from subsequent development of the language. The result, in Snell's study, is a vivid re-creation of certain aspects of Homeric thought such as the modes of vision. To concentrate exclusively on isolated words, however, produces an erroneous impression since, in fact, Homer is being judged according to his understanding of later general concepts. The assumption is that the only vehicle for concepts or categories is the individual word. We need rather to examine complexes of words to find the ways in which they relate to each other, and thus to find in their relations the general concepts. We may say that the Platonic *psyche* does not exist for Homer, yet there may be in Homer an apparatus that bears some resemblance to the Platonic *psyche*, although no single term like *psyche, noos,* or *thymos* may adequately represent that apparatus. By putting aside at first questions of linguistic (or philosophical) evolution, traced through selected words, and by using instead some of the structural techniques of modern anthropology, we may achieve a fuller view of the principles by which Homer (or Homeric man) attempts to impose unity on the flux of phenomena.

Homer expresses himself through detail and concrete image; his world is exterior, not interior. Most assuredly his is a sense-conscious mind. Yet it is a mind that has imposed unity through categories, particularly through structural relationships. The Olympian deities, to whom have been allotted both regions and operations of the world, are the clearest example of such structure realized in visible form. Their existence in itself is sufficient evidence of the symbolic nature of Homeric thought and, furthermore, of the unity the Homeric mind has imposed on the phenomena. But they are at the apex of Homeric structures. We need imaginative excavation at a lower level to discern the way detail in Homer is a manifestation of invisible principles.

The Homeric notations of time and space exemplify the visual imagination and that subjective quality with which the imagination invests them. Time is not an abstract, homogenous continuum but subjective experience, though not, for that reason, private confusion. Homer's temporal notations carry a wealth. of associations related to communal life, to daily human activity, and to the changing aspects of nature. In grammatical terms, time is still more adjectival than adverbial; temporal duration of a man's activity is an attribute of the man himself in such adjectives as παννύχιος, πανημέριος, "night-long," and "day-long." Time is measured in visible tokens: the progress of the sun during the day, the parallel progress of the stars by night (*Ody.* 14.483), the change of season, the human duties appropriate to those moments and seasons.

In lines moving in their simplicity, Achilleus says to Lykaon in the *Iliad* (21.111-113): "Someone will come upon me, it may be at the first light of dawn, or in afternoon's lengthening shadow, or in the fierce glare of noonday sun, and with Ares' help, with spear or speeding arrow, will rend my *thymos* from me." The context adds a particular resonance to the passage. Achilleus, implacable in his revenge, has only scorn for the warrior who is ignorant of the nature of war. With himself as paradigm, he attempts to give Lykaon the ideal of a heroism that comes with knowledge.

The lines, have, however, an intensity quite apart from what they gain at the particular moment in the drama. Even in themselves they are rich, almost beyond translation, because the three time notations are filled with concrete associations. Morning, noon, and night are three kinds of external phenomena and three corresponding kinds of inner experience. Dawn is a goddess arising from sleep, scattering rose petals across the sky, bringing light to gods and men, going as a herald before the Sun. Midday, *meson ēmar,* is that moment of equilibrium between Sun's slow ascent to midheaven and his downward path towards Ocean. Afternoon, *deile,* is the Sun's now faster descent, the lengthening of shadows, oxen unloosed from their weary labors, hungry judges arising from their seats of justice to make their way home to dinner after a day of litigation in the agora, a woodcutter with aching arms preparing his dinner on the mountainside. In the context of the *Iliad* these moments have special associations. Morning is the expectancy of battle, the hope of victory; midday is battle at its fiercest, hottest and brightest, battle, like the Sun, hanging in the balance, in apparent equilibrium – Homeric wars are never won or lost at noon – and afternoon is battle quickly running to a halt for another day. Each of the three moments, or better, seasons, has a joy peculiar to it. Translated into experience, Achilleus' words run: "Perhaps as I go out to another battle in glad expectation of victory, perhaps it will be in the melee of battle as I strain every muscle under the burning sun, or perhaps just as the armies separate for another night, then death will seize me." Death will come suddenly, but whenever it comes it will be when Achilleus is in the midst of life, whether his feeling be anticipation, exhilaration, or relief.

Time is not measured, however, only in momentary experience. Time can be measured in the larger blocks of nine-day periods, twelve-day periods, seventeen-day periods. These blocks of time occur rarely in the *Iliad* and when they appear they signify a period when events are held in abeyance. Expressions for numbered days are far more common in the *Odyssey,* and in that poem during the sea voyages, where normal human activities are no longer present to register time. On land, numbered days mark a waiting period; at sea, they are a measurement of space. To cross the sea is, in Homeric language, to measure it (*Ody.* 3.179); landmarks at sea are measured off in days.

Fränkel has seen in the Homeric use of the word *day* in such expressions as "day of freedom" or "day of slavery" the beginnings of the concept of an abstract sense of time.[6] There are, however, two temporal abstractions in Homer — one Fränkel dismisses, the other he ignores. The word ὥρη, which Fränkel does not discuss, represents a thoroughly abstract concept. Liddell-Scott Jones gives a misleading impression of the word by listing its first meaning as (*a*) calendar season, particularly spring, and its extended meaning as (*b*) *kairos,* the appropriate time for a particular action. The development is surely in the reverse direction. It begins as a term of general applicability to any set of events. Any point of time can be ὥρη in Homer: there is a *hora* for sleep, a *hora* for telling stories (*Ody.* 11.379), a *hora* for dinner (*Ody.* 14.407), a *hora* for marriage. *Hora* is not so much a point on a continuum as the simultaneous conjunction of several discrete factors. It is not time but timing, or timeliness. From its meaning as timeliness in the most general sense one particular kind of timeliness is singled out: spring (ὥρη εἰαρινή) is the season *par excellence;* it becomes, simply, ὥρη.

Underlying the lexicon's differentiation of ὥρα into a primary meaning of a fixed period or calendar season and a secondary meaning of appointed time are two assumptions about primitive thought: it is implicit in the lexicon that more general meanings develop from the concrete and that "spring" is the concrete and therefore the basic meaning of ὥρα. Homeric language indicates the contrary development. *Hora* is first a general concept, that moment when a variety of things function in unison, and then it can be applied to specific conjunctions, such as spring. The Horai who are the doorkeepers of Olympos in Homer (*Il.* 5.749; 8.393, 433) clearly are "Timeliness." We may call them goddesses of the seasons, but only if we understand seasons in the most general sense, as opportune moments. Hesiod's names for the Horai, Eunomia, Dike, and Eirene, are harmonious with Homer's Horai as thoroughly abstract concepts, of which the annual seasons are one specific application.

The movement, then, is from general structure to specific occasion. Even then, it is probably erroneous to consider spring something concrete for Homeric man. Spring is a concrete reality to the scientist who can define it precisely in astronomical terms as beginning at the moment when the sun crosses the equator. Prior to scientific understanding of the earth's rotation, spring is the general term to cover the conjunction of many discrete events. Spring is lengthening days, shorter nights, the sun moving northwards, animals mating, plants in flower, the return of migratory birds. Other seasons are also conjunctions of many processes, but none seems to explode with such energy, variety, and rapidity as spring. If *hora* is *kairos,* spring is *kairos* magnified and made most conspicuous. *Hora,* we can conclude, is one abstract concept of time in Homer. It is significant that *hora* appears most often in the *Odyssey,* a poem in which judicious timing is of the utmost importance.[7]

If *hora* is time when everything happens concurrently, *chronos* is close to the opposite. *Chronos* in Homer, as Fränkel rightly notes, has not the full range of meanings it acquires in later Greek; it is restricted to specialized contexts where it signifies duration of time.[8] It is time in which nothing happens, or at least nothing that can register passage of time. But the word is important as indicative of Homer's mode of thinking. Homer does possess this word for time more abstract than the word *day,* but it is a word he reserves for situations lacking all subjective or natural coordinates. His visual imagination clocks an event by relating it to another event in nature or man's daily habits; when such relations fail he falls back on *chronos.* *Chronos* is time without character since it is temporal space emptied of all visible relationships.

As with time, so with space. Space is not a linear continuum divisible into miles and furlongs, or stadia and parasangs, but a nexus of visual activities. Distance is measured by its relation to human experience. It is an unladen ship cutting through the sea daylong under full sail, a man's shout across the water, a day's ploughing, a mule team outpacing plodding oxen, a loom's shuttle at a woman's breast, a ship's mast, the cast of a herdsman's staff. The greatest distance possible Homer expresses in the proportion: Agamemnon's glory is as widely dispersed beneath the sky as the city was great which he destroyed (*Ody.* 9.264-5). Or, as a variant for global distance, Zeus assures Poseidon that the extension of his glory will parallel the dispersion of the light of *eos,* that is, it will spread throughout the world (*Il.* 7.458). These are the direct pictographic linear measurements similar to the pictographic representations of time.

There are other spatial terms of greater significance in Homeric thought since they cluster into more important categories. The terms for human orientation in the world, the expressions of direction, influence every aspect, every gesture, one might say, of Homeric life. As concrete as the linear measurements, they are yet filled with what we should call a more symbolic significance since they serve as an abstract schema of man's relationship to his universe.

The obvious directions are right and left, front and back. If we should ask Homer what he meant by *front* ($\pi\rho\delta\sigma\sigma\omega$) he would give us a catalogue thus: Dawn arising and casting her first light, Sun climbing into the heavens, morning, choral dances, life, *and the past.* His catalogue for behind ($\delta\pi\ell\sigma\sigma\omega$) would be the opposite: Sun descending into Ocean, disappearance of light, mist, Hades' realm, Tartaros, *and the future.* Life in front, death behind. The only good thing behind is Zephyros, the wind that blows your ship from the west to the east. Homer might well be astonished at the paucity of our conceptual thought which sees no direct connection between the disparate phenomena of a compass point, sunset, mist, darkness, death, and the future, when his *zophos* subsumes them all under a single category. To explain that our thought distributes compass points, death, and temporal progression into separate categories might not convince him of the superiority of our logical systems.[9]

It was Durkheim who first grasped the importance of polarity as the organizing principle of primitive thought.[10] G. E. R. Lloyd has drawn on such studies in his own analysis of oppositions in early Greek thought. He has recognized pervasive duality, shown in such pairs as male/female, right/left, darkness/light, in Homer and Hesiod, but his main concern has been with oppositions within the philosophical systems of the pre-Socratics and their successors.[11] Lloyd touched on only a few expressions in the early poets, but it is possible to see that the bipolar structure is far more comprehensive in Homer than he considered it.

The interpretation of the sociological school has been that societies have not deduced polarity first from nature but have rather created mental categories of opposition into which aspects of nature have then been fitted. The clearest exposition of this theory is in the study Durkheim's pupil Robert Hertz made of the value systems expressed in many societies in the opposition between the right hand and the left.[12] There may be a slight physiological predominance of the right hand over the left, but such predominance, Hertz claims, cannot account for the wealth of physical, moral, and religious associations subsumed under the opposition of right and left. Instead, it is because societies have already imposed a dichotomy that they, by sanctions and tabus of various sorts, impose that dichotomy in the particular instance of right and left. The sociologists would trace polarity back to dualist social organization or to primeval distinctions between sacred and profane. Neither of these original causes seems adequate for early Greek thought. We have no evidence of an original dualist social organization and although sacred and profane certainly yield one of the important oppositions in Greek thought, for almost any polar opposition we can discern deities presiding at both poles: Gaia and Ouranos are both sacred, to balance Zeus on Olympos there is Hades in the underworld. It is easier to defend the opposition of contraries as a principle derived from nature. Male/female, night/day, and summer/winter are immediately accessible oppositions. Need we suppose a hypothetical social organization as the primal dichotomy when real dichotomies are so visible in nature?[13]

Whatever the original impulse, it is clear that Homeric man sees the world through the structure of polarity and that for this structure the sun is his most definitive guide. The sun is his great measuring rod whose course measures time and divides space. From the character of the sun and its movement the whole of terrestrial space achieves definition. The sun's circuit creates polarities, but also relates them to each other. Its daily appearance, first, yields the primary opposition between *eos* and *zophos*. *Eos* and *zophos* are directions, but they are not equivalent to our compass points east and west and they express far more than mere compass points. They shape the world into a nexus of oppositions; our discrete sets of contraries, east and west, north and south, above and below, up and down, are all contained within the contrasting terms *eos* and *zophos*.

Eos herself is more than pretty conceit. She herself is a component, or rather several components of the sun which have been separated from the sun, hypostatized into a separate personification, and then related back to the sun. As the region of the sun's first appearance she is a spatial direction, the east. She is also a temporal direction, the morning, as her epithet *erigeneia* may suggest. *Eos erigeneia* is light first coming into being, she who appears first. Then her light is split into components that are harmonized by being related to her as her attributes. Her saffron robe is, as the ancients understood, the somewhat more somber first dawn, when day and night are still scarcely differentiated; her fingers of rose are daylight spreading and increasing in intensity. She is the forerunner of the day, heralding him on his way, imitating by anticipation his every step. Not only at the first break of day but throughout the whole day she accompanies the sun, scattering light ahead of him. The Homeric notation for the period from dawn to noon, "while it was *eos* and sacred day increased" (*Ody.* 9.56 et al.), suggests that *eos* climbs into the heavens and increases with the sun. Her dancing floors (*choroi, Ody.* 12.4) suggest movement also, in particular her variable movement as she accompanies the north-south progress of the sun through the year.

Eos precedes the sun spreading light ahead of him. He, in a picture suggestive of the Ionian lords trailing their long chitons, trails darkness as a robe behind him across the ploughlands (*Il.* 8.486) – a picture that makes it clear that darkness descends first in the east. As in movies in which the process of sunrise and sunset is speeded up, Homeric light is light visibly in motion except at the stillness of midday. It radiates outwards ahead of the sun and is gathered up behind it. Homer's relation of the sun to its light displays an acute observation of many particulars of natural phenomena, but they are particulars woven into harmony with each other by being transposed into the social dynamics of aristocratic society, in the figure of the sun proceeding on his lordly way, heralded by the goddess of light, and trailing a garment of darkness behind him.

Zophos is not as fully realized as *eos.* It is more a shadowy kind of substance than a person. [14] It is the exact contrary of *eos:* the region into which the sun and its light descends and eventually disappears. *Eos* is a rising, *zophos* a descent; *eos* is bright, *zophos* is murky; *eos* is movement, *zophos* stillness; *eos* sheds light, *zophos* encloses and hides it. *Zophos* is the sum of the attributes of the sun as it descends from its noontime meridian to its western disappearance.

North and south play no part in Homer as separate zones. There are really only two regions in Homeric space: the region of sun and dawn and the opposite region of sunset and darkness. Only between these does Homer draw his contrasts. [15] The Ethiopians inhabit the two extremities of the earth, some living at the setting of the sun, the others at its rising (*Ody.* 1.24). Odysseus, to indicate total geographical disorientation, says (*Ody.* 10.190-192): "We do not know where either *zophos* is or *eos;* neither where the light of the sun descends beneath the earth nor where it rises" (cf. *Ody.* 8.29). J. Cuillandre has argued that πρὸς ἠῶτε ἠέλιόν τε in Homer must mean not only the eastern point of rising of the sun but the whole terrestrial space that receives the sun's rays, namely, the zone that lies beneath and south of the sun's circuit. He reads πρὸς ἠῶ τε ἠέλιόν τε as the whole southern region extending from the eastern sunrise to the western sunset. [16] *Zophos* he interprets as the northern region extending from western sunset to eastern sunrise. *Zophos* is, as the west, that into which the sun descends, but when Odysseus sails towards Hades' realm he puts ashore on Kimmerian land "where the sun's rays never penetrate, neither when it rises into starry heaven nor when it turns from heaven towards earth, but perpetual night is stretched out over wretched mortals" (*Ody.* 11.16-19). This is clearly a description of the northern zone of earth, but we know from elsewhere in Homer that the dead descend beneath *zophos* (*Il.* 23.51; *Ody.* 20.356); *zophos* is also, therefore, the region where the sun's rays never penetrate.

Cuillandre's study has the advantage of presenting a coherent system of Homer's spatial orientation derived from the very obvious phenomenon of the sun. It is worth noting, in corroboration of Cuillandre's thesis, that the sun can supply three cardinal points from its circuit: its appearance, its noontime meridian, and its disappearance give an east, a south, and a west. North is the one cardinal point for which the sun offers no assistance. The northern region is defined by a wholly negative relationship to the sun and is characterized by the absence of sun, exactly as Homer describes the land of the Kimmerians: the land beyond the reach of the sun, whether in its rising or in its setting. Before the invention of compasses the only pointers for the fourth cardinal point were the stars, "the Bear which revolves around the same point and does not share in the baths of Ocean" (*Ody.* 5.274-5). Cardinal north is a night-time discovery. In one of those pleasing coincidences of nature, north, the one point not described by daytime pointers, except in a negative way, is also the one point most exactly described by night-time pointers. Homeric practice shows this to be no idle formulation. Homeric man orients himself by day according to the two solar directions, πρὸς ἠῶ τε ἠέλιόν τε and ζόφος, but when the sun disappears at night his eyes turn northward to orient him by the stellar constellations circling around the celestial pole. Kalypso gives Odysseus a set of three pointers by which to steer his ship: the Pleiades, Boötes, and the Great Bear (*Ody.* 5.272-275). Pleiades and Boötes would give a roughly east-west axis, but since Boötes would set shortly after the rise of Pleiades the most exact pointer would be the Bear as north.[17]

The zones are not fixed, absolute points any more than our terms east and west. They are always relative to the observer. When Odysseus leaves Hades' realm, rowing at first since no Zephyros is strong enough to carry you eastward from the furthest extremity of *zophos,* he soon reaches Kirke's island, "where are the palace and dancing floors of early-appearing Dawn and the ascensions of the Sun" (*Ody.* 12.1-3). We need not understand by this description that Odysseus has arrived in the western Aegean, unless we suppose that Homeric mariners always took their compass reading with Lakedaimon or Mykenai as center. For a person sailing from Hades' realm, the western rim of the world, any island he reaches will be in the east. Odysseus sails from darkness to light, from night to morning, death to life; more simply, from *zophos* to *eos.* When Odysseus arrives at Kirke's island he is back in the realm of day.

Even with a magnetic north and reliable compasses our own terms for compass directions are notoriously confused because they accumulate connotations in which geography is mingled with historical fact and social prejudice. For the citizen of Los Angeles, to go East is to visit New York, but to visit Japan in the opposite direction is to travel to the Orient, or to the Far East. The West for him is Europe, and the Western tradition a diachronic line drawn from Jerusalem through Athens, Rome, Los Angeles, and extending somewhere in the Pacific Ocean. By a set of historical accidents reinforced by prejudice the compass directions of his ordinary speech will on occasion be true to the compass, and on other occasions will turn diametrically counter to the true compass readings for his longitude. But the Angeleno lives comfortably enough in a world where east is sometimes east, sometimes west, where west is sometimes west, sometimes east. We have yet to see a study of Homeric geography that recognizes, as a first principle, the discrepancy between our compasses and our language, even in this age of science.

Homer's *eos* and *zophos* are not as abysmally off course as our east and west. When an American uses the word *west* it is quite impossible to know which direction he means; only context can reveal his meaning. Homer has to reckon neither with a spherical earth nor with a history of demographic dispersion around that sphere. His world is the Mediterranean and his terms are directly related to the visible phenomena in that limited area. There is a consistency in his usage that is lacking in ours. On the other hand, Homer's terms are complex because they systematize a large body of communal experience. It is no argument, for example, against the authenticity of *Odyssey* 11 that it makes no reference to a descent to Hades' world, whereas elsewhere in Homer Hades is situated beneath the earth. *Zophos* is the region of settings; it is both westerly and downward. If one follows a course towards *zophos* one will eventually descend. The associations of the word are varied, and no poet is obliged to stop and explain them on any given occasion. Another fact that contributes to the difficulty of interpretation is that Homeric terms are not points like our cardinal points but relationships to the sun (and to other visible phenomena). When we are told that the Ethiopians live πρὸς ζόφον and πρὸς ἠῶ τε ἠέλιόν τε, we can accept that as generally equivalent to our east and west. But a bird of omen flies πρὸς ἠῶ τε ἠέλιόν τε, literally towards the sun and the light. That might mean simply counterclockwise — against the sun, as people said before they had clocks — or clockwise from west (or north) to east, or clockwise from east to south. Unfortunately, no passage in Homer will solve the problem definitively. Hektor's words at *Iliad* 12.239-240 read like a definition of good and bad omens, but comprehensive as they are they offer no clarification. In fact, they compound the difficulty by adding ἐπὶ δεξιά and ἐπ' ἀριστερά, another two terms we know from our own culture to be heavy with cultural prejudice.[18]

The quest for Odyssean geography is a classic example of the difficulties inherent in assuming that Homer's compass is directly translatable into ours. Not that Homer's geography is purely fanciful or purely "spiritual." Odysseus visits fabulous peoples, but they are peoples set in real places to which Odysseus is driven by real winds across definable distances. His is a journey plotted on the map of reality yet difficult for us to reproduce, since Homer's sextant describes some angles that are roughly equivalent to ours, some that are the diametrical opposite, and others that no modern sextant can describe.

Scientific instruments, collaborating with scientific logic to refute our senses, supply an objective center that exerts a gravitational pull on our imaginations. However much our senses insist that the sky is revolving, we train ourselves to align our idiosyncratic experience along the astrolabe of science until, by habit and act of will, we come to believe that the visible motion of the heavens from east to west is the reverse image of the true terrestrial motion from west to east. For Homer, his senses and his logic are his only astrolabe, one that exerts no deviant force on thought as do modern instruments. The Homeric world, shaped by imagination, is not polarized into logical conceptions and visual impression: σώζειν τὰ φαινόμενα becomes a matter of urgency only when logic and the phenomena begin to diverge into apparently contradictory directions. In Homeric imagination both are in harmony with each other.

Homeric imagination, first dissecting external space along a polar axis to apportion the physical world within two zones, *eos* and *zophos,* then continues, by its own logic, to invest everything within those zones with the character of the sun as it appears in them. The region of *eos* draws its character from what happens in it. It is the region from which one takes one's orientation, therefore the front, the region of rising, of beginnings, of brightness, activity, vigor, joy. The region of *zophos* has the opposite character. It lies behind and below; it is murky, damp, mist-enshrouded, the region of settings and endings. Skylla's cave is πρὸς ζόφον and like *zophos* is mist-enshrouded (ἠεροειδές, *Ody.* 12.80-81). Kirke's pleasant isle lies near the dancing floors of *eos* and the ascensions of the sun. Odysseus' rapid return from Hades' realm to Kirke's island makes for a pointed contrast between western gloom and eastern light. Ithaka, as Odysseus tells his Phaiakian hosts, lies *pros zophon,* in fact it is the furthest island out towards *zophos;* it lies very low, literally close to the ground, while its neighbors lie toward the light and the sun — πρὸς ἠῶ τε ἠέλιόν τε (*Ody.* 9.25-26). It is isolated not only from the mainland but from its neighboring islands, as its royal house is somewhat isolated from the heroic mainstream. The ruggedness and isolation of the island are characteristic tokens of its westwardness. There is, for Telemachos, something of the same contrast between Sparta and Ithaka as there is for Odysseus between the underworld and Kirke's island (cf. van Leeuwen on Phaiakia). For Telemachos, Sparta is the very pinnacle of paradise. When he arrives, Sparta is the scene of great festivity; a marriage is being celebrated with banqueting, music and song, and tumblers dancing their accompaniment. The brilliant sheen of gold, silver, and bronze, the gleam of amber and ivory, the luxurious style of his bath and fresh robes make Telemachos suspect he has entered the palace of Zeus himself. His low-lying, obscure, little western island is, as Telemachos admits, rather a dour place by contrast. He compares the spaciousness and fertility of Sparta with the small area and barrenness of Ithaka. The soil of Ithaka is rugged goat pasture; it has no wide meadows for horse rearing nor open spaces for race courses. It is, in short, an unsuitable locale for heroic pastimes. Of all the islands lying in the sea, Telemachos ruefully confesses, it is the least well equipped for the gracious life. Even gifts to Ithakans must be small, scaled down to western topography (*Ody.* 4.600-608).

By yet a further extension, human character also is shaped by the character of the space it inhabits. Kirke is an eastern enchantress, with voice and ways as beguiling as her locale. Helen, for Telemachos coming from his rude western island, is an eastern enchantress too, as beguiling as Kirke. Ithakans are, by contrast, tough and resilient. Odysseus is gifted with powers of endurance and an intelligence to compensate for the natural gifts a hero like Achilleus possesses from birth. His is the success story of the self-made man; self-made because he learns to become, by wit and determination, what others are by birth. A product of discipline and training, he is a true native son of the western isles.

The description of Aiolos on his island presents a different kind of geographical situation, but it is an excellent example of the harmony of man and locale. The episode at his palace reveals how concrete detail links with detail to manifest something quite abstract. Aiolos is, notes Stanford, a "*Significant Name* for the ruler of the veering, swift winds," since the name embodies the nature of that which he rules.[19] The island's name, Aiole, is equally significant. "We came," says Odysseus, "to Changeful [Changeable, Changing] Island, where lived Changeful [Changeable, Changing], son of Hippotas" (*Ody.* 10.1-2). It is more than name as symbol, the island's nature reproduces its name: it is a floating island — πλωτῇ ἐνὶ νήσῳ (v. 3). The invisible is made visible in the form of an island shifting in accordance with the dominance of now one wind, now another. The transformation of abstract essence into concrete reality does not stop at the physical location and mobility of the island. Everything that happens on the island continues the dramatic representation. The six sons given in marriage to the six daughters of Aiolos, coming together in the palace for daily feasting, imitate the winds issuing from their respective poles and converging at the center. The winds are further realized in smells, sounds, and sights: savory smells rising from the palace, the moaning of flutes around the palace by day and the sudden stillness at night, these are the effects of wind in poetic image.

The king in his behavior is no less true to his name than the island he rules. One day he sends Odysseus on his way with a favoring West Wind to hold him straight on course for Ithaka. Ten days later, when Odysseus returns to the same spot — as he must if the winds are unloosed, since Aiole is where all winds converge — now a victim of those forces that Aiolos controls, Aiolos kicks him out of the house as a man accursed. One day Aiolos is a kindly Zephyros; the next a blustering Boreas.

A shifty king ruling a shifting island is a touch of Homeric humor, but there is more than verbal pun on *aiolos*. It is not even a question of metaphor. Rather, the behavior of the winds is observed with accuracy and felt so vividly that it finds expression in all correlative phenomena. In a few lines (vv. 1-75) Homer gives us much information about the nature of the winds and the effect of their counteraction on each other, although it is not information programmed in our terms. Homer could not give us as a formula that variable forces intersect at a variable focus, but that is the formula incorporated in his diagram. Furthermore, as Homer transposes the visible phenomena of sun and sunlight into the forms of his aristocratic society, in the stately procession of Sun and Dawn, so he transposes the phenomena of the winds first into a literal geography and then into social forms, in the persons of the king and his twelve children in whom is blended normal human character with the aspects of the phenomena they represent. The king and his children are totally human personifications, or so it seems at first glance. As authorities over the winds they live out their lives as Homeric aristocrats, enjoying daily banquets in their palace. In the capricious character of the king, however, in the closed society of his court, which neither loses nor gains any members but merely transfers them *in perpetuo,* and in that society's symmetrically incestuous marriage structure, we see the attributes of the winds. Aiolos and his court have the trappings of human society, the palace, the feasts, the entertainment, the hospitality, but they are only trappings for at a deeper level their institutions reveal a society impossible in the human world. Such blending of the natural phenomena with purely human social structure, a blending particularly common in the *Odyssey* where nature plays a large part, often disguises the sharp observation and the logic on which Homeric interpretation of reality rests.[20]

* * * * * *

The sun not only gives the two poles in space but acts itself as Homer's magnetic pole upon man's behavior. Man's daily schedule conforms to the rhythm of the sun. Man too has his daily rising and setting, his increase of strength to midday and his waning strength after midday. In the *Iliad* the progress of the war is several times an explicit imitation of the pattern of the sun's movement. "As long as Helios bestrode midheaven," says the poet, "the weapons fell on both armies and the people fell. But when Helios turned towards ox-loosening, then were the Achaeans gaining the advantage" (*Il.* 16.777-780). When Helios has one foot on each side of heaven the battle hangs in the balance, with weapons falling indiscriminately on each side. The moment Helios loses his balance the battle too loses its balance and begins to turn in the Greeks' favor. The parallel equilibrium of sun and battle at midday is given even sharper focus in another variant (*Il.* 8.66-74): "While it was light (*eos*) and sacred day increased, weapons fell on both armies, killing the people. But when Helios bestrode midheaven, then Zeus poised golden scales in which he put two fates, one of the Trojans, the other of the Greeks. He held the scales in suspension, and the day of fate descended for the Achaeans. The fates of the Achaeans sank down to nourishing earth while the fates of the Trojans rose up to broad heaven." In this passage the whole of the morning is the period of equivocal battle and noon is quite literally the moment of balance, the moment when parity must yield to disparity. Odysseus relates war to the two parts of the day, forenoon and afternoon, in the same way when he describes the battle between his sailors and the Kikonians (*Ody.* 9.56-59): As long as day was increasing, he says, his men held their ground, but when the sun turned towards ox-loosing the Kikonians routed them. In these expressions, and in the similar one which occurs before Agamemnon's *aristeia* (*Il.* 11.84ff.), morning is a period of tension that is resolved at noon. When the sun crosses the meridian there is a relaxation of energy on one side or the other and that side begins its descent.

The sun, however, is also the seasonal calendar. Its ascent and descent becomes an amplified visual representation of the whole annual cycle, of birth, growth, death, and eventual rebirth. The sun is the daily reminder of the process of the whole of nature. Thus still another set of oppositions is added to Homer's directions *eos* and *zophos*: *eos*, already synonymous with rising, that is, activity, now becomes synonymous with birth and life, and *zophos* synonymous with death. The poet can then say "As many as dwell ὑπ' ἠῶ τε ἠέλιόν τε as a periphrasis for the whole world of living men. To live is, in Homeric language, to look on the light of the sun. By contrast, humans at their death leave the light of the sun and descend, like the sun, beneath the *zophos*. When Odysseus goes to Hades' realm Teiresias asks him why he has left the light of the sun (*Ody.* 11.93) and the other shades are amazed that Odysseus has penetrated beneath the *zophos* while still alive, as if *zophos* were some sort of substance impenetrable except by noncorporeal shades. In Homeric cosmology "Hades received as his share of the world the murky *zophos*" (*Il.* 15.191). As Aiolos the shifty king is allotted the shifting island which reflects his nature, as Zeus is allotted the bright ether, so Hades, king of shades, rules that part of physical space which lies in shadow.

For all the multiplicity of detail, we can see in Homer's representation of space an attempt at systematization. Space is organized into the basic dichotomy, *eos* and *zophos*. That dichotomy subsumes many others: life and death, light and darkness, joy and sorrow, ascent and descent, mobility and rest. Space is thus invested with spiritual quality. External aspects of nature and the inner world of human experience function in indivisible harmony. Man's movement, his gesture even, is a declaration of that harmony between inner and outer. Gesture is space invoked, space imitated. Going eastward or westward, upward or downward, left or right, is a physical act, but an act significant of a person's character or emotion. It is because space has quality that we are entitled to find significance in Achilleus' gesture when he hurls the royal scepter to the ground and sits down himself (*Il.* 1.245-246) or to assert that when Agamemnon sits down to deliver his apology to Achilleus his posture is as important as his utterance (*Il.* 19.77).

Odysseus' father, Laertes, is the clearest example of orientation in space as an expression of psychological condition. His outward appearance is an alignment of both spirit and body along the appropriate axes in external space. Laertes has renounced the city, as Antikleia tells Odysseus, with the comforts of its beds and fine coverlets, and has retired to the fields (μίμνει ἀγρῷ, οὐδὲ πόλινδε κατέρχεται *Ody.* 11.187-188). Rags are his only clothes; the ashes of the fire his bed in winter. In autumn his bed is wherever he may be, any haphazard heap of leaves on the ground (*Ody.* 11.188ff.). In the autumn of his grief and old age he has moved both outward and downward. He has descended in every way, from the city to the fields, from beds to the ground. He has abdicated political authority and social order. He has exchanged riches for poverty, fine fabrics for ashes and leaves, growth for decay, order for dissolution. He has descended from the human level to the animal and even to the vegetable. Now one with the season's dying leaves, he is, like them, strewn on the ground, drifting at random in the wind. For us the autumn of life is metaphor and in Homer too spring and autumn are made metaphors for the progress of a man's life or the cycle of human generations. Here, in Antikleia's description, Laertes is metaphor personified. He has become Autumn, an embodiment, fully realized in all details, of the aspects and processes of the season of dissolution. An ember in a dying fire, a dry leaf spiralling at the rim of Homeric vision, Laertes is the political and moral dissolution in Ithaka since Odysseus' departure for Troy.

Antikleia's description of Laertes is a Homeric simile but for the lack of a word of comparison. Like a simile it blends the human figure entirely into its natural landscape. Had the poet said that Laertes had become like an animal finding warmth at the fire, or making its bed in the leaves under the open sky, the description would have been subject to analysis as another example of that sophisticated stylistic device, the simile. Since it occurs as a piece of naturalistic description it may receive passing notice on its touch of pathos, but its real importance, first for the method of Homeric thought and then for the *Odyssey* specifically, passes unnoticed. Laertes' location and mode of life are a graphic representation of old age and grief. His figure shows us, in the most literal way, what Homer means in his frequent expressions of the deterioration of the *menos* in old age, or the wasting of the spirit in grief. From his figure we can infer how Antikleia herself died a slow death of grief for Odysseus.

The solar season in Ithaka, as we shall have occasion to see (chap. 5), is the late autumn. The deterioration of conditions in Odysseus' absence mirrors the natural waning of the year and Laertes is the most expressive imitative metaphor both of the natural season and of the social condition. His person sums up, in a single dramatic image, the many tokens of loss of control and authority in Ithaka. It is interesting that Odysseus on his homeward journey is also assimilated to the season. When he is at sea the winds toss him about as the autumn wind gusts a burr across the plain (*Ody.* 5.328-330). The wind shivers his ship as it whirls a heap of dry chaff in all directions (5.368-370), and Odysseus is a fragment cast against the shore at Scheria. Once on land, like an animal in hibernation, he buries himself beneath the discarded leaves of autumn; as Homer says, he is like an ember that a man, living in isolation far from any neighbors, buries beneath the ashes at the boundary of his property (5.488-491). Throughout Odysseus' journey from Kalypso's island to Scheria the physical descriptions and the similes show Odysseus suffering the same kind of dissolution as Laertes. Like Laertes, Odysseus is scarcely an animate being but an object without control, at the mercy of the elements. Only at the end of Book 5, at his arrival in Scheria, is there an image that, though related to the description of Laertes, promises something more than the image of Laertes can promise. Odysseus hidden beneath the leaves is a "seed of fire," but Laertes is a dying ember. The "seed of fire" shows that winter can be not only death but also preservation and regeneration.

Homer's representation of abstracts, then, is like a nexus of relationships. Time is such a nexus, as is space, and the two are bound together in another nexus since they are both measured by the same phenomena, notably the sun. Homeric thought, seeing the whole natural world unified into a single complex of space and time, then attempts to have everything conform to that order. Aberrant or eccentric phenomena — winds, storms, earthquakes, lightning — are organized, first, each into its own miniature cosmos (as, for example, the cosmos of Aiolos) and then by relationship to the larger hierarchy of the Olympian deities whose province is the equilibrium of the whole. Homeric thought then integrates man into that order. Man, as a part of nature, is already of that order, but it is also his task to contribute to the maintenance of that order by imitation. Whether man structures nature with reproductions of his social forms, as Durkheim and his school have argued, or whether the situation is reversed and social forms are derived from nature, the important fact is that Homeric man *believes* that the natural order exists independent of man and man is but the copy of that external order.

Only when we understand that the external world is a coherent system for Homer, and that man is a microcosm by analogy, can we begin to talk of Homeric psychology.

Analogical thought is fundamental to Homer; it is through analogy that the various phenomena and experiences are attributed to one or the other of the polar oppositions. Even the simplest measurements are analogies. Two men running a close race fade into an image of a woman at the loom (*Il.* 23.760-763); the morning light is transferred into the image of a herald preceding her lord. The similes are the analogies that readers of Homer remember best, but they are only the most stylized example of a ubiquitous mode of thought.

Many signs point to the Homeric conception of the human being as a functioning unity. There is, first, the frequent association of the human life cycle with the cycle of nature. The human species, with its generations coming into being and passing away, mirrors the perennial continuity of nature, but the individual too progresses through his cycle of the seasons from spring to winter. The figure of Hermes as he appears to Odysseus on Kirke's island has all the attributes of spring; he is the youth with the first hint of a beard, in the season of freshest vitality (χαριέστατος ἥβη, *Ody.* 10.277-279). The verb ἡβάω is used once in the *Odyssey* of a flourishing vine, laden with fruit (5.69), and the noun ἥβη is used several times of persons, most frequently in the expressions ἥβης μέτρον ἵκεσθαι: to grow into full maturity. The *hebe* of a person is a point of time and a physiological state, the point of transition when the child blossoms into the adult and also the physical vigor manifested at that moment. Like *hora* it is the conjunction of many processes at a single moment.

If youth and first maturity are the spring season of a man's life, old age is, as we have seen in the case of Laertes, the autumn and winter. The aging process in man is a duplication of the process of withering and dissolution in nature. When Athena ages Odysseus she parches his skin, as weather parches the crops, and causes his hair to drop out (*Ody.* 13.398-99, 429-430).[21] Such phrases as ὀδὰξ ἐν χείλεσι φύντες or ἐν δ' ἄρα οἱ φῦ χειρί remind us of the constant Homeric propensity for visualizing in man's appearance or action a duplication of some aspect of the organic life around him.

When we come to Homer's anatomical vocabulary we find ourselves in difficulty, particularly as we try to define the seats of intellectual activity. We cannot even fix the location of the mental "organs." The *thymos,* when given a location, is generally described as being ἐν στήθεσσιν, but it is several times described as ἐν φρέσιν. The *etor* can be ἐν κραδίῃ, and the *noos* in the *thymos.* Once Andromache describes her *etor* as being in her mouth (*Il.* 22.452). Other, purely physical organs, do not float in and out of each other in this way. The instability of the mental apparatus suggests that we may not be dealing with physical organs at all but with something more abstract, something resembling mental orientation. In a word like *menos* the idea of mental orientation and a governing principle emerges clearly. *Menos* can mean simply physical strength (e.g., *Ody.* 21.426), but when Zeus breathes *menos* into Achilleus' horses to make them leave the corpse of Patroklos it is not strength he gives them. The horses have strength enough to stand solidly immovable against entreaties and the lash of the whip. The *menos* they receive from Zeus makes them willing to move. *Menos* here is a redirection of their will, a channeling of their energy into movement. It is a stimulant rather like *thymos.*

Thymos is perhaps the most complex mental word in Homer. It is located in the chest, or in the *phrenes,* or simply within (ἔνδοθι, *Il.* 22.242). It leaves a person (τὸν μὲν λίπε), or exits from his bones or his limbs. It can fall to the feet in terror (*Il.* 15.280). It can split into two within the *phrenes* when a person is in doubt. On one hand it functions as the receptacle of certain intellectual activity. A man can experience joy, anger, desire, and grief in the *thymos.* A man deliberates, smiles, admires, remembers, glares, recognizes, makes choices, gives answers in or with his *thymos.* A seer knows wise things in his *thymos* (*Il.* 12.228) or, like Helenos, can construct the plan of the gods in his thymos (*Il.* 7.44). A plan appears good in the *thymos* (*Ody.* 9.318); a man talks to his *thymos.* As an object, the *thymos* can be persuaded, can be eaten by weariness and grief, diminished or wasted by grief, filled or satiated with food, grief or weeping, can be storm-tossed, stirred up, melted, bewitched by *eros*. On the other hand the *thymos* is also something more active, a subject that orders, urges, hopes, restrains, flutters with anxiety, rejoices, exalts, forbids, has volition and daring, can be arrogant and intransigent, credulous or incredulous. It also functions in combination with other mental organs, commonly the *kradie*. *Thymos* and *kradie* together goad a man, or a man sees, knows something, or deliberates in his *thymos* and *kradie*.

Physical organs do not enjoy such versatility. A man's limbs are personified to the extent that they may rage for battle, but they do not ponder, express anger, joy, pride, achieve understanding, nor do they divide into two. Their function is simple and understood as simple. They move and their only experience is desire for movement or for rest. Animals possess *thymos* but their *thymos* shows no sign of possessing such an expressive range of experience as man's. One animal can rejoice or exult, another feel fear, but these elemental emotions cannot compare with the rich variety of man's *thymos*.

The error of most studies of the Homeric words for mental operations has been to treat them as in some way physical organs.[22] Parallels must be sought elsewhere. If we attempt a composite picture of the *thymos* derived from its various appearances and actions, what we find is not an organ at all but a *homunculus*. The *thymos* has the character of a man. It is pitiless or gentle; it suffers as a human suffers; it experiences emotions, is satiated or bewitched. It acts as a man acts; it hopes, boasts, orders, forbids, decides, dares, consults, believes. The visible models for the *thymos* are, thus, entirely human. It is a construct built from the observation of human activities and expressions and then projected inwards. Smiles, frowns, furrowed brows, groans, sighs of contentment, these are the stuff of the *thymos*. It may be a concrete entity in Homeric imagination, described in concrete images, but its function is abstract since it is a composite of all the facial gestures and bodily attitudes. It is the seat of the most varied, even contrary, expressions, the central locus where they are coordinated and directed, and from which they emerge to the surface.

Homer knows the function of physical organs, both the outer organs of sense, such as the eye or ear, and inner organs such as the stomach. Yet the *telos* of a physical activity never rests in these organs. Sensations travel through them, as if they were but channels, to penetrate to some deeper stratum, which Homer most commonly calls the *thymos,* but occasionally the *phrenes* or the *noos.* Hunger tears at the stomach, but the *thymos* prompts the stomach to hunger. Food and drink gratify not the stomach, or only secondarily the stomach, but primarily the *thymos,* the source of the stomach's original stimulation. Similarly, a word passes through the ear to the *thymos.* A person puts a word into his *thymos,* or even more significantly, *synthesizes* it in his *thymos.* On one occasion the *phrenes* assume this synthesizing function, when Penelope "put together the divine song of Phemios in her *phrenes*" (*Ody.* 1.328). Sight parallels hearing: the eyes may receive the image, but it passes through them to the *thymos,* which registers the image in some way that the eyes themselves cannot do. The *thymos,* far from being merely the locus for appetitive stimulation, is also the receptor, the governor, and the organizer of sensory data. It is the inner focal point of the total personality.[23]

The gods are, to some degree at least, a projection outwards of the human community, of individual characteristics and social intercourse. They represent the mind's power to discern human structures and magnify them in a form still more visible. When we look at the words for mental operations we see something of the same projection, but now inwards instead of outwards. Though the *thymos* and its congeners may be identified as organs, they are structures patterned first after the individual in all his actions, expressions, and feelings, and then after the social community. Homer may have had, in fact, an accurate knowledge of internal anatomy, but it is doubtful if he had a clear understanding of the workings of that anatomy.[24] It is reasonable to suppose that Homer would have drawn on whatever he knew of physiological mechanisms, but that he would have also looked to the external community for models that would help fill in where his knowledge was deficient.

Scholars who look for the single word that will express *soul* have failed to observe that the mental life of man is represented, in a shadowy and vaguer form certainly, as a replica of his social life.

The Homeric community is a hierarchy, but essentially a binomial one of kings who make decisions and their subordinates — followers, servants, and slaves, as for example Thersites who is permitted no say in the assemblies. Among the kings there is one acknowledged superior, but he is not the superior either in fighting ability or in planning; his superior authority is merely accepted. He is not a dictator. Decisions are formulated in council meetings and reached by something close to a consensus, marked by the general applause for the course the community will adopt. Within the rank of kings there is not much differentiation in personalities or skills. It is essentially a homogenous society, all are of equal rank and all are adept in the same skills. We have all developed for ourselves very clear portraits of the characters of Achilleus and Odysseus from the two Homeric poems, but it would be hard, in fact, to find cogent distinctions in the *Iliad* between Achilleus and Ajax, or Odysseus and Diomedes. Achilleus is the superior warrior, perhaps runs faster than others, and has an implacable pride; that is, he is an Ajax in extreme form. Odysseus is a better speaker than Achilleus, but Achilleus too was taught to be a speaker of words and a doer of deeds. Differentiation is within a stock of traditional heroic virtues which are the common possession. All have the qualities necessary for a warrior, but an individual might show some superiority over his peers in one or another particular. Since it is precisely around those slender differences that the two poems have been constructed, the effect is to render Achilleus and Odysseus as polar opposites. Polar opposites they are, but only within the circumscribed confines of Homeric aristocracy. They are the *thymos* and the *noos* of that homogenous, homonoetic community.

The individual intellect approximates that community. The words for the various intellectual parts are not exactly synonymous, but distinctions between them are difficult to define, at least within our linguistic system. The *ker*, like the *thymos*, can experience emotions; it can laugh, be weakened by grief, overcome with anger. Yet the *ker* seems a lesser version of the *thymos*, without its full range of activities, particularly the cognitive and deliberative aspects. *Noos* and *thymos* preside, it seems, over the hierarchy of mental organs. We can define *thymos* as emotion − though experience would better express its flexibility − and the *noos* as cognition, but we cannot insist on exclusivity any more than we can expect specialized division of labor among the Homeric kings. The *thymos* seems to perform almost every function of the *noos*, though the *noos* seems less able to duplicate the functions of the *thymos* or its subordinate, the *ker*. The *thymos* performs cognitive acts of knowing, deliberating, and evaluating, but the *noos* does not exhibit the emotional affects of the *thymos*. Possibly, as scholars have argued, the *thymos* takes over, as it were, the functions of the *noos* only when a strong element of emotion is present in the act of knowing or thinking. There is certainly some dichotomy between the *thymos* as the seat of passion and the *noos* as the seat of perception, but we may be led to posit a stronger dichotomy than actually exists, if we are influenced by the later development of the words, reinforced by the Latinate connection between motion and e-motion (see Snell's play on the words), and by a later anatomical theory which holds to an absolute differentiation of physical organs.[25]

If *thymos* and *noos* are Achilleus and Odysseus internalized, the other terms express the community around them. The *ker*, as we have seen, does much the same as the *thymos*. The *kradie* likewise. It is most often linked with the *thymos* and experiences the same kind of emotions. In the dichotomy between the *thymos* and the *noos* the *phrenes* are more closely aligned with the *noos*, having more to do with judgment than with passion. But demarcation in the functions of these various terms is as fluid as their bodily locations. The interchangeability of their functions and their frequent collaboration in experiencing certain sensations, making decisions, and initiating actions suggests that they are parts functioning in a harmonious whole.

No organ has become sufficiently individualized to become *Geist,* it is true (though *thymos* and *noos* at times come close to it). The *Geist* is rather the continuous collaboration of the various members of that interior society.[26]

If there is a harmony between the inner organs, that harmony becomes even clearer when we consider both the inner and outer organs together. At one point in the *Iliad* Poseidon comes to reinvigorate the two Ajaxes. He strikes them, with Homeric exactitude, both internally and externally, with words and with scepter, and fills them with *menos* (*Il.* 13.47-60). Their limbs become lighter, their hands above and their feet below. The one Ajax says to the other (vv. 73-75): "The *thymos* in my chest is more eager for battle; my feet below and my hands above strongly desire war." Telamonian Ajax answers (vv. 77-80): "Yes, the hands about my spear are eager, my *menos* surges, and beneath, with both my feet, I am impatient. I ache to do battle with savage Hektor." The poet than concludes (vv. 81-82): "So they spoke, exulting in the *charma* which the god had placed in their *thymos.*" A simple act of physiological renewal is treated in elaborate detail. The poet mentions first simple *menos* and the outer limbs. The Ajaxes talk of the *thymos* within reaching out for battle, their *menos* and their external limbs. Telamonian Ajax adds the *"I"* as a more comprehensive entity which feels the same desire as his limbs. Then the poet sums up all the sensations, inner and outer, the above and below, as expressions of a joy in the *thymos.* This kind of description, in which the sensations are first differentiated and localized and then related back to something like a central nervous system, is not that of a man who thinks only of the parts.[27]

The correspondence between a man's external limbs and his internal anatomy is commonly expressed in the opposite way, in the description of dissolution. "Do not tear your skin or waste away your *thymos* with weeping" Odysseus tells Penelope (*Ody.* 19.263). Mekistiades stripped the armor of Aisepos and Pedasos from their shoulders, loosed their *menos* and their limbs from below (*Il.* 6.27-28). It is in the descriptions of physiological dissolution, in fact, that we have the clearest representation of the living person as an organic whole. Andromache's panic and loss of consciousness at Hektor's death provides such a description rendered in explicit detail. Before she hears any news she is living her life in an orderly way; we come upon her weaving a garment (*Il.* 22.440-441). Then we are given a picture of progressive dissolution. In the first stage Andromache hears a wail and her composure is shattered; her limbs and organs no longer function as they should; she loses control. Her limbs are spun around and her hand drops the shuttle to the ground (v. 448). She tells her maids that her heart in her breast is palpitating, and palpitating, moreover, up in her mouth, and that her knees below have gone stiff (vv. 451-453):

$$\dot{\epsilon}\nu\ \delta'\dot{\epsilon}\mu o\grave{\iota}\ a\dot{\upsilon}\tau\hat{\eta}$$

$$\sigma\tau\acute{\eta}\theta\epsilon\sigma\iota\ \pi\acute{a}\lambda\lambda\epsilon\tau a\iota\ \mathring{\eta}\tau o\rho\ \dot{a}\nu\grave{a}\ \sigma\tau\acute{o}\mu a,\nu\acute{\epsilon}\rho\theta\epsilon\ \delta\grave{\epsilon}\ \gamma o\hat{\upsilon}\nu a$$

$$\pi\acute{\eta}\gamma\nu\upsilon\tau a\iota.$$

She rushes from the palace like a maenad, with her *kradie* palpitating (vv. 460-461). Complete dissolution comes when she sees Hektor's corpse on the plain below the city. Black night covers her eyes, she falls backwards, exhales her *psyche,* and her headdress falls to the ground far from her (vv. 462-470). Eventually she breathes again, her *thymos* is gathered back into her *phren,* and she begins her lament. From disorder to disintegration, the process is spelled out in order. Hands, knees, *etor, kradie, psyche,* eyes, even shuttle and headdress, all are affected by the shock. The poet's reference to Andromache's *thymos* returning (v. 475) is a summary much like his summary of the *menos* surging through the limbs of the two Ajaxes. Andromache's *thymos* is, like theirs, the central nervous control and when it is dissipated the various parts of the body cease their normal function. Andromache's syncope well expresses the Homeric concept of a living individual: *etor, stethos, psyche, thymos, phren,* and *kradie* function as a community of internal agents which together maintain life and consciousness.

Syncope is not the only occasion for the breakdown of the mental equipment. Hysteria can throw things awry, and wine too. Theoklymenos, when accused by Penelope's suitors of hysteria, gives a different image of the functioning organism (*Ody.* 20.365-367): "I have my eyes and ears and both my feet and a *noos* well constructed in my chest. With these I shall take my leave since I recognize an evil in store for you." Theoklymenos has healthy organs, mental and physical, all doing their work as they should. He describes his *noos* as τετυγμένος οὐδὲν ἀεικής, drawing his image from man-made artifacts. The mind itself is a construction that can be well made or poorly made, and the individual is a larger construction in which the parts fit together. Odysseus' description of Elpenor gives the same kind of image (*Ody.* 10.553-554): "There was a certain Elpenor, the youngest of the lot, none too efficient in battle nor well fitted together in his *phrenes* (οὔτε φρεσὶν ᾗσιν ἀρηρώς)." Elpenor's *phrenes,* a poor piece of carpentry in themselves, have a deleterious effect on the rest of the structure. He is clumsy in battle, says Odysseus, and we observe him to be equally clumsy as a dinner guest.

With these descriptions of the construction of inner organs we may compare the dissolution caused by fear, as when Priam's herald descries Hermes on the plain (*Il.* 24.358): "So the herald spoke and the old man's *noos* became fluid because he was in great fear." Priam's *noos* "flowed together" (σὺν δὲ γέροντι νόος χύτο); it collapsed and lost its shape. Compare the similar expression that Achilleus used to Phoinix at *Iliad* 9.612. μή μοι σύγχει θυμὸν ὀδυρόμενος καὶ ἀχεύων. A man's body is a piece of construction that disintegrates when struck at a vital point, or when subjected to violent emotional shock, as when Até took Patroklos' *phrenes* and unloosed his limbs (*Il.* 16.805). In the same way, the individual mental organs are imagined as structures that can disintegrate under shock.[28]

In addition, then, to whatever medical knowledge Homer may command, his picture of mental, or rather of mental-physiological, operations is built up from three basic models at least. The individual, the harmonious integrated community of peers who share in the same tasks, and the constructed artifact all go into the composite structure. Man is the sum of his parts. What happens to one part affects the whole. We can now better understand why *soma,* the Homeric word for the body as a whole structure, is reserved almost exclusively for the corpse. If we find it strange that Homer should use the word for the dead rather than the living structure, it is because we start from the opposite perspective. Locutions like "arms above and knees below" are not part of a modern scholar's usual vocabulary, whereas they are still vital in Homeric thought and language. We prefer the all-purpose prosaic generalization, but Homer's visual acuity and his own kind of logic lead him to locate things and events within the nexus of their relationships. The use of directional enclitics like -δε, as in ὅνδε δόμονδε, συφεόνδε, θωκόνδε, and -θεν, as in οἰκόθεν, and the great variety of untranslatable particles remind us that Homer is a poet who thinks in terms of structural relations.

In his portrait of the body the relationships catch Homer's attention: hands above, knees below, god without, *menos* within. Just as Homer has two kinds of abstractions in his temporal notations, so he has two anatomical abstractions. *Hora,* as the coincidence of everything at a certain moment, is significant time; *chronos* is time without relationships. In the body the *thymos* plays the part of *hora. Thymos* is the coincidence of energy, desire, will, thought, the harmonious function of all elements, and is manifested uniformly throughout all parts. *Soma* is the opposite; it is body bereft of relationships and therefore of functions. Only when Homer has nothing to say of the individual parts, when neither the *thymos,* nor the *psyche,* nor *noos,* nor *phrenes,* nor eyes, nor limbs have anything to convey, does the structure becomes *soma.* While the body is alive and active the parts as representative of the whole interest Homer's eye. Body in motion, time and space in motion, is what Homer describes, not the static model of the still-life artist.[29]

Analogous is the situation for the word for shadow, σκιή. Epithets for *shadowy* occur twelve times in the *Odyssey,* five times in the *Iliad*, but the substantive never appears in all of Homer except to denote the dead.[30] Should we argue some deficiency in Homer's conceptual apparatus that it cannot perceive *shadow* as an entity per se in the phenomenal world lying beneath the sun? Should we not rather relish the perception that invariably attaches *shadow* to some phenomenal reality in our world, but conceives of it as something separate, detached from its phenomena, in the afterworld? As *soma* is the entity detached from all its relationships that define it as a living organism, σκιή is what remains through eternity of a man when death has disintegrated all his vital forces.

So far we have considered how Homer assimilates various phenomena into a single complex, first in the ordering of the external world and then in the ordering of the interior world of thought, emotion, and will. It is useful to explore other analogical modes of thought in Homer, to gain a better understanding of the Homeric search for structure. Analogical thinking finds its most conspicuous expression in the Homeric simile. The similes, as H. Fränkel has argued, cannot be limited to a single point of comparison, the *tertium comparationis.*[31] Without the *tertium comparationis* there can be, of course, no simile — a poet must find some way he can relate two entirely discrete phenomena to each other. But Homer rarely thinks in single points of comparison. There is often a second *Vergleichspunkt,* a third, a fourth, until the simile becomes a composite picture, an assimilation of one unified structure into another. Studies that isolate epic similes entirely from other narrative devices do a disservice to both Homer's poetry and his thought. The method of expressing function as a unity in multiplicity, as structural pattern beneath the phenomena, is the Homeric mode of thought, repeated in every aspect of Homeric style. There is no essential difference in method between the vision that transposes warriors on the battlefield into a tableau of hunters and their prey and the vision that transposes the relationship between two runners into that between a woman and her loom. Homeric notations of time and space are in fact similes, and like similes they can be a brief statement or a detailed tableau with important emotional implications.

The most pertinent feature of similes is that they almost always relate human appearance, human attributes, or human action to the world of nature. Men are likened to leaves, to animals, to natural elements, sometimes to deities, and, less commonly, to other men. Some nonhuman objects receive their similes: horses are compared to birds (*Il.* 2.764; cf. 16.149); the Phaiakian ship is as swift as thought (*Ody.* 7.36); two rivers are compared to oil on water (*Il.* 2.754); bristling weapons are like the bristling sea (*Il.* 7.63); Achilleus' shield shines like the moon or the light from a shepherd's hut high on the mountain side, his helmet gleams like a star (*Il.* 19.374-383), the point of his spear like the evening star (*Il.* 22.317-319). Such objects that are compared to other objects are directly part of human action, as conveyances or weapons, as some aspect of an individual's, or group's, motion or appearance, an organic attribute of the person. Achilleus' weapons gleam like stars, but he himself stands forth as baneful Sirius. At times the individual, at other times one of his attributes is described in a simile.

The similes are mostly a one-way intellectual process. They see the patterns in external phenomena – the action of wind on waves, on leaves, or forest fires, the relationship of heavenly bodies, the movement of birds and animals, the annual cycle of change – and draw man's life and activity into the orbit of these natural events. The simile attempts to make visible the human order by finding a correspondence between it and the order of nature. Similes assume order, reality, and quality in the natural world and human action gains through simile not only visibility but significance. When Achilleus is likened to Sirius his action achieves a particular significance because the star already has its meaning. Modern poetry generally works in the opposite way. It attempts to save the phenomena by endowing them once again with the human quality that has been abstracted from them. Homeric poetry sees in a bivouacking army a field of stars, but post-Homeric European poetry might well see in a field of stars a bivouacking army, as if the external world became more visible when graphed by human coordinates.

Vergil's simile comparing the uncontrolled winds to a frenzied human mob (*Aen.* 1.148-154) sharply emphasizes the change in perspective between Homer and his successors. In the perspective of the Homeric simile the human world receives its pattern from that already established in the natural world.[32]

Some scholars are insistent that Homeric similes have but a single point of comparison and that their primary appeal is a simple visual scene. The most strenuous advocate of the single *"heftig und tief diskredierte Vergleichspunkt"* is G. Jachmann, who devotes a long excursus in his study of the Catalogue of Ships to an attack on Fränkel for introducing the kind of symbolizing and allegorizing that is alien to the spirit of Homeric poetry.[33] Symbolism is the property of the naive, more so than of the mind of the modern sophisticate. An unlettered peasant finds more symbolic representations in a day than a literary critic does in a month. We could talk of the obvious symbolism in the representation of the gods in Homer and Hesiod. Or we could look at the folk sayings, proverbs, animal fables from all cultures, ancient and modern, and find there both symbolism and allegory (the perimeters are hard to locate precisely). If further defense were needed, Claude Lévi-Strauss gives us an excellent example of symbolic and mythic imagery among modern "primitives" in his discussion of the incantation delivered by a medicine man over a woman suffering a difficult childbirth.[34] So thoroughly have physiological facts been translated into myth in the incantation that if we had only the incantation and knew nothing of its function, we might perhaps assign it to some theogony. The event of childbirth is cast in the incantation as a titanic battle between stout warriors and malicious demons; the mythopoiesis at work here makes us think of Hesiod. The difference between naive symbolism and modern symbolism is that the modern poet does not quite believe the symbol. He writes his symbols in the subjunctive mood: Let X be the symbol for Y. Even when he believes in the psychological or poetic reality of his symbol he still thinks subjunctively, since whatever reality he ascribes to his symbol is not the one that exists in science. His symbolism has only a contingent reality; it expresses his personal hypothesis on the nature of the universe. The naive symbolist, on the other hand, has not erected a barrier between symbol and reality, nor between poetic and scientific reality. X, because it shares some characteristic with Y, is an aspect of Y. The human interpreter can deduce from X the shape of Y, even though X be but a fragment and though X and Y lie in separate spheres. The naive symbolist lets his mind roam freely through the realm of symbol, ever on the lookout for the significant detail, and undistracted by doubts about the reality of the relationships he sees. Thus, superstition is but hyperthyroidism in the symbol-building faculty.

Homeric omens are clearest proof that symbolic logic is as native to Homer's characters as to the poet himself. Omens, as another kind of analogical thinking, are like similes, but similes that are the property of the characters in the poem rather than of the poet. Omens are interesting because they permit us to watch Homeric characters practicing the structural and analogical thought we have hitherto only deduced from the language of the poems. Both simile and omen view the relationship between man and nature in much the same way, though the occasions for their use are, of course, quite different. The Homeric omen assumes order and meaning in the external world, and sees in one small event a paradigm of that order. It is man's part to discern that structure from a single clue and then to modify his behavior in accordance with it. Where the simile is descriptive, the omen is prescriptive.

Characters within the Homeric peoms find what we should call "symbol" in any phenomenon at all, in a word, an exclamation, a sneeze, a dream, a shout, in thunder or lightning, in the movement of birds, in any chance coincidence of two events. Their practice should present a problem for those who find "symbolizing" alien to Homeric poetry. Homeric omens give us leave to interpret Homeric similes as more than sensual image; they not only make interpretation of the similes permissible but also show us the method of interpretation. Like similes, the omens range from a brief note to a complex image.

They can be an involuntary sound, an elaborate dream, a word, or a whole speech. Even in its simplest form, however, the omen is more than just a sound, a word, or a movement. It achieves efficacy because it is part of a larger structure which it makes apparent. It occurs within a context and thus illustrates a natural order or some deviation from order. It is not birds per se that are omens, but the particular species of birds, their kind of movement, the direction of their movement, the appropriateness of their appearance at that time of day or year. A bird omen, however briefly stated, is a complex picture of many relationships. The interpreter, in calling it a good or bad omen, is analyzing those relationships and synthesizing them again in human terms. When Telemachos sneezes, Penelope first interprets the sneeze as a disruption within the context of normal human activity and then transfers the whole relationship into another context, that of her present circumstances. A disruption in one context always means disruption in another.

Odysseus gives us the fullest example of an omen as a set of relationships when he asks for an omen on the day of his vengeance (*Ody*. 20.92-101). Just before he falls asleep on the eve of his vengeance, outside his palace, Athena appears at his head to give him encouragement; just before the following dawn he hears Penelope's lament (literally, in Homer, "he put together her voice") and imagines that she has recognized him and is standing at his head. Athena and Penelope appear like two dream figures but with contrary import. Penelope weeping seems to be a bad omen which annuls Athena as good omen. It is a further complication that the good omen appears at night, the bad one just at dawn. Odysseus is already in a state of anxiety but the confusion in omens disturbs what little equilibrium he still possesses; he resorts to a direct invocation of an omen, a rare practice in Homer. He takes the coverlets that lay over him during the night and places them inside the house on a *thronos;* he puts the oxhide, on which he had slept, outside, on the ground. He then prays to Zeus: "Give me one omen from inside, another outside. Let someone who is awakening inside utter a good word [*phēmē*], and let another sign appear from Zeus outside." The polar tension of the Athena-Penelope omens is resolved by invoking polarity; Odysseus demands an omen that will draw the polarities back into harmonious order. He demands that a whole set of contrasts should coincide: inside and outside, sound and sight, *phēmē* and *teras,* above and below, man and God. He himself imitates polarity by exploiting opposition in preparation; he makes a twofold division of his bed clothes and asserts the division by their location. The one set, which had been above him, he places inside and above, on a chair; the other, which had been beneath him, he places outside, on the ground.

The double omen Zeus sends in response is a statement in polarity (vv. 103-119). The one omen, thunder from Olympos, comes from Zeus, from nature, from the king of gods, from outside, at a distance, high above. The other is from inside, close at hand, close to the earth, a human voice, a remark from a woeful female servant, the feeblest of all Odysseus' household. One is the expression of power, the other is the helpless cry of servitude. The two omens together comprise an astonishing set of polarities: nature-society, God-man, male-female, sky-earth, power-infirmity, distance-proximity, outside-inside. But even that does not exhaust the content of the passage, since the old slave woman sees, and then exploits, polarities in the single omen of the thunder. Thunder from a cloudless dawn is an unnatural collocation of opposites which spells doom, and she resolves the opposition inherent in that event by fending its import from Odysseus on to the suitors. She pursues the oppositions vigorously. She contrasts her lot with that of the suitors, her labors with their luxurious feasts, the omen of dawn with their last night. The disorder in that sign from nature she projects on to the suitors, hoping thereby to guarantee a balancing order for Odysseus and his household.

The passage is extraordinary for its exploration of the structure of polarity as a mode of thought. It begins with Athena's appearance and Penelope's cry, two events of opposite import (deity-human, outside-inside, day-night, encouragement-despair). Odysseus than acts out opposition in the disposition of his bedding, and solicits further opposition in a double omen. Zeus sends his half of that omen, which is itself a polarity, and a slave woman completes the second half of the omen when the thunder provokes her to utter her own set of apotropaic oppositions. Contraries are resolved by the homeopathic use of one set of contraries after another, as if only by burdening fate with the accumulation of contraries can Odysseus elicit a truly reliable prognostication. This is structural thought in its most elaborate form. [35]

Odysseus' double omen is somewhat specialized. No one else in Homer solicits such an omen in which oppositions are so strenuously and deliberately exploited. Birds, meteorological phenomena, or words are generally less ambiguous omens, or ambiguous in a different way. They are good or bad; they must be interpreted, but they are not as complicated. In Odysseus' situation the pattern is neither good nor bad. Odysseus sees a set of phenomena — Athena's consolation at night and Penelope's cry at dawn — as a unified structure that is somehow a statement of his circumstances. But it is a structure that needs clarification. To force the contradiction to yield its meaning he invokes it by deliberate intent, both in his own person and in his double omen, submerging himself in the contradiction to become master of it rather than victim.

Dreams are another kind of symbolic thinking in which Homeric characters indulge. They can be of the simple kind, in which a messenger delivers some warning or advice, or they can be an elaborate *mythos* with a structure that must be related to that of the everyday world. Even the simple dreams, however, are fraught with ambiguity. Agamemnon's dream in *Iliad* 2 is quite unequivocal, but an unequivocal message can mean its opposite — as Nestor seems to hint when he hears of the dream, and as is, in fact, the case with this particular dream. Manifest content is not always the true content. It is interesting to see how Agamemnon deals with the latent ambiguity. He himself publicly adopts the latent content of the dream by proclaiming that the Greeks should return home. He becomes the dream's polar opposite with the hope that in the articulation of the contradiction meaning may emerge. The irony is that he read the dream correctly — that is, by acting as if it were false — and the troops accept his reading with enthusiastic support, but Odysseus and the other heroes refuse to accept such a reading and the war continues.

Penelope's dream of the geese and the eagle (*Ody.* 19.536-553) is a *mythos* in wholly symbolic terms. It is a symbolic drama which must be translated into human terms point for point. To us the meaning of the dream may seem transparent; indeed, the eagle acts as interpreter within the dream (vv. 548-549): "Before I was a bird [omen] for you but now I have returned as your husband to dispense doom to all the suitors." Odysseus, hearing Penelope's account, also finds the meaning transparent (vv. 555-557): "There is no way to rotate the dream in any other direction since it was Odysseus himself who declared how he is working fulfillment." But the dream may mean its opposite, as was the case with Agamemnon's dream. Penelope recognizes this possibility, but in her reflection on dreams she seems to recognize that it is the complexity of the total *mythos* which makes interpretation difficult.

A pertinent complication is the presence of Penelope herself as one of the *dramatis personae* in the dream. She sees herself taking pleasure in watching her geese eating, and when they are killed she and the Achaian women gather to keen shrilly at her bereavement (vv. 537, 541-543). Her emotion is an important part of the *mythos*, for it orients us in a particular way: the characters are not geese and an eagle, but her geese, eating grain around her house, and a bird óf prey with a cruel beak which swoops down from outside to destroy her property. The intrusion of her subjective response into the dream adds the disturbing implication that the eagle, which claims to be her husband, is in fact a vandal bent on destruction. So disturbing are the contradictions that the eagle returns as his own interpreter, to orient the dream in a favorable direction, but his metamorphosis only adds to the complication. Even Penelope's syntax reveals her perplexity. There is a fine ambiguity in her

use of the first person pronoun: χῆνές μοι (v. 536) and ὅ μοι
αἰετὸς ἔκτανε χῆνας (v. 543).

Penelope illuminates the interlocking worlds of symbol and
reality when she tells Odysseus that on waking from her dream
she looked out and found the geese pecking grain from the
trough just as before (vv. 552-553). The eagle in the dream had
identified the geese as the suitors, but her first waking thought
is for her real geese. Has she lost all ability to discriminate
between symbolic geese and real geese? She knows the
difference well enough, but her categories are more complex
than a simple dichotomy into real and symbolic. She looks to
the real geese for some kind of confirmation of the dream. It is
as if she thought in two stages of symbolism. If Penelope's
barnyard geese, the earthly counterparts, conform to the dream,
then this increases the probability that their more symbolic
counterparts, the suitors, will follow suit. Or, since the entire
conversation is in wholly symbolic terms – first Penelope's
dream, then Odysseus' interpretation, and finally her evaluation
of dreams – it would not be straining credibility to say that
Penelope in talking of her barnyard geese is using still the
symbolism of her dream. She woke and found the suitors were
still there.

It is not surprising that Penelope's response to Odysseus'
confirmation of the dream is that dreams yield to no easy
formulas (*amechanoi*, v. 560) and that they speak in a bewildering syntax (*akritomythoi*, v. 560). In an extended image of her
own she explains that dreams are refractions through the
opaque lens of horn or ivory (vv. 560-570); that is, all dreams,
true or false, are opaque. The vocabulary Odysseus uses in
interpreting the dream and Penelope's explanation is applicable
to all the forms of symbolic thought, dreams and omens.
Dreams are in a language where the elements are not clearly
arranged, they must be sorted and put into intelligible syntax
(*hypokrinasthai*, v. 555). The structure of the whole image must
then be oriented in the right way (*apoklinant'*, v. 556), as if it
were a diagram to be superimposed upon reality.

Penelope, in her attempt to define the nature of dream, resorts to a mythical image which is itself close to a simile: there are gates of certain substances and dreams emerge from them that partake of the quality of those substances. The substances, horn and ivory, become embodiments of the most abstract principles, plausibility and implausibility, frustration and fulfillment, deception and truth. In her definition, ivory is first a substance, then a gate made from the substance, then dreams that issue from that gate, and then a quality of a dream. Penelope's image of the gates of dreams is definition by analogy, where a concrete substance becomes characteristic of a certain kind of dream. That she has given mythical definitions rather than scientific ones, that she has defined dreams etiologically — that is, by explaining their results, whether they come to fulfillment or not, in terms of their points of origin — should not distract us from the process of intellectual analysis her image represents.[36]

Penelope's dream is, for her, a true representation of reality, hence the mental connection she makes between dream geese and real geese. Her myth of the gates of dreams is also a representation of reality, her symbology of dream. Her myth is thus itself a symbol, a symbol used to define a symbol. Both myths, her dream and her definition of dream, characterize Homer's kind of symbolic thinking; they show that his characters think in images and similes as he does, though their similes appear as dreams, omens, and myths.

Characters within the Homeric poems also have another kind of simile which is peculiarly their own. The paradigmatic myth, which is so constant a feature of the characters' thought, is, in fact, the most extended kind of simile in all of Homer. Like similes, however, the paradigm can appear as the briefest reference or be elaborated into a lengthy and detailed story. The hypomnesis in prayers, as in Thetis' prayer to Zeus, "If ever in the past I served you well in word or deed, grant me this request" (*Il.* 1.503-504), or reminders of past character, as Hektor taunts Paris, "Is this the sort of man you were when you braved the open sea to carry off a foreign bride?" (*Il.* 3.46-48) are paradigms in miniature. But the longest simile in the *Iliad* is the story of Meleager which Phoinix tells to Achilleus in Book 9. Paradigm is but historical simile. It relates a contemporary event to a recent historical, or a distant mythical, past. Paradigm can be a hortatory myth like the story of Meleager, or Achilleus' story of Niobe weeping for her children (*Il.* 24.602-614), or self-justifying, like Nestor's digressions into his former deeds of prowess or Agamemnon's etiological explanation of the appearance of Delusion in the world (*Il.* 19.78-133). Characters resort to a paradigmatic story to explain some present event, to defend their position, to accuse, to advise, to warn someone else or themselves. The past is cogent because it is human experience fixed and structured. Homeric heroes find in paradigm a permanent pattern which can give shape to their ephemeral lives and actions. Paradigmatic stories are thus a system of classification put into historical terms. They form a large and diverse body of categories to cover types of behavior, types of character, and types of situations.

The short paradigm makes a simple comparison. "You were brave once, you should be brave now" is Hektor's message to Paris. The extended paradigm, however, like the extended simile, involves a whole range of correspondence. The appositeness of the Meleager story to Achilleus lies in the total *mythos,* in the similarity in both circumstances and character of the two protagonists, just as the appositeness of Penelope's dream of her geese lies in the total *mythos.* Agamemnon's paradigmatic story of Atē's deception of Zeus is just such a simile of multiple comparison (*Il.* 19.78-144). It gains depth and complexity because while Agamemnon uses it as a vehicle to make some very conscious comparisons between himself and Zeus, the poet is also using it behind Agamemnon's back to signal to us certain comparisons to which Agamemnon remains oblivious. Agamemnon's comparisons are sufficiently transparent. As the king of gods was deluded in thinking he could have his way, so the king of men admits his delusion. As the god was foiled by one of his subordinates, Hera, so was the human king foiled by his subordinate Achilleus. And as the god can plead the excuse of external persuasion, so can the human. It takes no great perspicacity, however, to notice that Zeus' "deception," that is, his *atē*, was his failure to deceive others. What he can call *atē* was really his careless lack of foresight; the invocation of *atē* neatly obscures the simple truth that Zeus was hoist with his own petard. Zeus hurls Atē from Olympos in a great show of recognition of his error, but it is in fact only a show since the error he admits is his falling victim to Hera's superior intelligence and not the more significant error of his attempt to outwit the other gods. What was Zeus doing practicing *atē* on others? Agamemnon too blurs the simple fact of his own greed by invoking Atē as external persuasion, for what he invokes is really nothing but "human nature." Agamemnon's admission of guilt, in putting his *atē* aside, is also only a half-hearted pretense of recognition. He admits only that he miscalculated; that is precisely the admission Zeus makes. Finally, in the paradigm, Herakles, laboring as a hired hand for Eurystheos, can blame Atē, and perhaps then not notice that he owes his ignominious life (*ergon aeikes*, v. 133) to his father's machinations and feeble intelligence. So too the Greeks can perhaps overlook the truth that the prolongation of the war is Agamemnon's personal and sole responsibility. Great god and great king, both fade discretely behind *atē*, that smoke bomb which conveniently disguises simple egotism and sheer mental incompetence. *Atē* may be for Homeric man a legitimate explanation of human error, but other heroes do not resort to such flagrant conscience salves. Achilleus painfully recognizes and assumes his responsibility — with his consciousness of his part in the death of Patroklos how could he deliver a pompous homily on atē? Agamemnon, in contrast to Achilleus' behavior, offers only an ersatz apology which attempts to camouflage more than it reveals. To make his equation between the king of men and king of gods more secure — the only equation in which Agamemnon is seriously interested — Agamemnon pointedly remains seated to deliver his homily.[37]

Both Homer and his characters, then, think continuously in structural analogies but they represent the structure through visible particulars rather than in scientific formulas. The animal world and the human, the physical and the spiritual, the organic and the social, the contemporary and the historical, all are part of a single unity and any fragment from one sphere can act as a paradigm both for its own sphere and for any other sphere. There are no wasted words or gestures in Homer, since every gesture reveals something else. An outward gesture reveals an inward attitude, an inward attitude will express itself in an outward gesture. The personalities of Homer's actors are a duplication of the unity of the world seen in microcosmic scale. Through word, action, even the slightest shift in posture, the character of the actors reveals itself as a consistent whole. Agamemnon remains seated when he lectures his troops on até and thereby dramatizes the significance with which he views the similarity between him and Zeus. That Odysseus should crouch in the ashes at the hearth when he comes as a suppliant to the Phaiakian court (*Ody.* 7.153-154) is as indicative of his character as his finest oratory or his cleverest stratagem. Penelope weaves a shroud by day and unravels it by night as she weaves and unravels promises or hints of promises for the suitors. Her promises, which hold them until Odysseus' arrival, are the web in which she entangles her suitors, and their final shroud. When Odysseus returns the suitors have discovered Penelope's trick; Penelope has, that is, exhausted all possible prevarications but one: given one last day of weaving, she weaves the Contest of the Bow. Helen's weaving in the Iliad is similarly paradigmatic of her character (*Il.* 3.125ff.). She weaves into a robe the struggles the Greeks and the Trojans suffer for her sake, just as she afterward thinks of the songs later poets will sing of her (*Il.* 6.357-358). Her woven tapestry of the Trojan War is her mnemonic device, the master pattern that future bards, weaving into their own medium, will transmit from generation to generation. In the *Iliad* Helen is, literally and figuratively, the weaver of sorrows; in the *Odyssey* she has become also the anesthetist of sorrows. Helen prepares a literal anodyne for her guests in Sparta when grief overcomes them, but she herself is the true Nepenthes when she begins to divert heavy hearts with encomiastic stories of Odysseus' cunning (working herself again, we might add, into her own tapestry). As Penelope's weaving and unraveling is her gift for beguiling fiction made visible, so Helen's pharmaceutical *nepenthes* is the visible token of her gift for making men endure and forget their heaviest sorrows.

Homeric thought is pervaded with symbolic thought. Paradigm, omen, and simile are all expressions of such symbolism, but they are only the most overt expressions. They exemplify the kind of thinking that looks for relationships between one object and another, between persons, between events, between an individual's separate actions. Mythical imagination can tolerate the most extravagant metamorphosis – suitors can become geese, Odysseus an eagle – because it is, specifically, a structural relationship for which such imagination scans the horizon. Mythical thought, in fact, expects at every instant metamorphosis at the corporal level but stability at the deeper level of relationship. One *Vergleichspunkt,* whether it occurs in myth, simile, or omen, always implies a complex set of correspondence. Homeric staging may be at times paratactic but his thought is always syntactic.

Interpretation of Homer is not only permissible but necessary. Interpretation can help bridge the distance between us and Homer, but it is not distance alone which makes interpretation necessary. Homer and his *dramatis personae* are always making their own interpretations of reality, transposing event into symbol, symbol into event, present into past, past into present. The unity that their acute observation leads them to assume embraces the cosmos from the highest to the lowest, from the earliest to the latest; their imagination searches the world for tokens that will affirm anew that unity. Imagination that sees in any fragment the shape, and indeed the decisive proof, of the whole is symbolic imagination. The Homeric poems will always remain only graceful naturalistic tales unless we can ourselves enter into their kind of symbolism. The sensitivity of the Homeric seers, which can detect the invisible canvas from a single visible brushstroke, is the same sensitivity Homer demands of his interpreters. The *Odyssey* is, after all, a poem, one of the central themes of which is the contrast between those who notice tokens and put together meanings and those who do not — the danger is not of reading too much into Homer, but of reading too little. Better the perspicacity of Theoklymenos than the myopia of the suitors.

"Pre-history is nobody's childhood."[38]

III

Intimations of Order

High decorum is one of the most salient traits of Homeric narrative. Whether it be a noble scene like Priam's meeting with Achilleus in the *Iliad* or a more mundane description – Agamemnon's scepter, an arming scene, preparations for morning's battle or the evening meal – everywhere there is the sense of the processional: orderly arrangement of events within a sequence, stylized exaggeration of gesture, a reverence for detail. There is truth to Matthew Arnold's words on the rapidity of Homeric style, but that style is never precipitate. For all the flow of the hexameter, Homer sculpts the furniture of his scenes with unhurried care. It may come to seem an ironic vagary of literary criticism that Homer's elaborately stylized repetitions, the very hallmark of the ordered temperament, were once read as *vestigia* of that shamelessly plagiaristic *Bearbeiter*. It may puzzle later generations too that Homeric formulas, the absence of which would reduce the *Iliad* to something just above war journalism, were once read as metrical crutches rather than as the vivid mimesis of that decorum which Homeric characters seek and enact in their every gesture. What are formulas but the invocation of order on the linguistic level, comparable to the formalism of larger stylistic structures?

We have come to recognize ring-composition as an important structural device in early Greek poetry. But we miss its importance unless we see it as an expression of mental perspective. Hesiod's "Hymn to the Muses," with which he opens the *Theogony,* is a masterly example of ring-composition, or rather of spiral composition, since one ring glides into another, as Hesiod moves from invocation to narrative, thence back to invocation, and then on to further narrative. In the first lines of the hymn Hesiod depicts the Muses' dance around the fountain of Helikon and the altar of Zeus as "they flowed nimbly with their feet" (ἐπερρώσαντο δὲ ποσσίν, v. 8). Hesiod's spiral composition is his verbal mimesis of that ring dance the Muses perform when they sing and inspire mortal singers. The structure of his proem is, therefore, what they are executing with their nimble feet, while their voices relay the information that becomes the content of his song. His description of the Muses and their circular dance puts in visual form his concept of inspiration; the structure of his description reinforces that visual experience by making the inspiration felt as well as seen.

Homer illustrates in another way how style represents experience. In Homer too, ring-composition figures prominently as a device for framing a speech, a scene, a book, and even to frame the poem, as Books 1 and 24 of the *Iliad* thematically and structurally balance each other. Scholars have seen in this technique the verbal expression of the symmetries of Geometric art, or the formal conveniences for structuring a long oral poem. When we look closer, however, we find ring-composition to be indeed a way of life. Homer's characters are often attended by their complement of two persons of inferior rank. Ladies are accompanied by two handmaidens, kings are attended by two heralds or squires, Telemachos by two dogs, Penelope is courted by two principal suitors, Odysseus can rely particularly on two faithful servants, Eumaios and Eurykleia. The framing formulas for Homeric speeches, and the balancing panels for Homeric scenes, reproduce in their way a distinctive feature of Homeric social organization. The lowly formula, when all is said about its utility in hexameter composition, has yet a deeper level of utility, which is to reinforce the idea of dense and textured order, making manifest for us that which the Homeric characters themselves attempt to realize in every aspect of their lives.

Thus, order is of ubiquitous concern in both the *Iliad* and the *Odyssey*. The *Iliad* certainly has much to say on the effects of disruption of social and cosmic order. But order is singled out as the main burden of the *Odyssey*. Restoration of order in Ithaka is the subject of the poem — on this at least Analysts and

Unitarians can meet in convivial agreement. The theme appears unequivocally in Zeus' opening speech in Book 1 on the blind folly of men and the justice of the gods, and it continues through the poem until Athena's pacification of the warring parties in Ithaka in Book 24. The moral is unambiguous – how could it be otherwise in a tale where honest folk are pitted against unredeemable villains? That good triumphs over evil is a moral both obvious and unashamedly primitive, in itself more primitive than the subtle examination of human failures in the *Iliad.* But the *Odyssey* is considerably more sophisticated than its moral, for it has used that simple fairy tale – that the good are rewarded and the bad punished – as but the surface for another poem which is on the nature of order and the interconnection of different kinds of order, moral and psychological, natural and physical. The achievement of the *Odyssey* lies not so much in its bald philosophical premise, if we can dignify' it by naming it thus, as in the poetic subtleties with which it attempts its definition of order.

The *Odyssey* is structured in the form of a travelogue, but this is no Baedeker of some private traveller recording random curiosities in the world of men and nature. Rather, it is a collection of systems that function as paradigms of social and natural order, through which Odysseus and his imitative son pass on their way to the final re-creation of order in Ithaka. The cities and minds of men that the proem advertises as the content of Odysseus' journey prefigure, some directly and others as faint overtones, the possibilities for action in Ithaka. They are Odysseus' preparatory education, as Sparta and Pylos are the schools for Telemachos. The *Odyssey* reveals, through the progressive stages of Odysseus' journey, a hierarchy of order ranging from simple to complex and encompassing both society and nature. The *Odyssey*'s hierarchy is not the Aristotelian set of categories, much less Dante's perfectly calibrated realization of the distance separating utter chaos from absolute order, but comparisons are nevertheless viable. No less than the *Divine Comedy,* the *Odyssey* sets itself the task of realizing experience through a rational system of categories distinguishable from each other by their increasing complexity.

The simplest systems in the poem are those representations of purely natural phenomena. The tidal monster, Charybdis, scarcely anthropomorphized, is distinguished by her permanent and regular schedule. Three times daily she vomits up the sea, and three times swallows it again (12.104-105). By his knowledge of her recurrent and predictable schedule, Odysseus is able to excape past her threat to safety. In the description of the doves that fly past the Clashing Rocks we perceive a similar regularly recurring schedule (12.62-65). Whenever the doves fly between the rocks bearing ambrosia to Zeus, one falls victim to the rocks, but Zeus always sends in another to make up the full complement again. It is inviting to accept the later identification of Homer's *peleiai* with the Pleiades, which are traditionally seven in number although only six are visible to most observers. Homer hints nowhere at such an identification, and other possibilities have been conjectured. An argument in favor is that some feature that reveals a permanent cyclical nature is the defining characteristic of natural phenomena in the *Odyssey*. As Charybdis maintains a permanent cycle of operation, so the doves of Zeus maintain their permanent cycle, although theirs is an oscillation between loss and renewal. Whether the *peleiai* are the Pleiades or not, the regularity in their pattern is their claim to be some form observable in the seasonal and natural world.

We reach a higher level of complexity in the representations of natural phenomena that are endowed with anthropomorphic form. The winds are realized in an intricate system on the island of Aiole, where every aspect — the location and movement of the island, the behavior of the king, his family organization, and their form of entertainment — conjures up a particular aspect of the winds. Sociologists who have argued for the divine world as the replica of human social organization have failed to see how frequently humans erect divine societies that, although mirroring human society in many aspects, will yet contain certain features that mark them off as specifically nonhuman. King

Aiolos may behave as any bad-tempered human king, but his island behaves as no known island does. Its special behavior is an ad hoc creation, a mythic principle to embody something in the special nature of the winds. But more important than that floating island, there is once again the cyclical pattern which marks the world of Aiolos as part of nature; here the feature is incorporated into the marriage arrangement. Aiolos has six sons and six daughters who live always with him, and the six sons are married to the six daughters (10.5-9). What can this permanent incestuous union, from which there issues no offspring, be but the representation of twelve winds, which never increase in number, but always pass back and forth? The north wind blows south, the south north; the east wind blows west, the west east. Homer depicts that perpetual reciprocity as six marriages, with each male offspring in an inviolable bond with his female counterpart. Into the fabric of a human society are thus woven the clues that reveal the nonhuman nature of the phenomena described.

Thrinakia is similar to Aiole in being a representation of natural phenomena expressed in a mythic system. Again we begin with the human disguise. Helios is the cattle owner on the island, with seven herds of cattle, fifty head to a herd, and seven flocks of sheep, fifty head to a flock (12.127ff.). His daughters Phaethousa and Lampetie (the shepherdesses Brilliance and Radiance) keep perpetual guard over his property. Aristotle and others in antiquity understood the 350 cattle and the 350 sheep as Homer's image of the days and nights of the year, in fact of the lunar year. To some his interpretation might seem anachronistic allegory, and yet others with a good memory for numbers may interrupt at this point to ask the significance of the 360 male porkers that Eumaios guards for Odysseus. To this we can reply that if the image of the winds translates into visual form so many aspects of the winds' behavior, is it anachronistic to expect as much in Homer's description of the sun? When Phaethousa and Lampetie are so clearly hypostases of aspects of the sun, should not his cattle, which are protected by the direst tabus, embody as much significance? The property of the sun, in mythic terms, surely can be nothing but the days of the year (though we need not press, perhaps, for a hidden lunar-solar equation here). Helios' cattle are, moreover, unlike any herds owned by man. They are always fixed in size, neither producing any increase (*gonos*) nor suffering any diminution (vv. 130-131). We are not told explicitly, but are left to assume that the herds replenished themselves to their full complement after the destruction inflicted on them by Odysseus' sailors. Once again the cyclical pattern appears, of loss and renewal, and once again we see the feature that reveals beneath the human trappings the specifically nonhuman forms of behavior found in nature.

There are, then, a series of mythic representations for the elements or elemental forces: Skylla, Charybdis, Proteus, Aiolos, and Helios' cattle. They have their laws which must be learned if Odysseus is to survive. Some, like Skylla, cannot be outwitted at all . Others can be outwitted by a prior knowledge of their cyclical pattern, as Odysseus turns Charybdis' schedule to his eventual advantage, as Menelaos does likewise with Proteus, whose polymorphous transformations he anticipates. Others have laws that are expressed as tabus. But even the tabu is not mere superstitious prohibition. Aiolos' bag of winds, which Odysseus must not open, is a perfectly lucid pictograph of the skill with which the mariner binds the winds to his control. It is a metaphoric representation for a rational process of experience and skill, for holding on course with a favorable wind and blocking out contrary winds – or else, says Homer, you'll find yourself right back where you started. We can be sure that the Homeric sailor had knowledge of weather and sea of a thoroughly practical sort, with the bag of winds and magical tabus replaced by entirely realistic technical advice on tacking to the wind. Homer chooses not to supply that kind of information; instead he presents the story of Aiolos' winds.

From the thirteenth century A.D. comes an excellent document to illustrate the mentality that operates simultaneously on both mythical and technical levels. The Old Norse work, *Konnungs Skuggsjá* (*The King's Mirror*) is unwittingly a rich commentary on the *Odyssey*. It purports to give, in its first part, practical advice for navigation, and in fact gives a wealth of information of great precision on the length of lunar cycles, the influence of the moon on tides, and the periods between solstices. Then it gives a long description of the action of the winds, in which the author abandons the technical entirely for the mythical. According to his description, the winds go through a perpetual cycle, again a representation of loss and renewal, forming a covenant, breaking it, and then forming a new covenant. No sailor could derive much practical benefit from this picture of the winds, yet it is clearly as much part of the seaman's lore as the table of tides. Similar in its use of imagery, the *Odyssey* adopts the mythical to represent that most practical sailor, Odysseus, losing control of his craft in a storm. There is, besides, another storm in the *Odyssey* which parallels even more closely the *Mirror*'s conception. Poseidon, seeing Odysseus sailing for home, raises a violent storm in which the winds, Euros and Notos, Zephyros and Boreas, fall simultaneously on the sea (5.291-296). This storm, as we shall see later, marks the end of the sailing season, and at that moment the winds, hitherto accommodating, fall into disharmony, behaving exactly as *Konnungs Skuggsjá* predicts they will at the onset of winter.

Before Odysseus the sailor can discover the minds and cities of men he must conquer the natural perils at sea, by discovering and turning to his advantage the systems by which they maintain themselves. He must make his way through storms and past whirlpools. What part can Helios play in this drama of man against the elements? Odysseus' primary duel is with Poseidon, but his duel with Helios occupies a prominent second place. The Thrinakian catastrophe reverberates through the poem. A reference to it appears first in the proem when Homer reminds us that Odysseus' comrades brought about their own destruction by eating the cattle of Helios. It is the only incident that happens after repeated protreptic warnings. First Teiresias and then Kirke warn Odysseus against putting ashore on Thrinakia. Odysseus warns his men too against landing there; when

Eurylochos insists on doing so, Odysseus makes them swear a
solemn oath to leave the cattle intact. Their slaughter of the
cattle is thus sacrilege of the most deliberate sort, and it has
devastating results. Zeus, threatened by Helios with a sunless
heaven and a sunless earth, causes the death of Odysseus'
comrades, and accomplishes almost as much for Odysseus.
Odysseus is bereft of ship and crew, is forced into a near fatal
encounter with Charybdis, and is banished from sight for seven
years. Helios vies with Poseidon as Odysseus' personal fury.

To resort to a theory of the conflation of two sagas, one in
which Helios was Odysseus' enemy and the other in which
Poseidon played that part, is in reality no explanation, since we
are still left pondering on that original Helios myth. Why should
there have been such a myth in which the sun pursued a sailor
with relentless fury? More than that, why should that myth
have seemed so appropriate to the story of Poseidon's fury
against Odysseus that it could be joined to the Poseidon story
and treated, in fact, not merely as another adventure but one
fully as important in Odysseus' travels as Odysseus' blinding of
the Kyklops? If conflation is at work here, we must assume that
during the centuries of the poem's transmission the poem's
audience was content to see any adventure at all inserted into a
sailor's yarn, whereas Aristotle, who saw the plot of the
Odyssey as a structural unity, was expressing a purely idiosyncratic view. If, like Aristotle, we admire the poem's discretion in
narrating only the significant events in a man's life, we shall
have to search for the connection between Helios and Poseidon
elsewhere than in the faults of transmission.

The surface meaning of the myth of the attack on the cattle
of the sun — reverence for the sun — is readily apparent. But
Ikaros fell to his doom in striving to emulate the sun. Odysseus'
comrades' sacrilege is of a different sort. They desecrate the
property of the sun or, as Aristotle noted, the days and nights
of the year. Theirs is in some way an attack on, a negation of,
time. To see the connection of this attack with the poem's
themes we must retrace our steps back to the opening lines
where we discover that time plays a prominent part in this

poem as it does not in the *Iliad*. This is the judicious moment for Odysseus' return, says the proem; the circling seasons have brought around the year that the gods in their spinning have marked for his return (1.16-18). Poseidon is absent from Olympos, feasting with the Aithiopians who live at the boundaries of the world, which is to say he is nowhere in sight (vv. 22-25). Zeus, musing on Orestes' vengeance on Aigisthos, is in a receptive mood for Athena's request for the man whom she considers to have sufficiently expiated any wrongdoing he may be guilty of. All things conspire to make this the right moment.

As the poem progresses we find that the proem's words on the judicious moment are not idly said. This is not simply the optimum moment, but the necessary moment. Odysseus has, though he does not know it, a precise timetable to adhere to, which will lead him to his revenge in Ithaka on the most important day of the year. His timing will be crucial to his success. Odysseus, exiled for seven years by his comrades' assault on Helios' property, is ready when the poem opens to make his reentry into the cycle of time.

Just as he is about to make that reentry, Kalypso makes one final attempt to seduce Odysseus. She offers him, quite literally, timelessness. Her temptation, "the euphoria of eternity," far from being unique, is one of the besetting trials of Odysseus' wanderings. In one way or another many other figures offer him a similar release from time. The Sirens promise memory total and intact, mind liberated from the barriers of past and future, mind thus transcending time. Only Odysseus is privileged to endure this transcendent temptation and he survives it only by being bound to the ship's mast. His comrades, on the other hand, fall easily to the temptation of the Lotos-eaters, which is mind delivered from memory altogether. Whoever ate of the lotos wished to forget his return (9.97). Saved from the lotos they then fall victim to Kirke's baneful drug which makes men forget their homes and turns them into swine – perhaps Homer's picture of the amnesiac's lot (10.236ff.). Saved from Kirke, Odysseus' sailors choose oblivion by incurring Helios' anger. Their suicidal wishes are finally granted: "they contrived their own destruction, the fools" (1.7). The lotos, Kirke's drug, Helios' cattle, each is different, but there is a clear sequence in which Odysseus' comrades attempt to forget their return, and finally succeed.

Thus there is a series of psychological threats encountered in Odysseus' travels, forms of psychic destruction, culminating in the incident on Thrinakia, where psychological and physical destruction coincide. Modern psychology is well aware of the relation of memory to time. "In its first stages," writes Paul Fraisse, a contemporary psychologist, "the temporal horizon is simply a manifestation of memory, and it develops with the latter" (*The Psychology of Time,* p. 153). Memory is not merely the repository of experience but the constructive activity that creates our sense of time as a sequence of events and forms our sense of order. Clinical experiments that relate perception and memory only document one of the first axioms of Homeric psychology, that memory is survival and order. To remember is to be, as in the phrases "remember your *arete,*" "remember your strength but not your panic" (*Il.* 13.48), or "they saw the bird sent from Zeus and remembered their warcraft" (*Il.* 8.252). Alkinoos says (7.192-194): "Tomorrow we shall remember our escort, how the stranger may reach his home safely under our escort." Here remembering comes close to making a plan for the future. Since memory is so much part of what a man is for Homer, the properties of the lotos and Kirke's drug, which cause forgetfulness of home or of the return home, are really statements on the dissolution of identity.

Odysseus himself makes clear how dependent survival is on memory. Odysseus, though he was not turned into a pig, succumbed to Kirke's spell anyway and suffered amnesia for a year until his sailors roused him (10.472-474): "Now remember your paternal soil if indeed it is the gods' will for you to be saved and to reach your home and your ancestral soil." That is Odysseus' only lapse. Thenceforth he clings tenaciously to the memory of his soil. Our first sight of him in the poem is as he sits on the shore of Kalypso's island wearing his spirit away in weeping for his return (5.151-153). To Kalypso's final offer of immortality Odysseus replies (5.219-220): "Even so, I wish and yearn every day to go home and to look on my day of return." At the Phaiakian court Odysseus expressly attributes his survival to his desire for home. He begins the tale of his adventures with a fulsome proem on the beauties of one's own land. "For my part, I cannot look upon anything sweeter than ancestral soil," so Odysseus concludes his description of his rugged island (9.27-28). He continues by describing Kalypso's and Kirke's attempts to detain him, and explaining their failure (vv. 33-36): "But that did not at all persuade the *thymos* in my chest since there is nothing sweeter than ancestral soil and parents, not even if a man dwells in a prosperous home in a foreign land far from his own parents." Only after this preamble on the choice he has made between eternity in Kalypso's prosperous house and that miniscule point in time and space of his own island home is Odysseus ready to begin the tale.

Against the background of these incidents concerned with the attrition or preservation of memory, the cattle of the sun will assume their full significance. The sea is chaos. That chaos is represented in a variety of ways through the poem. Those who would locate precisely in the Mediterranean all the sites Odysseus visits overlook that passage where Odysseus himself records the moment when he sailed out of known geography into the primeval disorder of the sea. There at the Cape of Maleia "we would have reached our homes," says Odysseus, had not the north wind come up and thrust him into *terrae incognitae* (9.79-81). This is not to be the simple mariner's yarn of expeditions to Egypt, but the poetic statement of the experience of the sea. That experience becomes at one point the picture of the winds unloosed from a bag, at another point a storm of winds that Poseidon arouses to hurl Odysseus to an island far even from the gods. It appears also in Odysseus' description of reaching an unknown island during a moonless night. These are all forms of disorientation. The disorientation can be simple spatial disorientation, as when Odysseus tells his comrades (10.190-192): "We know not where *zophos* is nor *eos,* neither where Helios goes beneath the earth nor where he rises." But it can be other forms of disorientation, as in Proteus' manifold transformations or in the strange forms of life the sea engenders, like Skylla and Charybdis and Poseidon's son Polyphemos. One simile, in which the sea is the epitome of chaos, links both Penelope and Odysseus in a single fate, she suffering on land the same threat of disintegration he had suffered at sea (23.233-240): "As the sight of land brings joy to men swimming, whose ship Poseidon has smashed into the sea . . . in joy they touch land, escaping evil, so the sight of her husband was joy for her and she would not release him from the embrace of her fair arms." The full simile is a capsule description of Odysseus' landing on Scheria, but now the brine-laden, ship-wrecked mariner touching soil is Penelope. Both sailors are at last home from the sea.

When Odyssus first sights Scheria there is another simile descriptive of disintegration at sea (5.392-399). Odysseus lifted high by a great wave saw land: "as when to children the life of a father appears most welcome, when he lies suffering and wasting away in sickness . . . but the gods free him from the illness and bring joy, so to Odysseus it was a joy when land and woods appeared." Odysseus himself will credit his survival to his desire to see his fatherland. It is appropriate here that the land is his father, and he at sea becomes the child disoriented by his father's withdrawal into sickness but suddenly joyful and oriented again when he discerns his father returning to life. Out of sight of land is to be reduced to the child's destitution when bereft of parents.

If Odysseus' voyage is one of disorientation, spatial disorientation is matched in the psychological sphere by amnesia, and not only the amnesia of the mariner. A watery death is a particularly vile fate because the lack of funeral rites and a monument to mark the burial threatens even that vestigial existence which survives in others' memory. "We would not grieve so much," says Telemachos, "if Odysseus had died at Troy and received full burial rites. But now the harpies have carried him away without glory, and he is gone unseen and unheard" (1.236-242). The psychological disorientation of amnesia is translated into the temporal sphere as an attack on Helios' days and nights. Melville's Ishmael suffers vertigo at the seductive prospect of the infinite expanse of ocean. What is the killing of Helios' cattle but the mythic representation of Ishmael's vertigo, transferred from the spatial dimension to the temporal? A more vivid description of vertigo at sea could hardly be found than Odysseus' sailors' refusal to heed the direct warnings and their slaughter of the sun's property, which is to say their slaughter of themselves, since for Homer life and sun are so closely associated as to be virtually synonymous. Odysseus' sailors negate time and are banished from time altogether; Odysseus disappears from time, exiled to Kalypso's hiding place for seven years of inactivity. Odysseus almost succumbs, but the memory of home is the one stable and enduring landmark in that maze of time and space that is the uncharted sea.

If we are dubious about applying symbolic interpretations to Helios' role, many indications later in the poem make the interpretation both permissible and necessary. When Odysseus is cast ashore on Ogygia he disappears temporally and spatially, from geography and time. When he starts his homeward journey from the island we get a whole constellation of signs and images which determines the time of his return. He sails from Ogygia following the stars, which are the navigator's compass (5.272-277). But stars are also the main determinants of the seasons, chronometers as well as compasses. The constellations listed contrast with Odysseus' earlier admission of disorientation — "we know not where *zophos* is nor *eos*." Now with sleepless eyes he guides himself by the Pleiades, Boötes, and the Bear in their circling paths. He is oriented again, but we know from those constellations not only his spatial direction but the time of year. Or rather, those constellations hint at a certain time of year, and then subsequent similes and descriptions of weather corroborate their evidence. Those constellations are proof that Odysseus has aligned himself once more in harmony with time.

In Homer's portrayal of order and disorder there are, then, certain representations, like whirlpools and storms, that are of purely natural phenomena. There are others, like Helios, in which psychological and natural elements begin to blend. Helios provides a transitional mythos taking us from raw elements to elements that are represented as anthropomorphic cultures. In these cultures the connection with the natural elements remains, and in all there is clear evidence of superhuman powers. Kirke is the daughter of Sun and Ocean and has the power to transform men into animals. The Kyklopes are the sons of Poseidon and have almost invincible brute strength. Alkinoos is Arete's uncle (an incestuous marriage which in itself suggests a nonhuman society), both are descended from Poseidon, and their people have superhuman navigational skill. They seem in many respects to be a variant of the Aiolos myth, being the calm of the sea when all the winds are in harmony. Kalypso is the daughter of baleful Atlas and inhabits the island that is the navel of the sea. In all these there are features, in genealogy and powers, that proclaim them as representatives of the natural world, in particular of the sea, but they become vehicles principally for the study of anthropological systems.

Again there is a hierarchy from simple to complex, and the range of systems gives us something of Homer's idea of culture as measurable by the increasing complexity of social structures and by the degree of interaction between society and nature. At the lowest level are brutes like the Laistrygonians, but they need hardly detain us since in the Kyklopes, their next of kin in the evolutionary family, Homer has given a full portrait of the primitive. Polyphemos is by no means destitute of order. In his solitary world he is in fact addicted to system, though his system is, to be sure, no wondrous creation. A courtyard surrounds his cave, built up with stones, pine trees, and oaks (9.184-185). The organization within his cave would pass the most meticulous inspection. There are folds for the two kinds of young animals, lambs and goats, and each species is carefully subdivided into three groups according to age, the spring-born, the "middlings," and the newborn (9.219ff.). Two kinds of containers, pails and bowls, hold the whey. Polyphemos, when he returns at evening from the pasture, carries out his duties in a methodical way. He leaves the male goats and rams in the courtyard outside, drives the females inside and barricades his door with a stone (vv. 237ff.). He milks the sheep and goats, all in order (*panta kata moiran*, v. 245), then gives the young to their mothers. He then curdles the fresh milk, scoops the curds into wicker baskets, and puts the rest into pails to sit ready for him to drink. With his chores taken care of he turns his attention to his own comfort and lights a fire. This is a regular daily schedule from which he makes one significant deviation the following evening when he brings all his flock, male and female, into the cave with him (v. 338).

Gigantic oaf he may be, but Polyphemos has his *techne* and within the sphere of that *techne* he loses his clumsiness. He has the skills essential to his *techne:* he can build a wall and pen for his flocks, he can fashion pails for the whey, crates for the cheese, and plait wicker baskets for the curds. His *techne* is, of course, dairy farming; the whole dairy farm has been transported into his cave. Polyphemos' proficiency, whether in fashioning the necessary utensils or in performing his chores, is impeccable. Within the sphere of his craft he is an artist, as devoted to formal symmetries as any Geometric painter.

What Polyphemos lacks is not technical proficiency but the intelligence to go beyond his subsistence economy. Homer's portrait of Polyphemos is a vivid documentary on life without reason. Polyphemos suffers from two intellectual defects which prove to be his undoing: he has a total lack of curiosity and, as the corollary, a total lack of converse with other intelligent beings. The paradigmatic tale is woven around these two essential attributes of the Kyklopean character.

The Kyklopes, Homer says, had no shipbuilders, but this cannot be because of their lack of technical skill. Rather, they lacked shipbuilders because they had never thought of going to sea. Polyphemos shows himself, in his questions to Odysseus, acquainted with ships and marauding pirates, but to construct some conveyance which could carry his folk across to the island at the entrance of their harbor is an idea that has never occurred to Polyphemos or any of his clan. If the Kyklopes are indifferent about the possibilities on that island, they are positively obtuse about the possibilities of even their own land. They live in an agricultural paradise where everything grows in profusion without need for seeding, ploughing, or artificial irrigation. While fertile fields lie around him, laden with perpetual crops — wheat, barley, and grapes are specifically mentioned — Polyphemos blithely cultivates a dairy farm instead. Across the bay is the island that would be more suitable for men who eschew agriculture. Its soil is fertile but still uncultivated; it is the home of goats which, as we know, Polyphemos prefers to grain. Everything conspires to encourage the exploring instinct: the island is only a short distance off, it is unclaimed territory, it has besides its abundance of goats a good water supply, and, final irony, it has the absolutely ideal harbor where stern cables are never necessary and sailors can rest at their ease until their spirits prompt them to move on. The nautical technology necessary for crossing from the mainland to the island would be the very minimal. Even Kyklopes could have negotiated that placid bay if any possible motive for doing so had crossed their minds. But the paradise across the bay is not even a mystery for them; they have never noticed it any more than they have noticed the luxuriant crops on which their own flocks graze. Through this lack of curiosity about cereal agriculture Polyphemos falls victim to the potent wine Odysseus serves him. Though he claims that the Kyklopes are familiar with wine (9.357-358), we suspect he is merely boasting; he seems to be strictly a milk-drinker. Again, his lack of curiosity leads him to assume that he would be deprived of his eye by someone as large as himself. He had never given the prophecy much thought, there being little of the reflective in his temperament.

The limitation of intelligence extends to their social life. The *themis* of the Kyklopes is as limited as their technical skill. What they have is idiorrythmic; each Kyklops lays down the *themis* for his own wife and children but there is no common code that binds the individual families into a larger community (9.114-115). Polyphemos as a bachelor has not even the nucleus of a community. There is no other person to receive or share his *themis* and that is why he in particular knows neither *dikas* nor *themistas* (v. 215). The lack of a community restricts the Kyklopes forever to a low level of proficiency. Homer spells out the advantages of community in verse 112: there are among the Kyklopes no decision-making assemblies (ἀγοραὶ βουληφόροι). Decision-making assemblies are among the most important features of Homeric life. Without them no Kyklops will urge another Kyklops to action, none will collaborate with another in planning or executing some action, there will be none to prevent another's rash mistake, to propose a better plan, to offer professional expertise or the lessons learned with greater experience. There is, simply, no tradition; each Kyklops starts afresh, truly a *tabula rasa*. In Homer, where so much motivation is external, issuing as much from a man's comrades as from his gods, where, even when a man develops a plan on his own initiative, he generally lays it before someone else before putting it into action, the Kyklopes' abhorrence of each other's company assumes ominous significance. Their isolation from each other and, apparently, from the gods means in effect a perpetual lack of motivation. Homeric men rarely suggest things to themselves when in isolation, but merely repeat old habits. Achilleus has no initiative once he retires from the Greek army, he can merely sing lays of ancient heroes. It is in the community that proposals are made and new actions taken. Polyphemos' cry of pain stirs some faint interest in the other Kyklopes, but they are quickly satisfied with his reply that Noman is killing him. Men with greater experience of communal life would have remained puzzled by Polyphemos' answer, would have found it as nonsensical as it was. Anyone with the slightest communal sense would have investigated further to discover the true cause of Polyphemos' pain.

Polyphemos' intelligence, adequate when he ranged along the pastures, becomes vastly deficient when he is confronted with another intelligence. He is an easy prey to Odysseus' cunning because he has never had to develop his wits in competition with another. To use men for food is a gory mistake, but only one of his several elementary mistakes. To preface his question on the whereabouts of Odysseus' ship by a boast that he pays no reverence to Zeus himself (how then expect him to reverence mere mortal strangers?), to promise Odysseus a guest-gift after he has already devoured six of Odysseus' men, to block up his doorway against trespassers from without before checking for possible trespassers already within, all these are most telling proofs of the hazards of life lived in isolation. The so flagrant pun in the name *Outis* escapes Polyphemos because he has never had the opportunity to learn what *tis* was. To a person with no acquaintance with names one name is as good as another. It takes only a rudimentary social converse to distinguish names from jokes, but that rudimentary level lies above Polyphemos' range of experience. Polyphemos' pathetic attempt at a pun on *xeinion,* his guest-gift to Odysseus, is but his gross admission that he has no knowledge of the social relationships that *xeinia* symbolize.

The story of the one-eyed giant is one to delight a child's sense of the absurd, though its too obvious gusto brings an occasional frown to the adult scholar's brow. What Homer has done is to transform the tale into a moral for adults, while retaining all the elements of the traditional tale. The pun on the false name undoubtedly is part of the tradition. In Homer, the pun still induces its childlike glee — Odysseus prides himself almost excessively on its wit — but it becomes only one particle in a more sophisticated exposition. Since we are given several preliminary indications of the character of Polyphemos before the pun occurs, his failure to see through the pun is not only consistent with his mental acumen elsewhere but is also the culmination of the portrait the poet had been carefully painting stroke by stroke. Absurd as the pun on *Outis* is as Name-No Name, Homer's success is to make it plausible. Homer's description of the Kyklopean character, their indifference to the utilitarian potential of the crops at their feet or of the island that fairly begs them to cross the bay and their lack of social converse, becomes the background for the pun and for the Kyklopes' reaction to Polyphemos' cry. How could a person who never associated with other men, whose life was a Sisyphean round of shepherding flocks in isolation, of milking goats and making cheeses, how could he know anything of those other categories of experience that names, true or false, represent? For names presuppose communities and social relationships — only Jehovah has no name. How could he know that every question he asked Odysseus decisively betrayed his ignorance of social forms, betrayed, in short, his lack of *experience,* and therefore made the trap that was to ensnare him that much easier to set? The other Kyklopes' failure to make sense of Polyphemos' nonsensical cry is as absurd as his original mistake, but Homer makes it plausible by his earlier references to their indifference to communal responsibilities. They too are caught in the same trap as Polyphemos, although he mistranslates *Outis* as a real name while they translate it correctly back into the negative pronoun. It is a nicely double-edged pun, a trap whether interpreted correctly or incorrectly.

The old folktale of the small man who uses cunning to outwit the clumsy ogre has become a comprehensive examination of two kinds of intelligence. Polyphemos' life is diligent and methodical but hardly more humanized than that of the flocks he tends, a continuous repetition of daily habits never questioned and never changed. His dairy farming, so *perversely* methodical amid the profusion of natural cereals, his indifference to the island across the bay, and his intelligence unwhetted by contact with others are all directly contrary to Odysseus' desire for exploration, for experimentation, for testing himself, for expanding the range of his *techne.* The contrast is pointed between the Kyklopes' lack of curiosity, evidenced particularly in their ignorance of shipbuilding skills, and Odysseus' insistent need to cross over from the island paradise to explore the unknown mainland. Odysseus' foresight, first in taking a skin of potent wine on the chance that he might meet a wild man, later in anticipating the drift of Polyphemos' interrogation, and then in plotting his revenge so that Polyphemos should also aid in Odysseus' deliverance, is also in explicit contrast to Polyphemos' stolid inability to anticipate anything. Polyphemos can scarcely see what lies at his very feet, much less reflect on future possibilities. The giant's grotesque single eye, again a traditional element of the tale, becomes more than a convenience for the exigencies of the plot. Everything we are shown about the Kyklopes, everything they do and say, proves them to be monocular. Polyphemos' single eye sums in one poetic image the whole of the Kyklopean character.

To move from Polyphemos' cave to Kalypso's island is a distinct matriculation. The description of her cave displays a landscape painter's eye such as no Geometric vase ever revealed. The growth on her island is luxuriant but not unbridled. All is symmetrical. As a frame for the picture there is an encircling forest, flourishing with alders, black poplars, and fragrant cypresses, the home of owls, hawks, and cormorants (5.63ff.). The woods open on to an expanse of meadow, also framing the cave (cf. *amphi*, v. 72), carpeted in soft violet and celery and watered by four springs. Set in the meadow is the cave around which grows a wild vine, heavy with grapes. At the very center of the whole composition is Kalypso herself, singing and working her loom. It is a carefully constructed ideal landscape set in concentric balance: trees, springs, meadow, cave, nymph. Perhaps it is a poet's even more than a painter's landscape since it is a harmonious blend of shapes, colors, textures, sounds, and smells. The smell of burning wood wafting from Kalypso's hearth over the whole island is the true frame for the composition. The sound of Kalypso's voice, the plash of fresh springs, the contrasts of texture and color between the tall somber trees and the flat meadow of delicate flowers are all part of the composition. Within the composition each separate segment is itself a unified composition of diverse elements — not simply a grove but a grove of three kinds of trees, not simply birds but three kinds of birds, a meadow of two kinds of plants, the smell of two kinds of burning wood. This is catalogue poetry at its best, where variety within a species and the variety of species are shaped into a dramatic whole. Bird contrasts with bird, tree with tree, and the discrete elements fuse into larger components which then contrast with each other, forest with meadow, meadow with cave. Sketched in only a few lines, the order around Kalypso's cave is far more intricate and subtle than that in Polyphemos' cave. In both descriptions there is the same kind of pictorial technique, a diversity of species combining into larger contrasting units. In Polyphemos' cave there is the contrast between male and female animals, between young and old, the contrast of one species with another, and within the species further contrasts, between three kinds of young animals, three kinds of milk products. Kalypso's island is an amplification of the formalism in the cramped cosmos of Polyphemos' cave, his cosmos expanded into more majestic proportions in the open air and including the nature that he specifically excluded.

Kalypso's ecology differs profoundly from that of the Kyklopes in exuding a life shaped by intelligence. Kalypso is a deity and her landscape has idyllic perfection, but her divinity means only that she has the human attributes in a more potent, idealized way. She can accomplish by will what humans must labor to achieve – she sings, for example, at her weaving as mortal women do not – but her aesthetic values are not essentially different from human values. Where Polyphemos obtusely cuts across nature to labor stoically at his dairy farming instead of living at his ease off the fruits of the earth, everything around Kalypso is marked by harmony. In her external landscape each element – trees, flowers, water, smells, sounds – harmonizes with the others to form an integrated composition, and Kalypso herself is integrated into the whole. The landscape outside the cave is as much an artistic creation as the fabrics Kalypso melodiously weaves inside the cave; both are the expressions of her personality which is that of a sensitive and aesthetic human.

The harmonies in and around her cave are visual tokens of Kalypso's character, hints that receive confirmation in her personal behavior towards others. The portrait of Kalypso, although hardly more than a thumbnail profile, is one of the most sympathetic in the *Odyssey*, though modern taste has ignored her in preference for Nausikaa's budding adolescent sexuality. Kalypso's character has a restraint that suggests a depth and a poignancy scarcely matched in the poem except by Penelope. Kalypso's dialogues with Hermes and Odysseus are models of delicacy and understanding even though both bring only hurtful news. She suspects that Hermes' extraordinary visit to her bodes no good; in fact, she suspects quite well his exact mission, but she receives him with great courtesy and promises to accomplish whatever is his wish. When Hermes has partaken of the *xeinia* she sets before him, the ambrosia and nectar of the gods, he reveals his mission. Kalypso shudders and bursts into an angry diatribe on the gods for their jealousy, and then pretends to have no resources to send Odysseus on his way. Hermes insists on Zeus' order and she acquiesces. Angry as she is at Zeus' command, in her subsequent behavior towards Odysseus she disguises her deepest feelings and in a tone of gentle pity tells him she will send him on his way. She smiles at his fear of some deception on her part, scolds him in a playful way for his suspicious mind, but readily swears the oath that will put his mind at rest. Later, at their last dinner together, at that communal board which is itself a poignant reminder of the issue that separates them, as she eats the nectar and ambrosia of the immortals and serves him the food "such as mortal men eat," she broaches for the last time the possibility of his remaining with her. Her appeal, even with its overt comparison of the respective charms of a mortal Penelope and an immortal Kalypso, remains underplayed. It is not really even a direct appeal but a final blessing ambiguously worded to offer Odysseus a last chance to change his mind (5.203-213): "If you truly wish to go," she says, "go with joy. But if you knew what lies ahead of you you would choose to stay here and become immortal in spite of your longing for your wife. And I, an immortal, am, surely, in no way inferior to her." When Odysseus declines her implicit offer she never reverts to the subject again but devotes herself to expediting Odysseus' return to her aging mortal rival.

Kalypso is a powerful goddess in the grip of a powerful passion, as her outburst to Hermes reveals, but she defers to others, even to Penelope, with urbanity, hides her passion, and expends her superior intelligence and power in furthering an action entirely antithetical to her own interests. Her *thymos* is not made of iron, she tells Odysseus (5.191), though it could easily have been so. She has the passion that could steel her heart and we have indications enough of the supernatural forces she could, if she chose, harness to her passion. There is no evading Zeus' command, it is true, but the generosity of Kalypso's acquiescence goes far beyond Zeus' imperative. Her last conversation with Odysseus shows her acquiescence to be as much influenced by Odysseus' desire as by Zeus' command. In spite of the mysterious and alien elements in Kalypso — her magical powers, her deep seclusion within the forest, her isolation from gods and men — elements that might lead one to expect a barbaric person, she lives according to the forms of humane society. The civilized landscape of her island, where natural elements are shaped into aesthetic order, mirrors the civilized landscape of Kalypso's character, where natural emotions are so governed that the unobservant scarcely discerns them. The wild vine embracing Kalypso's cave, sinuous tendril in a rectilinear landscape, is an apt token of island and lady: everywhere order and control, but here and there a reminder that the order is an act of will.

Kirke, the intermediary between the barbarism of Polyphemos and the refinement of Kalypso, is the barbarian princess whom Kalypso chooses not to be. Like Kalypso, she has magical powers, she lives in seclusion on a solitary island, she sings as she plies the loom, weaving delicate and beautiful fabrics. Kalypso is the daughter of Atlas, "who knows the depths of all the sea" (1.52-53), whereas Kirke is the daughter of Helios (10.138). Once again, in the similarity between the two seductive nymphs we have an indication that both sun and sea play an equal role in this tale.

In other respects, however, Kirke shares traits more in common with Polyphemos than with Kalypso. Specifically, she acknowledges no laws of hospitality, though she is no cannibal. She first transforms men to animals, and presumably eats them in that form later. Once she is outwitted and conquered at the point of a sword she becomes the picture of hospitality, showing herself as well acquainted with social forms as anyone else. Her four handmaidens busy themselves with setting the table, mixing wine, preparing food, heating water for Odysseus' bath. They bathe and clothe him, seat him at the table and serve him a choice meal. Everything is impeccably correct but for one thing which reveals the difference between Kirke and Kalypso. It does not occur to Kirke that Odysseus should be unable to enjoy his dinner while his comrades grovel in the pigsties outside. Kalypso has a generous character but Kirke's generosity appears only under compulsion. Once Odysseus mentions the cause of his distress she is immediately solicitous; she transforms his comrades back into men and has Odysseus return to his ship to bring the rest of the crew to her house. Thereafter she remains benign. She is hospitable, and when Odysseus wishes to leave she makes no attempt to hinder his going. With our knowledge of her ambivalent character, however, we cannot but feel a momentary qualm with Odysseus when her first response to his request to leave is to send him on an expedition to Hades' realm. The expedition turns out to be no trap, she had already sworn an oath to devise no tricks, but there is a touch of the sinister in her jocular greeting when Odysseus returns from the underworld (12.21-22): "So you did it, you rascals; you went down alive to the house of Hades. Now you are the twice-dead; other men only die once." Kirke's intentions are not altogether to be trusted. Kirke has, then, the refinement of Kalypso but without the humaneness. Under compulsion she is civilized, as Polyphemos is not, but her civilization is, one feels, a fragile veneer.

At the opposite end of the spectrum from the Kyklopes are the Phaiakians. With them the symmetrical balance, the aesthetics of contrast, so evident on Kalypso's island but only germinal in Polyphemos' cave, come into full flower. The formalism is repeated but with appropriate modification and in far greater detail. Odysseus, as he walks through the city, marvels first at the harbors, the ships, the meeting places, and the high palisades fitted together (7.43-45). This artificial forest of stakes and masts gives way to a view of real trees in a spacious four-acre orchard enclosed on both sides (7.112ff.). In the orchard are pears, pomegranates, apples, figs, and olives. Set in the orchard is also a vineyard which is, in its turn, as Stanford notes, elaborately symmetrical (vv. 122ff.). In the background is a flat, dry area which catches the sun, subdivided into two smaller areas, one for collecting grapes and the other for the winepress. In the foreground is the vineyard itself, again subdivided into two areas, with green grapes on one side and nearly ripe grapes on the other. At the edge of the orchard are well-ordered (*kosmetai*, v. 127) vegetable beds yielding every variety of produce. There are two springs, one irrigates the orchard and the other runs towards the palace to supply water inside.

In the center of this most formal of all Homeric landscapes stands the palace, splendid with the sheen of precious metals. Bronze-plated walls run the length of the palace, decorated with a frieze of lapis lazuli (v. 86ff.). Gold doors are set in silver lintels on a bronze threshold. Gold and silver dogs sit on guard on each side of the doorway. Against the walls, running the length of the palace from the threshold, are rows of thrones draped with delicate *peploi*. Golden youths stand on pedestals with torches in hand. Fifty women busy themselves in the palace, some grinding grain in handmills, others working looms and carding wool.

The schematic similarities between the descriptions of Scheria and Ogygia are evident. In both there is the fascination with variety shaped into unity. Kalypso's grove of different kinds of trees finds its parallel in the Phaiakian orchard with its different fruits, in the Phaiakian vineyard squared off with separate areas for various stages of viniculture, and in the palace itself which is a composite of bronze, gold, silver, and lapis lazuli. The framing design around Kalypso's cave – trees, meadow, cave — is repeated in the Phaiakian tableau of orchard, vineyard, vegetable garden, and palace. There is in both scenes the contrast of the larger elements with each other, horizontal lines balanced against vertical, dark against light. In Scheria the sets of contrast are multiple: mechanical male servants — the golden sconces sculptured as youths — contrast with the live female servants, the female household staff contrast with the feasting male aristocrats, the hard surfaces of thrones with the texture of fabrics thrown over them, the oily sheen of fabrics with the glitter of metals, the shipbuilding skill of the men with the weaving skills of the women. Within the separate elements there is also the play of contrast. The description of the walls and doors of the palace is an amplification of the contrast of the light of the sun and moon in the simile at verse 84: first bronze and gold (vv. 86, 88); silver and bronze (v. 89), silver and gold (v. 90), and finally the gold and silver watchdogs. The women too are subdivided into two groups, each group acting in unison, with grindstones providing counterpoint to the hum of the looms.

The scene in the palace is framed by two similes drawn from nature. The first, a comparison to the bright sun and moon, introduces the metals, emphasizing their brilliance, their hard surfaces, and their solidity (7.84ff.). But the statuesque rigidity of walls, doors, carved dogs, and sconces gives way in the second half of the description to the mobility of the women at their tasks, to their close-woven, pliant, and oleaginous fabrics. The rustle of poplar leaves in the second simile is an appropriate signal of the contrast the women with their nimble fingers provide to the static monumentality of the palace itself (7.106).

Stanford in his note on the Phaiakian vineyard (7.122ff.) suggests Oriental or Minoan influence in the formal proportions, which are, he finds, unparalleled in Greek literature. Minoan influence there may well be, but we cannot isolate the Phaiakian landscape from the other landscapes in the poem without violating the sense of the poem in the manner of earlier aleatoric criticism, which read the poem as an encyclopedia of ideas, tales, mores, and devices culled from disparate sources.

The Phaiakian landscape has its unique features. Its symmetries, most succinctly represented in the vineyard, are striking but they are not different in kind from the symmetries of the other landscapes. Scheria, the most highly elaborated example, is the culmination and perfection of the idea of landscape in the poem.

In this poem landscape and the uses of landscape are functions of personality and intelligence. The Phaiakian landscape and their palace decor mirror the complexity of their social economy. Cheesemaking exhausts Polyphemos' imagination, but the Phaiakians can work in any material – stone, metals, or wood – can build ships and palaces, carve statues, sail the seas, turn night to day. They are supreme artisans. The polychromatic, polymorphous scene in Alkinoos' palace reveals an organically functioning community, the first *polis* Odysseus has seen since leaving Troy, just as the monopolistic industry in Polyphemos' cave reveals the monocular character of its inhabitant.

There is a statement in the Polyphemos episode on the dichotomy between nature and culture, but it is not a simple contrast drawn between the two figures, Polyphemos the man of nature and Odysseus the man of culture. Rustic as he is, Polyphemos is far from being integrated with nature. Rather, it is an indication of his obtuseness that, in ignorance of nature's potential, he works against nature, cultivating a dairy farm when he might be raising crops. The wise man in the *Odyssey* is one who knows how to exploit nature with his own *techne*. Scheria is the paradigm of the ideal community, in which human craftsmanship is united with natural advantages. Alkinoos' gardens are blessed with continuous crops and a perpetual favoring west wind, but utopian advantages in themselves do not explain the success and beauty of his orchard and vineyard. Polyphemos has as much if he but knew it. Alkinoos' orchard is man's artifact utilizing nature's gifts. It is not magic that squares off the land into orchard, vineyard, and vegetable garden, nor magic that cultivates the grapes, dries them in the sun, and treads them in the winepress. The whole description of Scheria is a play on the complementary opposition of man and nature. The palace gardens are a prize exhibit of the effective collaboration of man and nature, but then the palace, a purely human construct, becomes in its turn a foil to the nature outside. Hephaistos donated the ornamental watchdogs at the palace gates because he too enjoyed imitations of nature, but the rest of the palace is a piece of Phaiakian imagination, human *techne* in competition with the natural fertility of the orchard.

Within the palace the contrast between natural and artificial is constantly present, as it is, in a different way, outside the palace. Ornamental dogs, imperishable like the harvests of the orchard, substitute for mortality-prone live dogs. The *kouroi* who serve as lampbearers are likewise ornamental statues, imperishable in themselves and making light imperishable, turning night into day. Ornamental dogs and youths, standing forever motionless and unwearied, contrast with the mortal women whose fingers flicker restlessly over the loom. The precious metals and the statues are man's attempt to re-create the permanence of nature, man's imitation of the sun and moon as the simile suggests, and the women at their looms and mills are imitative of the dynamic creativity of nature.

From the Kyklopes to the Phaiakians the increase in intelligence is obvious. Polyphemos is bumbling and crude, his every word and deed a travesty of social norms. Kirke becomes human when compelled, and remains so, but we see little of her as a personality except in her jest made to Odysseus when he returns from his journey to the underworld. She is still more incident than person. Kalypso, by contrast, is a personality. In her conversations, first with Hermes in her cave, then with Odysseus on the shore, and finally in her dinner with Odysseus, she reveals herself a fully human character, with emotions and the style to convey them. Odysseus must act now not through tabus or magical rites or cunning but as he would act towards another human, through conversation that respects the other's rights and desires. The intelligence that begins to emerge in the character of Kalypso becomes yet more elaborated among the

Phaiakians, whose behavior reflects the orderly disposition and the intricate harmonies of their palace and grounds. The Phaiakians worship the gods and sacrifice to them; they know and respect the laws governing guest-host relationships; they gather in assemblies to formulate decisions in the same kind of feudal democracy the Homeric heroes practice. They have the aesthetic sensibility of Homeric heroes, which they express in art, song, dance, and athletic competition. In their midst Odysseus is truly in the world where the ideals of human society operate, and he must behave accordingly.

The Phaiakians demonstrate their intelligence through their crafts, through agriculture, seamanship, weaving, carving, and metal work. But Homer does not leave it at that. Their speech and their personal behavior are also their artifacts. Their lives are regulated by the laws of ceremony and this ceremony best illustrates their intelligence. When Odysseus makes his appearance in the palace, appeals for help, and assumes a humble position by the cinders, the wise old councillor Echeneos says to Alkinoos (7.159-166): "Alkinoos, this is neither beautiful nor seemly, that a stranger should sit in the ashes at the hearth. Come, set him on a *thronos,* have the heralds dispense wine so that we may make libations to Zeus who attends suppliants, and have someone set a meal before the stranger." Echeneos' advice not only reassures Odysseus that he is among people who share his moral code but it sets the dominant tone for the rest of Odysseus' stay on the island. Alkinoos is quick to respond to Echeneos' courteous verbal gesture with his own physical gesture. Taking Odysseus personally by the hand, he sets him on a chair right beside his own, though this means displacing his son Laodamas from his customary favored position.

Courtesies abound throughout the next two days, extended to Odysseus by his hosts and reciprocated by Odysseus. When, in conversation with Odysseus, Alkinoos is critical of his daughter for her breach of propriety in leaving Odysseus outside the palace, Odysseus deftly returns the courtesy by assuming all responsibility for Nausikaa's decision. Only one nasty slip occurs in their cordial relations, when Euryalos goads Odysseus into athletic competition by suggesting that he looks more like a merchant seaman than an athlete, but reparations are quickly made for the insult. In fact, the occasion proves fruitful for a shower of courtesies. Odysseus proves himself superior in contests of strength, Alkinoos' readily concedes his superiority and has the Phaiakians put on an exhibition of dance and song. Odysseus cooperates with the Phaiakians in the recovery of their self-esteem by paying them a liberal compliment on their dance, whereupon they return his compliment by liberal donations from their private treasuries. Later when Demodokos, in an unwitting compliment, sings the song of the Greek capture of Troy, Odysseus repays that compliment by sending the bard a special cut of meat.

The courteous exchange of compliments back and forth between host and guest betokens a harmonious community in which each individual recognizes the skills of the other and spontaneously defers to the other. Gifts and heralds, symbols in concrete form of social harmonies, both play an important role in Scheria. Gifts are compliments made tangible, memorials of esteem and friendship, and heralds serve in somewhat the same way to personify a compliment. The herald who accompanies Odysseus to his ship, who waits in attendance on blind Demodokos – setting food before him, putting the lyre in his hand, guiding him in and out of the palace – or who takes Odysseus' gift to the singer is the public celebrant of the group's deference to a particular individual.

Within the ornate harmonies of the Phaiakian composition there is what seems at first one discordant note: the burlesque tale Demodokos sings of the adultery of Ares and Aphrodite. Can a society as preoccupied with the observance of forms as the Phaiakians find it congruous to burlesque the gods whom they otherwise reverently worship? Social context is always important in Homer, but here without an understanding of the social context Demodokos' song seems almost meaningless and absurd. It is, in fact, a song about disruption within a social context. We may note in passing that, apart from its paradigmatic themes, the song itself is a harmony of song and dance, of words and movement, illustrative not only of the Homeric propensity for transposing action into song, song into action, but also of the particular Phaiakian delight in balance and contrast. Youths danced around Demodokos, says Homer, while Demodokos took up the song of the love of Ares and Aphrodite (8.262-266). Stanford, in his note on the passage, cautions us that the suggestion that the dance was a mime of the story is only surmise, but can we suppose that the youths were dancing something other than the story which Demodokos sings? That would be an even bolder surmise. The dance, the earliest reference in Greek literature to some kind of dramatic performance, is also the earliest reference to a performance in which males enact female parts. That the performers are male has direct bearing on the nature of the song Demodokos sings, for they remind us that the audience too is male. The sports Alkinoos arranges for the day are exclusively male. When women play so prominent a role in the Phaiakian court it is not merely coincidence that there is no reference whatsoever to any feminine presence at the games, which are introduced by a catalogue of sixteen male names, of spectators and participants (vv. 111-119). Only when the men return to the palace in the evening do women reappear on the scene.

The song of Ares and Aphrodite is sung and danced by males for an exclusively male audience. The theme of the song, a wife caught in adultery and the cuckold's revenge, is one to obsess the male mind and perhaps to amuse a male rather more than a female audience. The gods as the song's *dramatis personae* emphasize this point clearly enough. One male deity is wronged by another, a third male deity considerately reports the wrong, and two male deities gather around to enjoy the joke. When the cuckold calls the gods to witness the adulterous pair caught in his trap only male deities appear, Poseidon, Hermes and Apollo, but the female deities all remain at home out of a sense of *aidos,* embarrassment for Aphrodite and their sex (8.324).

The Greek attitude towards their gods always remained large enough to embrace the burlesque and the reverent, just as blasphemy has remained a durable and integral part of Christian practice, but Demodokos' song goes beyond the comic touches in the portraits of the gods elsewhere in the Homeric poems. Hera's scolding in the *Iliad* or her seduction of Zeus have a quiet humor, but Demodokos' song reaches beyond comedy to the point of lewdness. The uninhibited exchange in the song between Apollo and Hermes, genteel perhaps by our contemporary standards, is certainly obscene by Homeric standards. Nowhere else in Homer is adultery, whether human or divine, the object of such mirth, nor are ever sexual innuendoes plainer than in Apollo's question of Hermes, "Would you like to be forced this way to sleep in chains with golden Aphrodite?" and in Hermes' smirking reply, "Ha, would I indeed, lord Apollo!" (vv. 335-342). Demodokos' song, a male joke for male company, is appropriate in its place out on the playing fields, but would be vulgar if sung in the palace.

The song has its burlesque humor but also has obvious significance in the larger frame of the whole poem as a paradigm, set in jocular style befitting the Phaiakians, of the grimmer event that will take place within the week at Ithaka. Odysseus will, like Hephaistos, return to ensnare and exact vengeance from the would-be adulterers in his palace. The humor too is not merely gratuitous. The song is about the loss of dignity that even gods can suffer who transgress the proprieties. Hephaistos exacts a pledge of reparations from Poseidon for Ares' outrage, but the truly dire penalty for the guilty pair, as the song depicts it, is humiliation. What humor there is in the song exists solely in proportion to the high value the gods place on their personal dignity. Aphrodite becomes an object of ridicule only because as a goddess she has natural dignity. Poseidon, playing the patriarchal role in the story, demands to have the lovers released because he finds the public show an intolerable affront to the divine decorum, and the goddesses, placing the same value on decorum as he, refuse to add by their presence to Aphrodite's shame. Among mortals consequences can be more tragic, but among gods exposure to laughter is punishment enough. A song with its theme the public disgrace attendant on a breach of the social conventions is an apt one in the repertory of a people whose primary stress is on form and manners. Nausikaa did well, in bringing Odysseus into the city, to show a modicum of concern about the gossip of the townfolk. The Phaiakians, professional aesthetes, are jealous custodians of form.

Dexterous representation of form is the hallmark of the Phaiakian character; though related to the Kyklopes their character is totally antithetical. The Kyklopes know nothing of social life, but the Phaiakian is totally social – nothing, in fact, but social amenities. The Phaiakians function as an integral community and the advantages of communal life are many and obvious. Where the solitude of the Kyklopes keeps them at the level of crude improvisation, their Phaiakian cousins are craftsmen whose gardens, ships, palaces, dances, and banquets abundantly reveal their creative élan. They have also that curiosity so noticeably and disastrously absent from the Kyklopean nature. They are genuinely interested in Odysseus' tales, and in the stories of heroic deeds at Troy, and press him to continue even when he is, or feigns to be, ready for rest. They are knowledgeable about travellers' tales and find that Odysseus' narrative is greatly superior to the ordinary run. In aesthetic accomplishment, says Alkinoos, Odysseus' story rivals a bard's song (11.363-368). In comparison with the other societies in Odysseus' Apologos the Phaiakians stand out as the richest, most productive, and most imaginative.

When we turn our attention to Ithaka we understand the function of these prior documents of order, natural and human. Affairs in Ithaka are in complete disarray and the societies Odysseus passes through on his way home, and in a lesser way those his son visits at Pylos and Sparta, are paradigms for the restitution of order there. The situation in Ithaka is abnormal and unnatural, as Athena notes in her first appearance when she asks Telemachos (1.25-29): "What is this, a wedding feast perhaps? It is an ugly thing to see licentious men like these at the banquet table. A man of sense would be revolted at such behavior." The unnatural is noted in a score of ways. Athena came upon Telemachos, says Homer, sitting with the suitors but his mind was with his father (1.114-115). While the mother is besieged by suitors, her son sits among them thinking of his father, while they think of his mother. Telemachos actually apologizes to Athena for the entertainment, an occasion remarkable for being the unique instance in Homer of an apology for what Homer elsewhere calls the ornament of a banquet. When Phemios takes up the lyre to sing, Telemachos dissociates himself from the suitors by engaging Athena in conversation throughout what he claims is their song, not his (1.158-160): "You will forgive me, guest, but the lyre and song are their pleasure, a luxury they can well afford when they dine at another's expense with impunity."

The feast Athena comes upon is a parody of a wedding feast, and Phemios' song a parody of song, being not the host's customary offering to his guests but a servitude inflicted on both bard and host by the guests. It reminds Telemachos, the host, of the embarrassing truth that the guests are not guests but pirates, and the hosts their prisoners. Guests who have become pirates, hosts who have become unwilling prisoners, a presumptive widow, a presumptive son − that is Ithaka when the poem opens.

Uncertainty as to the status of Odysseus forms the central dilemma for Telemachos and Penelope, and the dilemma is such as to force them into despair. If Odysseus is dead the suitors are legitimate suitors; Penelope must choose among them and Telemachos, as head of the house, should be arranging his mother's remarriage. But if Odysseus is alive the suitors are vandals and Telemachos should be protecting his mother from their illegitimate suit. Telemachos shows his ambivalence by associating with, and alternately dissociating from, the suitors. He repeats the pattern in his behavior towards his mother, now defending her before the suitors, now siding with them against her when Penelope requests that Phemios change his song. Though he had apologized to Athena for the song, to Penelope he can say (1.346-359): "Mother, why do you begrudge the singer who takes his pleasure where his mind prompts him? It is not singers who are responsible but Zeus. . . . The *mythos* will be men's concern, but especially mine." It has now become his song. In the very extremity of ambivalence Telemachos confesses himself unsure of his own parentage (1.215-216): "My mother claims that I am Odysseus' son but I do not know." As is apparent from the genealogical boasts before battle in the *Iliad*, he who knows not his father knows not himself either. Telemachos is a young man of undefined status, undefined purpose, undefined role.

Penelope suffers in the same dilemma. She equivocates between resignation to Odysseus' death and hope in his imminent return, weaving her procrastination by day and unravelling it by night. One moment she is the dutiful wife outraged by her suitors' courtship – "You dare to pursue the wife of your benefactor" she reproaches Antinoos (16.418-433). A short while later she has the inexplicable urge to play the role of the courted lady (18.158-168).

Laertes' physical abdication from the palace to a corner of the estate epitomizes the vacuum in the center. Penelope and Telemachos, though remaining physically in the palace, have abdicated psychologically, trapped by their indecision and both awaiting the miraculous epiphany of Odysseus to deliver them from evil. Into the vacuum step the suitors, who quickly exchange whatever legitimacy their courtship may have had initially for criminality. They commandeer the best of the livestock; they dictate the hours for meals and the kind of entertainment to be provided; they appropriate the host's authority in deciding whether to extend hospitality to strangers who may come to the house. So habituated are they to their perverted conduct that they bite their lips in anger when Telemachos issues his first firm command, and Antinoos reproaches him for violent talk (1.381-385). They abuse, both verbally and physically, the suppliant at the hearth and go so far as to attempt assassination of the heir of the estate. Prophecies from Halitherses and Theoklymenos, omens from Zeus, pleas from Telemachos, Penelope, and Odysseus himself, only harden the edge of their arrogance. They are the Kyklopes in the human realm, ignoring their hosts' requests, making a travesty of hospitality, priding themselves on their cleverness while being blind to the doom they themselves are helping to construct. Like Polyphemos they know nothing of *dikai* and *themistai*.

The role of the slaves in Ithaka accentuates the abnormality in a striking way. In the *Iliad* slaves are almost invisible and none is treated as a dramatic character except Briseis in the one brief moment of her lament over the corpse of Patroklos. Otherwise they are merely supernumeraries. Eumaios, by contrast, is more fully drawn than several of the lesser heroes of the *Iliad*. Behind this difference between the two poems is certainly a differing emphasis on character. We might posit a link between the *Odyssey* and pastoral, between the *Odyssey* and comedy too, which, whether Aristophanic or Menandrian, occupies itself, as tragedy does not, with manners (i.e., *ethos*) and hence with domestic servants as representatives of one level of manners. That the *Odyssey* has its roots in both the pastoral and the comic is undoubted, but those traditions alone cannot account for the emphasis on menials in Ithaka. Outside Ithaka the Phaiakian bard Demodokos is the only figure to receive emphasis comparable to that given to deities or members of the aristocracy. Helen's household staff, or Nestor's, or Alkinoos', are as invisible as menials in the *Iliad*. Nowhere else in Homer does a lady look to her maid for approval, as Penelope looks to Eurynome when she thinks of appearing before the suitors. Even Odysseus' comrades are mostly nonentities who emerge from anonymity for brief moments to act as foils for Odysseus, being craven when he is adventurous, careless when he is cautious, willfully sacrilegious when he is pious. Eumaios and Eurykleia, however, are full characters in their own right. Others too, Eurynome, Philoitios, Melanthios, and Melantho, are as much characters as several more elevated persons in the poem.

Eurykleia and Eumaios, in particular, have dramatic parts to play precisely because of their masters' abdication. It is the servants, not the masters, who retain some vestige of order in the face of general anarchy. While the one does what he can to preserve the estate the other plays her parallel part in the domestic economy of the palace. We are by now accustomed to expect landscape and architectural descriptions to be as much a formulaic theme for the *Odyssey* as arming scenes are for the *Iliad.* When the islands and caves of the Kyklops, Kirke, and Kalypso, the harbor and palace of the Phaiakians, and the palace at Sparta are described in detail, we are struck by the conspicuous absence of Odysseus' palace from this portfolio. Telemachos and Odysseus may dilate on the character of their island, but Odysseus' palace itself receives none of the customary *amplificatio.* What replaces his palace in this scheme are the domains of Eumaios and Eurykleia.

Eumaios' hut, lowly as it is, is as striking as a palace for its architectural detail, its symmetry and its craftsmanship (14.5-28). It has a court, lofty and beautiful, says Homer, delineated by a wall of stones and wild pear. Outside the court Eumaios has built a palisade of oak beams set close together. He has subdivided the inner courtyard into twelve sties, in each of which are fifty sows with their litters, while the male hogs are kept outside. He has reared four watchdogs and has four assistants working for him. When Odysseus first sees Eumaios he is sitting alone because his assistants are out on their tasks; but Eumaios, far from being idle, is shaping sandals from animal hide. How different from our first sight of Telemachos idly daydreaming among the suitors.

While the palace falls into disrepair Eumaios holds firm, stalwart paradigm of order and a quiet reproach to his less industrious masters. Like Laertes, he has withdrawn from the contamination of the palace to his own corner of the estate — apart from his mistress and old Laertes, says Homer (14.9) — but unlike Laertes he struggles, in his corner, to conserve what he can of the estate against the depredations of the suitors. He is the builder, the craftsman, the accountant, the guardian in Ithaka, insofar as his lowly station permits him such functions. The description of his quarters makes a poignant contrast between the wastrel suitors and Eumaios the conservationist. The forecourt of his hut is a fortress in reduced scale: within it the 600 sows amble about with their litters, prosperous and secure. Outside the court is contested territory, where the male hogs are kept, fattened by Eumaios but under lien to the suitors (14.13-20): "They were much fewer, only 360 in all, for the ravenous suitors were depleting their number as Eumaios was ever sending them the prize beasts of his sleek stock." Eumaios' formal responsibilities extend over only one small part of the estate — he is the swineherd — but he exercises a proprietary concern for the whole estate as we see when he catalogues Odysseus' holdings in livestock, the twelve herds of cattle, twelve flocks of sheep, twelve of goats, and twelve of pigs on the mainland, and the eleven flocks of goats elsewhere in Ithaka (14.96-106).

The industry and orderliness Eumaios demonstrates in the construction of his home and the management of the estate are matched by Eurykleia's administration within the palace. As Eumaios has assumed by default responsibilities that should be exercised by Laertes or Telemachos, Eurykleia has assumed the management of the palace because Penelope cannot exert the customary authority of Homeric ladies. It is Eurykleia to whom Telemachos applies for provisions for his journey, Eurykleia who readies the palace for the feast of Apollo, Eurykleia who dispenses tasks among the household staff. There is one room in the palace that is orderly and secure, the storage chamber, with its supply of gold and bronze, its chests of garments, its jars of olive oil and wine stacked against the walls. That chamber is Eurykleia's domain and her jealously guarded prerogative (2.345-347): "The housekeeper used to be in there day and night, a woman of experience and intelligence, who kept account of everything, Eurykleia, daughter of Ops son of Peisenor." When Telemachos tells Eurykleia, on the eve of the vengeance, that he is moving the armor from the great hall to protect it from smoke damage, Eurykleia exclaims (19.22-23): "Ah child, if only you would have the discretion to think of the house and to watch over all its possessions." Hitherto it had been Eurykleia who kept accounts and guarded the family's possessions, and her response to Telemachos reveals how abnormal the situation had been.

Eumaios and Eurykleia provide the most effective revelation of the disorder in Ithaka. Eurykleia's efficiency must counteract Penelope's vacillation and withdrawal; Eumaios' carefully structured organization of the livestock offsets, to some degree, the disintegration of his two masters, the young master who sits daydreaming in the palace and the old master out on the estate, drifting in surrender to the elements. Odysseus' task is not merely the expulsion of usurpers but the re-creation of an original order that had existed in Ithaka. He must excavate, as it were, down to the almost obliterated foundation and then reconstruct on that old edifice. No wonder, then, that he finds his footing first with Eumaios and Eurykleia, working through Eumaios to Telemachos and through Eurykleia to Penelope. Eumaios and Eurykleia are his foundation, the one securing a stockade on one small area of the land and the other securing a single room in the depths of the palace against the depredations of the suitors and the negligence of his family. Through his faithful servants Odysseus must rebuild what once was his.

It is not true to say that there is no description of the architecture of Odysseus' palace. The landscape formula is there, but abbreviated and in a form that deviates so strikingly from the customary theme that it emphasizes the disparity between Ithaka and the orderly community on Scheria. When Eumaios and Odysseus first approach Odysseus' palace together, the poet mentions only the sound of the lyre within, but Odysseus casts his eye over the building and deduces from its exterior that this must be the fine house of Odysseus (τάδε δώματα κάλ', 17.264). Odysseus then proceeds to describe the building for us (vv. 266ff.). It rambles, with building attached to building, its court boasts a wall with finished cornices and it has stout double doors. Despite Odysseus' claim that the house would be easily identifiable even among many houses, the building seems to be one of no great pretensions, certainly not comparable to the splendor of the palaces at Sparta and Scheria. Odysseus merely observes the obvious, that the building is no swineherd's hut but is distinguishable from more rustic dwellings by its size, its more expensive outlay in the construction of

walls and doors, and by that final aristocratic clue, the sound of
a lyre gracing a banquet within (as singing voices are elsewhere
the clue to the presence of nymphs at work). But in one
sentence Odysseus reveals the drift of his thought. Noting its
size, its court, and its sturdy doors, Odysseus concludes (v.
269): "This is not a house a man could storm from without."
The tactician scans the establishment for its military possibilities. The house must, of course, be stormed from within.

Our spy, revolving thoughts of infiltration and guerilla
combat, fixes his attention on the security of those banqueting
at their ease inside rather than on the dimensions of the palace
or the splendors of the material. With good reason Homer
allows Odysseus to assess the architecture, while refraining
himself from the customary kind of description. Architectural
portraits elsewhere betoken organization and stability, even if it
be only the stability of Polyphemos' microcosm. The kind of
portrait appropriate to Scheria, which would emphasize harmonious integration of the elements and human craftsmanship
utilizing natural material, would be incongruous in Ithaka where
instability reigns. Thus Odysseus may note that the building is
an impregnable fortress, but Homer picks out one feature for
elaboration as an emblem of the general decay. What we
remember most vividly of that entrance to Odysseus' palace is
the heap of manure that has not yet been carted away from the
door, and a cast-off, flea-ridden dog lying barely conscious on
that manure (17.291-304, 318-322). Such is the scene that
replaces, in the landscape formula, the orchards, carved beams,
and polished metals that greet our eyes elsewhere. No other
edifice in the poem has so ignominious an approach.

Hermes stands in awe at the beauty around Kalypso's cave;
Odysseus stands in awe at the threshold of Alkinoos' palace
which shone forth like the sun or moon; Telemachos gazes at
Menelaos' palace and wonders whether he has wandered into
the palace of Zeus. But a dungheap confronts the visitor to the
palace in Ithaka as an ugly proof of present neglect. Eumaios'
apology explains the intrusion of this seamy realism into the
poem: without a master over them, he says, servants no longer

have the will for their tasks (17.320-321). The juxtaposition of dungheap and the dying dog with Odysseus' observations on the security of the building points the contrast between the craftsmanship of the past and the present abuse. This contrast is further reinforced by objects in the palace that the poet selects as examples of craftsmanship. Odysseus, entering the palace, sits at the threshold and leans against a cypress column. Suddenly a single column looms up in that hall as a remembrance of the past (17.340-341): "A carpenter in bygone days had polished it with a practised skill and evened it by the line." It is a formula, but the formulaic character only accentuates its force, since it is a description used of two structures for which Odysseus himself is the carpenter. The formula is used for Odysseus when he is shaping the timbers for his ship (5.245 = 17.341), again for the building of his bed (23.197 as a variation of 17.341), and one further time to describe the threshold of the storage room where Odysseus' bow is kept (21.43B-44 = 17.340B-341). Isolated objects rather than the whole palace are singled out for their sturdy construction − when Odysseus leans against that carefully finished cypress column, the description signals that the carpenter has returned.

The full landscape and architectural description is lacking when Odysseus arrives at his palace. Instead, it is transferred from Odysseus' arrival to Penelope's entrance into the store-room in the inner recesses of the palace (note ἔσχατον, 21.9). That is the moment in Ithaka most directly comparable to Odysseus' arrival at Scheria. It is Penelope's entry to another world, the world of the past which she may well be leaving forever. Her step across the threshold into that *Erinnerungs-raum,* so full of tokens and memories of Odysseus, is stylized in the way characteristic of significant arrivals elsewhere in the poem. The solemnity of the moment is marked by a description that for detail rivals the moments of Odysseus' arrival at Alkinoos' palace and Telemachos' arrival at Menelaos' palace. The description extends over some fifty lines, in which physical description is interrupted by the story of how Odysseus obtained his deadly arrows (21.6-57). Through the course of that description we are told of the key to the chamber, of the oak threshold, with its doorposts and shining doors that bellow like a bull in pasture as they open, of the treasures within, gold and iron and the chest filled with fragrant clothes, and finally of the shining bowcase hanging on its hook.

Amid the wealth of oaken beams, gleaming doors, chests, and precious metals, the key, most unpretentious of objects, becomes imbued with extraordinary beauty and dignity. Now it is another token of the craftsmanship that once prevailed and is the object that provides access to the inner room which, together with its contents, has resisted the disintegration outside (vv. 6-7): "With resolute hand she grasped the well-carved key; beautiful it was, bronze, fitted with a handle of ivory." The most important of all objects within the chamber that key unlocks is the bow. When Odysseus handles it later he turns it this way and that, examining it with a practiced eye for possible termite damage in its owner's absence (21.393-400). But the chamber's sturdy structure and Eurykleia's faithful management have done their work well. What is stored in the chamber remains there undamaged. Preserved intact, the bow emerges from its hiding place, as its owner does from his, to become the pivotal object, not only memorial of the past order but the fatal instrument by which the old order is renewed.

BIBLIOGRAPHICAL CODA

Placing the meridians of modern structuralism as a grid over Odysseus' Apologos, I set out in this chapter to draw a preliminary map of a hitherto almost uncharted sea. Map-makers for Odysseus' journey have existed in prolific supply from classical antiquity to the present moment. Can there be a single island, cove, or escarpment on the whole Mediterranean littoral as yet untrameled by the nets of cartographers in pursuit of Odysseus' nautical lore? Ignorance alike of the Mediterranean and of the sailor's art bids me beware of tangling my own net where a hundred others already lie cast.

Other cartographers, eschewing littoral geography, point their instruments inward to reveal in Odysseus' journey the map of the soul. This kind of investigation particularly resonates in the modern fancy, although it too has always had a strong appeal. We may see its coordinates graphed in Charles H. Taylor, Jr., "The Obstacles to Odysseus' Return: Identity and Consciousness in the *Odyssey*," *Yale Review* 50(1961):569-580, and yet more clearly limned in Charles P. Segal, "The Phaeacians and the Symbolism of Odysseus' Return," *Arion* 1, no. 4(1962):17-64, who writes of Odysseus' Apologos "as the private, inner world of the soul, closed to external reality, having an imaginative structure and content of its own; and as the subjective, inward aspect of external experience" (p. 25). Within the limpid pools of Odysseus' tale we are to discern coral reefs of *Urfiguren,* the Great Mother, the Seductress, and other primordial daemons, whose spells confound daily lives but compose eternal art. Behind such modern exegesis stretches the venerable tradition of allegorists, whose discourses give us theories not so very different, with due allowance made for the intervention of Freud and Jung upon the vocabulary of morality and literary criticism. For both kinds of symbolists the journey of Odysseus is a series of temptations, but the ancients still believed in the cardinal sins that have given way, in the post-Freudian age, to such entities as the ego, superego, and id, and to the frustrations dependent thereon. That the elements of the *Odyssey* represent archetypal symbols of the human mind is true. But to call Odysseus' Apologos, as Segal does, "a world closed to external reality," is to make a modern separation between an object and its symbolic value which would be unthinkable in Homer's world. It is a fallacy to which we, ensconced amid our lexicon, scholia, and commentaries, too easily succumb to reduce Poseidon, Helios, and Kalypso merely to masks for internal impulses. The sun and sea were not symbols for Homeric man, any more than the Nile could be mere symbol for the Egyptians, but whatever symbolic value they contained derived from their physical powers which defined human existence. The cosmic exegesis of Heraclitus Rhetor is more in tune with

Homer's psychology than modern exegesis which circumscribes the poet by eliminating or diminishing the primary physical realities behind the symbols.

Ancient allegorists and modern symbolists have at least perceived that there is some kind of universal statement contained in the Apologos, some motivation in the telling of greater import than the leisurely occupation of a feudal society's time in the vacant night of winter. In this, they help to dispel the fairly prevalent view of the disorganized prolixity of the *Odyssey*'s narrative style. C. H. Whitman, commenting on the *Odyssey*'s landscape descriptions, writes in *Homer and the Heroic Tradition* (Cambridge, Mass., 1963): "Here simple delight in the setting has tempted the poet to sing on and on, regardless of symmetry or waiting issues. New fields of content have revealed themselves, and the older concept of form has become attenuated amid the new preoccupation with the immediacy of life" (p. 293). The *Iliad*'s formal superiority over the *Odyssey* is an arguable proposition, but that proposition aside, allegorists of whatever stripe would find untenable Whitman's reduction of the mysterious potency of the Apologos to artless pleasure in parataxis. For many of us much of the power of the Apologos lies, on the contrary, in the economy with which it can express the essential character of so wide a variety of lands, people, and experience. For persons of such persuasion it is the *Iliad* that must seem prolix.

Whitman's succinct appraisal of the Odyssean style, however, points up an aspect of the Apologos excluded from allegorists' interpretations. Allegorists may discern significance in a name like Kalypso, in genealogical relationships, or in an event like Kirke's transformation of Odysseus' men, but they have not concerned themselves with the larger formulas, with the style, that is, and structure of the various episodes. Here is where we can add to the symbolists' insights those of the modern structuralists, of such scholars as Ernst Cassirer and Claude Lévi-Strauss, into the *logos* of an episode or a particular description. In the structure lies the significance, the structuralists tell us. Even if we avoid Lévi-Strauss's proposition that the content is of meager import relative to the form, we can agree that the structure, the interrelation of *topos* to *topos,* is as much part of the symbol as those aspects of an episode such as dialogue and action.

Homer is an ample thesaurus for structural analysis. The modern myths or social habits that have been the stuff of Lévi-Strauss's research, however pregnant with mental templates, seem but the bric-a-brac of a culture compared to the spacious Homeric edifices. Despite Lévi-Strauss's caveat that a consciously artistic product may obscure the patterns of primitive mythopoiesis, it seems perverse to ignore the edifice in which a culture sees reflected and validated its idea of order. The Gothic cathedral is surely as true a manifestation of a culture's subliminal structures as might be the names given to dogs and horses. If a distinction must be drawn between the mythic and the aesthetic working of the mythic, Homerists have the good fortune to be able to fall back on some two centuries of Analytic scholarship which has so loudly ridiculed any claims the Homeric poems may pretend to aesthetic greatness. The poems are, so we have heard, reiterated in a dozen different ways, the genuine and unconscious products of the Folk, edifices built brick by brick, year by year, a toolshed added here, a coping wall there, rambling like ivy through time and space. For Analysts, the Homeric poems have been the very acme of synchronic and diachronic *bricolage,* a structuralist's Garden of Eden.

Of classical scholars, G. S. Kirk is one who has examined the relationship between structural theory and Greek myth. In his Sather Lectures, *Myth: Its Meaning and Functions in Ancient and Other Cultures* (Cambridge, Berkeley, Los Angeles, 1970), pages 162 to 174, Kirk turns his scrutiny on the Kyklops episode in the *Odyssey,* using the episode as an experimental case for Lévi-Strauss's dichotomy between nature and culture. Since Kirk's concern is with the nature of myth in general, and with modern interpretations of myth, his examination of the episode makes no attempt to see its patterns as part of the recurrent patterns of the *Odyssey.* In this chapter I have tried to follow Kirk in using structuralism on the poem. Unlike Kirk, I read the Kyklops episode not as an isolated morpheme but as integrated in the larger syntax of the poem. In contrast to Whitman, I read the landscapes and architectural descriptions not as diversions from the "waiting issues" of the poem but as, in fact, part of those very issues and ideas that prompt the song.

Though a specifically structural approach to the *Odyssey* has scarcely been attempted, I am indebted to various studies on the natural phenomena in Homer and on man as artisan in that natural world, both imitator and creator of order. For the phenomena, no study has superseded E. Buchholz, *Die homerische Realien,* volume 1 of which, *Homerische Kosmographie und Geographie* (Leipzig, 1871), has been particularly useful for my purposes. His concern is more for the individual descriptions of natural phenomena than for the relationship of man and cosmos as presented in the *Odyssey*. His work remains, however, the most complete tabulation and analysis of cosmographical data in Homer, an indispensable prolegomenon for any structural investigation. Charles Mugler, *Les origines de la science grecque chèz Homère* (Paris, 1963), also collects the evidence for Homer's acquaintance with natural phenomena and traces the efforts in Homer at systematization of the phenomena. He concludes that although Homer demonstrates a keen observation of nature, the Homeric penchant for enveloping observations in religious garb produces the effect that "cette réceptivité sensorielle dans les poèmes homériques est un état d'angoisse continuelle" (p. 203). The anxiety Mugler perceives is certainly present in Homer (what great poem, we may ask, is free from that anxiety?), but Mugler, in unduly emphasizing Homer's "perceptions sensorielles et ses impulsions effectives" (p. 209), overlooks the human search in the *Odyssey* for the *logos* with which man can at least adapt to, if not master, the phenomena. H. de Farcy, "Homère et la campagne," *Les études classiques* 4(1935):626-635, gives a brief sketch of Homer's sense of nature and man's place in nature. R. Hennig, "Kulturgeschichte, Naturkunde und Homerlektüre," *Rev. Études Homériques* 2(1932):18-27, has good observations, though his is an attempt to dispute earlier views as to the extent of Homeric acquaintance with world geography beyond the confines of the Mediterranean. A useful but brief consideration of order, natural and human, is in H. Diller, "Der vorphilos- phische Gebrauch von κόσμος und κοσμεῖν," *Festschr. B. Snell* (Munich, 1956):47-60.

To move from the phenomena to human *techne,* W. Helbig, *Das homerische Epos aus den Denkmälern erlaütert* (Leipzig, 1887), provides the kind of systematic tabulation of human artifacts – houses, weapons, dress, armor, conveyances – that Buchholz gives of the natural elements. Helbig's emphasis on the purely technical processes and products precludes any analysis of the interconnection between human *techne* and the laws of the natural world, but like Buchholz's study, his is an invaluable source book. Felix Jacoby, "Die geistige Physiog- nomie der Odyssee," *Antike* 9(1933):159-194, though a rather general article, has good observations in pages 175 to 178 on the interest of the *Odyssey* in geographical and anthropological knowledge. E. Fuld, "Quelques remarques sur les sciences naturelles et médicales dans Homére," *Rev. études homériques* 2(1932):10-17, while commending Homer's perception, finds his knowledge of geography, astronomy, and the like too much permeated by myth to be science. It falls short, in his words, of "une somme de connaissances par des règles et des qualités spéciales, notamment une ordonnance systématique" (p. 10). Fuld's criterion would equally incriminate Milton, whose theory, in Book 10 of *Paradise Lost,* of the 23 degree axial tilt of our planet is thoroughly mythic, but rarely do we press Milton's poetry for scientific principles as vigorously as we do Homer's. Structuralism helps here to an understanding that the mythic is not antagonistic to "une ordonnance systématique," but is itself a system which our empiric sciences believe themselves to have discarded.

Of some general interest for the *Odyssey*'s emphasis on human labor, a subject relevant to an understanding of the Apologos, are two articles by André Aymard, "Hierarchie du travail et autarcie individuelle dans la Grèce archaique," *Rev.*

d'histoire de la philosophie 33(1943):124-126, and "L'Idée de travail dans la Grèce archaique," *Journal de psychologie* 41(1948):29-45. More germane to my study is Jean-Pierre Vernant, "Travail et nature dans la Grèce ancienne," *Journal de psychologie* 52(1955):18-33. Vernant's concern is mainly with Hesiod, but many of his observations on agriculture and technical *poiesis* are valid for the *Odyssey* too. Worth quoting is his conclusion on agricultural and technical labor (p. 38): "De facon générale, l'homme n'a pas le sentiment de transformer la nature, mais plutôt de se conformer à elle." In discussing the word *rhapsodos* in "Griechische Wörter," *Glotta* 14 (1925):1-13, Hermann Fränkel offers useful remarks on human *techne* in Homer. He is a scholar who sees both the emphasis on the creative process behind the various kinds of *techne* and the direct link between the *techne* of building or weaving and that of the *rhapsodos*, who is "der Meister seines Handwerks" (p. 5). Perhaps most useful for my purpose has been Wolfgang Schadewaldt, *Von Homer's Werk und Welt* (Stuttgart, 1944), which has much to say on structural dynamics in Homer. His section on the Shield of Achilleus (pp. 368-374), in which he talks of polarity as an ordering principle of Homeric art, and more particularly his "Die homerische Gleichniswelt und die Kretisch-Mykenische Kunst" (pp. 130-154), have observations valid for all of Homer. He restricts his analysis of nature in Homer, and man's observation of nature, to the similes, but the dynamic aspect of nature and the human search for the *logos* behind phenomenal experience, which he sees operating in the similes, are as true of the Apologos as of the similes. "Das was Homer in der Erscheinungen seiner Gleichnisse darstellt . . . ist gar nicht das Sichtbare an den Erscheinungen, sondern grade jenes Unsichtbare, das *in* den Erscheinungen erscheint" (p. 145). It is from Schadewaldt that I have borrowed the term *logos,* extending it from its application to similes to the interrelation of landscape, character, and intelligence in the *Odyssey*.

In attempting to decipher the *logos* of the *Odyssey*, I claim adherence to no one scholar's method. Lévi-Strauss, *The Savage*

Mind (Chicago, 1966), page 17, talks of the mythical process of thought as intellectual *bricolage.* If I understand his term aright, Lévi-Strauss, as a student of mythical patterns, is himself a *bricoleur,* one who builds new sets from the debris (*des bribes et des morceaux*) of the old. If this is so, if myth and the pursuit of myth are alike *bricolage,* then eclecticism here is no heresy.

IV

From Cities to Mind

᾿Ἄνδρα μοι ἔννεπε, Μοῦσα, πολύτροπον, ὃς μάλα πολλὰ
πλάγχθη, ἐπεὶ Τροίης ἱερὸν πτολίεθρον ἔπερσε·
πολλῶν δ᾽ ἀνθρώπων ἴδεν ἄστεα καὶ νόον ἔγνω.

                                                    — Odyssey 1.3

Mind, the works of mind, and that well-versed man who can
observe their correlation — this is the declared theme of the
Odyssey. In the first three lines the poem comes as close as
Homer's Greek permits to announcing the poem's intent to
explore man's discovery of mind.

The poem looks first at the evidence of man's mind at work
on the external environment. Man must know how to navigate
by the stars, how to build a ship or beach it, how to arrange a
sacrifice, transform wood into furniture, wool into garments.
Professionalism is everywhere lauded; craftsmen are named and
honored as individuals throughout the poem, whether their
craft be prophecy, medicine, carpentry, or song. Even the
carpenter Ikmalios is remembered for all time for the sworls of
ivory and silver which he laid in Penelope's chair, and in the
footstool he made, in Homer's words, to grow out of it
(19.55-58). There are no unions or guilds in this world, only
individual makers. Strange retaliation, that this poem which
raises so unequivocal an encomium to the excellence of the
individual craftsman the critics should impute to a committee
of clerks or coffee-house guslars.

Every individual, it seems, must be a skilled technician in
Homer's world, but individuals are never only individuals living
in isolation. The Odyssean man is as much a political animal as
the Greeks of Aristotle's time, and individuals come together to
share in a community of professionals. Homer moves in his
observation from the individual object and its maker to the

179

more complex integration of skills in the social organizations that the poem collects in its category of cities (*astea*). In a variety of ways Homer shows the degree of intelligence in a community's social organization. He pauses to note the landscape, and the community's use of that landscape. He notes architectural design, the kinds of crafts within the community as expressed in the structure of the walls or the fabrics, in the condition of the livestock or the agricultural products. By such external tokens Homer shows individual minds in their relationship to their natural environment and to the other minds in their community.

But the poem does not leave us contemplating externals only. Like Hermes on Kalypso's island, we stop first to read the message the externals can transmit to us by their shape and arrangement, the quality of their material, the coordination of their parts, the harmony of their aesthetics and utility. Then, when we have had time to let our senses glide over the rhythms of those external formulas, Homer invites us to step into the rhythm ourselves, to cross the threshold and to proceed to the organic center where those formulas are first molded into rhythm. Each of the complex communities of the poem has at its center a court, and at the center of that court resides the intelligence that emanates through the community and governs the whole outer complex. If we are to understand what Homer means, in the deepest sense, by cities and mind, we must spend our time at court, observing the actions and relations there, learning with Telemachos and Odysseus, and through them to hear and then to practice the subtle rhythms of those social organisms.

The events at the courts are almost all words and thoughts. In the *Odyssey* as a whole, but particularly in the court scenes, conversation is the action. There is a yawning chasm in critical discussion of the *Odyssey* caused by the simple failure to recognize that the *Odyssey* is a poem about words, about the use of language. There is a confusion in criticism between the poem itself and the saga that provides the poem with its external events. What purports to be literary analysis of the poem turns out on inspection to be, often, a discussion as to whether one version of the saga or an event in the saga is early or late, good or bad. While we indulge ourselves in the quest for the original, and perfect, saga, the poem passes us by.

Insofar as the *Odyssey* is related to saga, it is a poem about attitudes towards a saga. It is the account of persons whose lives are shaped by a saga and who in their turn shape it for succeeding generations. From the poem itself we have a clear enough statement on the impossibility of knowing the original saga. The tradition, as the poem depicts it, is totally an oral one. The saga comes to us only in fragments, large and small. Some fragments come from singers who have received the tale from others, others come from the participants in the events; a large fragment comes from the protagonist himself. All these are deposited into the reservoir of oral tradition, and from that reservoir Homer himself draws a piece here, a piece there, to collage them into his poem on the human mind.

When Odysseus first meets Nausikaa he wishes for her "a husband, a home, and like-mindedness [*homophrosyne*], for nothing is stronger," he says, "than when a man and a woman hold a house, both thinking alike in their thoughts [*homo-phroneonte noemasin*]" (6.181-184). The ideal of harmony between two persons is the keystone of the poem, the *telos* to which it moves. The main action is the process by which Odysseus and Penelope recover their spiritual and psychological harmony. The important Scene of the poem is thus the conversation between Odysseus and Penelope in Book 19. So pivotal is the scene that it generates a family of allomorphs. A queen's entertainment of a stranger becomes the *topos* of the poem. The queen's hospitality towards the vagrant in Ithaka sets a pattern which another queen will rehearse before her in Scheria, and yet another queen will rehearse with the stranger's son in Sparta. In each of these three instances an anonymous traveller arrives at the queen's court. The community receives him and interrogates him. He conceals his identity at first but slowly becomes integrated into the life of the community. When his integration is sufficiently complete he reveals his identity and his mission. In each case the traveller learns to adapt himself to a variety of persons in the community, but the figure on whose goodwill he most depends is the queen.

These three scenes, around which grow the three acts of the poem, we can for convenience label as follows:

1. Helen's entertainment of Telemachos in Sparta
2. Arete's entertainment of Odysseus in Scheria
3. Penelope's entertainment of Odysseus in Ithaka

By analyzing the dynamics of these scenes, and the correspondences between them, we can learn what Homer has to say about mind discovering its own rhythms and about the harmony it creates with the rhythms of other minds.

HELEN AND TELEMACHOS

Telemachos' journey has a thoroughly practical purpose. He is to ascertain information on his father's whereabouts which will govern his future decisions at home. Factual information, however, comprises but half his mission, if as much as that. At a deeper level Telemachos' journey is his education. He must become the young hero capable of sustaining a hero's role in Ithaka, and for that it is necessary for him to be initiated into the heroic world represented by Nestor and Menelaos. But his education requires more than simple exposure to heroic culture. Telemachos must be educated to become the son of Odysseus. The son, in order to become spiritually like the father, traces out a reduced, and to some degree symbolic, journey in imitation of his father. Telemachos duplicates in important ways the kinds of experience Odysseus undergoes. He too must brave the sea to visit unknown peoples; he too will see cities and come to know mind. There will be a powerful king and queen to receive him, as there will be for Odysseus. Like the father, the son will arrive incognito at a magnificent palace, his identity will be recognized, and he will prevail through his charm and find there what he needs for his return. The Telemachy is, as my friend Julie Lamont first pointed out to me, a brilliant example of sympathetic magic. The son imitates the father in a literal fashion first in order to become the father, but the sympathetic action goes further than that. Telemachos also imitates his father in order to secure his father's return. He completes a journey abroad as a magical spell that will ensure that his father too will complete his journey.

The parallels between the two journeys, that of the father and that of the son, are numerous, as we should expect in a poem that understands education as imitation. So numerous, indeed, and so varied, ranging from large thematic structures to minute correspondences in verbal patterns and physical gestures, that mathematical probability should argue against a *Bearbeiter*'s later interference. If the Telemachy is credited to a *Bearbeiter* who has stitched together such an organic prelude from fragments appropriated from the *Odyssey*-poet's oeuvre, we can only praise the Lord that Homer left his papers in such competent hands.[1]

Among the more obvious parallels we note that both father and son must consult a person who is *pepnumenos,* someone with his wits intact. Athena urges Telemachos to address himself first to Nestor, since he is *pepnumenos* and will not lie (3.20), and then Nestor advises Telemachos to consult Menelaos since he too is *pepnumenos* and will not lie (3.323-328). Kirke sends Odysseus to Hades' realm to consult Teiresias, the only person in the underworld whose mind remains *pepnumenos* (10.494-495). Another parallel is that a substantial part of both journeys is given over to tales of the returns, the *nostoi,* though Telemachos is the initiate who hears them from his hosts and Odysseus is the initiated who narrates them to his hosts. Both father and son find themselves in similar predicaments from which they must extricate themselves gracefully. Both, that is, are entertained royally and are importuned to extend their stay in a rich but alien palace, but must reject the invitations in order to return to a lady whom they have left unprotected at home. Both make the final stage of their return journey accompanied by persons of magical powers: Telemachos sails from Pylos to Ithaka accompanied by Theoklymenos, a distant relative of his Pylian host and a seer with extraordinary mantic powers, and Odysseus is conveyed home by his Phaiakian hosts who have extraordinary navigational powers. Both father and son must look to an imposing king and queen to achieve their objectives, Telemachos to Menelaos and Helen, Odysseus to Alkinoos and Arete.

One parallel is a stellar example of Homer's love of balance and rapport in even the smallest gesture, and an illustration of the psychological essence the poet can concentrate into a gesture. In Sparta, Telemachos is recognized when Menelaos' references to Odysseus, whom he presumes dead, have prompted Telemachos to tears (4.115-116): "Telemachos drew his porphyrian cloak before his eyes. Menelaos recognized him." Helen, entering the hall at that moment, remarks (vv. 141ff.): "I say that I have not seen either man or woman more like the son of great-hearted Odysseus, I mean Telemachos, the baby whom that man left at home when the Achaians went beneath Troy for me, bitch-faced, and they pressed ferocious war." To which Menelaos replies, of the young man hiding his features behind his cloak (vv. 148ff.): "I too am just conceiving that same likeness which you notice. There are Odysseus' feet, these his hands, the glance of his eyes, his head, and his hair above. And here I was just remembering Odysseus in my conversation." Potent indeed is conversation, in which a reference to the person of Odysseus can summon forth his personification.[2]

Odysseus is recognized in a parallel as exact as his differing situation permits. At the Phaiakian court someone has been remembering Odysseus in story, namely Demodokos. Demodokos' remembrance has taken the form of the story of the Wooden Horse, which the visitor to the court had requested, just as the young visitor in Sparta utters a remark that prompts Menelaos' reflections on Odysseus. As Demodokos sings Odysseus bursts into nothing short of a funeral wail, as if (so goes the simile at this point) he were a widow mourning her husband killed before the city walls while protecting his city, his people, and his family (8.532ff.): "He escaped notice of all others but king Alkinoos, who alone remarked him and *recognized* him, as he sat beside him groaning copiously."

Whereupon Alkinoos, rather than display bad manners by revealing the name of the stranger in his palace, calls Demodokos to put aside the sweet *phorminx* since the tale he sings is not a *charis* to everyone (vv. 539ff.): "From the moment when the divine singer took up the song our guest has not ceased from shrill lament. A great grief indeed has surrounded him." If Demodokos' *charis* at this point must be to forgo his song, then Odysseus too must grant a *charis* in turn, says Alkinoos (vv. 542ff.), for by the mutual exchange of *charis* everyone, guest and host alike, will enjoy himself, and that would be much better. The *charis* Alkinoos requests from Odysseus is to restrain his tears and to reveal himself, to reveal, that is, his connection with the subject of Demodokos' song. Alkinoos asks that Odysseus should spell Demodokos awhile and continue the tale from the participant's point of view. Odysseus then reveals the name of the man who, on the occasion of Demodokos' earlier song, had "with stout hands drawn his great porphyrian cloak and shielded his head, and hidden his handsome features" (see 8.84-85). Odysseus then tells/sings a song such as the Phaiakians had never heard, and Alkinoos understands why this man can never stay to become his son-in-law.[3]

Amid the prodigal correlations between the journeys of parent and child, the one most apposite here is that both journeys show a distinct progression in complexity of physical and social structures. Telemachos and Odysseus both move from fairly elementary social milieus to highly organized and sophisticated ones, the progression visible not simply in the external arrangements of life in each culture, but also (and most important) in the psychological subtleties in the characters' speeches. Both father and son move from a situation (or situations, in Odysseus' case) that requires elementary responses to one that demands the highest concentration of finesse and discretion of which they are capable.

Telemachos has only two sites to visit; his journey has, therefore, a simplicity that perhaps makes the structure clearer and prepares us for the more complex pattern in Odysseus' journey. Telemachos' hosts at Pylos and Sparta belong to the heroic world; both Nestor and Menelaos participated in the Trojan War, both have stories to tell of Odysseus. Despite the obvious similarities, a wide contrast is drawn between the two sites, as if they were two opposing poles. Life at Pylos is curiously rustic. Though Nestor has a palace and what seems like unlimited wealth, we hear and see almost nothing of the palace, or of the life lived therein. All the events in the Pylos episode occur outside, on the shore or in the meadow. Similarly, description of social organization is minimal. We know that Nestor has a large household; we see his son Peisistratos play a minor role beside his father, and in the preparations for the great sacrifice to Athena we see something of the community life. All the same, life in Pylos seems strangely solitary and isolated.

In Pylos Telemachos meets a man who can teach him the right attitudes towards gods and men. Nestor is courteous, hospitable, cooperative, not to mention being a good raconteur. He strikes us, however, as a person of limited perception. He entertains unaware a goddess and the son of the man whom he calls his most trusted counselor. He recognizes Athena only after she has assumed her bird shape and flown away.[4] He comments on the similarity in speech between Telemachos and his father (another reminder that words are action in the poem), but this only after Telemachos has already revealed his identity.[5] Nestor can tell Telemachos nothing of Odysseus' whereabouts; the best he can suggest is that Telemachos visit Menelaos. Nestor's role seems to be a preparatory one, as is Nausikaa's role in the Scherian act, or Eumaios' role in the Ithakan act. Nestor points Telemachos in the direction of a more important scene.

The scene in Pylos is important as Telemachos' introduction to the civilized life that has been lacking for many years in Ithaka. The episode, however, remains straightforward and relatively unsophisticated. The contrast between Pylos and Sparta is remarkable. At Sparta, Telemachos is thrust into a more urbane society of a greater complexity and intelligence, where the demands on him are proportionately higher. No longer the rustic feudalism of Pylos. Now the setting is a palace, and the palace itself becomes a significant part of his experience. Telemachos was slightly bashful when first approaching Nestor, but timidity becomes utter astonishment when he views Menelaos' palace. It is so far outside the range of his experience that he is led to compare it with Zeus' palace on Olympos.[6] The communal life in the palace is as elaborate and impressive as the architecture. The whole palace is a hive of activity; a wedding feast is in progress when Telemachos arrives, with a singer, dancers, and acrobats providing entertainment. The magnificence of the palace, of the feast and its entertainment, the abundance of precious objects in the palace (Telemachos receives no guest-gift from Nestor, but only the loan of a chariot), and the presence of two powerful and equal rulers (rather than a single one as at Pylos) all conspire to suggest technological and political achievements far in advance of those found on the sandy shore of Pylos.

There is, as we have now come to predict, a correlation between technological achievement and mental acumen. Menelaos and Helen exceed Nestor in sophistication as much as their palace exceeds his in splendor. Menelaos is sufficiently alert to overhear Telemachos' comparison, made *sotto voce* to Peisistratos, of Menelaos' palace with Olympian architecture. At Pylos, by contrast, Athena prays, aloud presumably, to Poseidon to grant "Telemachos and me success," but Nestor is apparently distracted since he must ask the strangers' identity immediately thereafter (3.60ff.). We do not customarily place Menelaos among the shrewdest of Homeric heroes, yet in the *Odyssey* he is quick enough to recognize Telemachos without prior knowledge; his discretion leads him to debate whether he should reveal his awareness to Telemachos (4.116-119). Menelaos demonstrates his discretion further the next day when he searches out Telemachos and asks him, in private conference, the real reason for his visit.

Helen is drawn as a person even more perceptive than her husband. She too recognizes their young guest, and her recognition is instantaneous and sure, whereas Menelaos gives the impression of some vacillation. Though Helen had never seen the baby born to Odysseus, she recognizes in the person before her the exact image of Odysseus as he was when he went to Troy twenty years before (4.141-146). At a later point in the first evening she demonstrates her graciousness by supplying the drug *nepenthes,* and she herself becomes Nepenthes who turns remembrance from sorrow to joy by relating old tales of Odysseus' stratagems.[7] When it is time for Telemachos' departure from Sparta, it is Helen who is quick to interpret the bird omen as propitious for Telemachos and his family. Odysseus is warned that his passage home from Scheria depends specifically on Arete's approval. There is no formal statement to credit Helen with such preeminent authority in the Telemachy. Her role, however, is certainly the dominant one. She recognizes Telemachos before he identifies himself; she has the ability to turn the evening's lamentation into good cheer; she can interpret an omen favorably for Telemachos. In such acts, indicative of her dominance, we see the evidence of Penelope's influence extending even to the structure of the Telemachy.

The poem's first exemplars of family *homophrosyne* are the king and queen of Sparta. As hosts they are impeccable — solicitous and discreet. But more remarkable is their unanimity. They have the same thought, as we have seen, on the identity of their still anonymous visitor. They have the same thoughts when it comes time to change the lugubrious mood of Telemachos' first evening at their court. To change the mood, each tells a story about Troy, and in their stories they show themselves as perfect complements for each other.

The stories they tell have to do with Odysseus' cleverness, and both are of the Greek penetration into the city of Troy. Nestor had talked of Odysseus as the most gifted of orators. Menelaos and Helen now give paradigms of Odysseus as the most gifted at inventing and executing schemes. Menelaos tells the story of the Wooden Horse that Odysseus had devised. Helen tells of Odysseus' spying mission, when he had entered Troy disguised as a beggar. In giving their fragments of the

Odysseus saga they fulfill their social obligations towards their tearful young guest. At the same time, however, they use the stories as the medium through which to speak to, and about, each other. An important element in Menelaos' tale is Helen's counterstratagem for testing the Wooden Horse, a stratagem that would have doomed the Greeks had it not been for Odysseus' ability to control even that emergency. What emerges from his story is that Helen too is a person of clever strategies, the only peer, in fact, of Odysseus. Helen's tale is also of strategy and counterstrategy, and again the principals are Odysseus and Helen. In her story, Odysseus planned another strategy for gaining entrance into Troy, but once again she was capable of penetrating the disguise. Her story· is as much self-flattery as it is flattery of Odysseus. She takes pains, however, to give Menelaos his due. She compliments him by claiming that her desire was to leave Troy and to return to him. Her interception of Odysseus was prompted, so we are to understand from her version of the tale, by her desire to be reunited with her husband. Whether true or not, it is at least a nice reflection on the marital *homophrosyne* that figures so large in this poem.

With what delicacy those two masters of tact touch on the catastrophe of which they were the joint sponsors. Even while admitting their responsibility, how deftly they can temper it so as to caress each other's sensibilities, Helen by acknowledging Menelaos the equal of any man in both looks and intelligence (cf. 4.264), Menelaos by acknowledging Helen as the only peer of Odysseus, and by crediting her with the gift of impersonating every man's wife – an admission that seems to mitigate, to a degree, Paris' mistake in abducting her.

Menelaos and Helen are ideal hosts in all practical ways, but hospitality in the *Odyssey* includes more than keeping conversation and wine flowing. It requires an intuitive understanding of the hidden meaning behind spoken words, an understanding even of unspoken thoughts. Homer has endowed Menelaos, and more especially Helen, with such gifts in ample measure. It is interesting to see Telemachos responding in reciprocal fashion to their hospitality. He becomes more adept in social forms. When Menelaos presses him to stay and promises prize horses and a chariot as his guest-gift, Telemachos replies in such a way as to elicit Menelaos' highest admiration. Telemachos declines the offer by appealing to the fictitious impatience of his friends waiting in Pylos, but at the same time he compliments Menelaos and depreciates himself and his little island home. With good reason Menelaos has to laugh, grasp Telemachos by the hand, and exclaim: "You are of good blood, my son, by what you say" (4.609ff.). A second time, at the end of Telemachos' stay in Sparta, Menelaos presses him to tarry longer and offers him a tour through the mainland, but Telemachos declines, again with a white lie, though this lie is a refined shadow of the truth. Telemachos pleads his fear that in his own and his father's absence from Ithaka he may lose some precious object from his halls (15.90-91). His meaning could not be clearer, even though propriety forbids him from putting his real meaning into words. Nor could Odysseus himself have framed his anxiety in so delicate a manner. The straightforward but bashful young man of Book 1 has achieved, by the time he leaves Sparta, an elegant self-possession.[8]

Telemachos will give ample proof in Ithaka that his physical journey abroad has increased his mental powers. Just how great the increase will be we can deduce from his behavior when he decides on the disposition of the seer Theoklymenos to whom he had given asylum on his ship. On the shore at Ithaka, Telemachos first suggests that Theoklymenos stay with his archenemy Eurymachos, Penelope's most aggressive suitor. In Sparta, as we have seen, Telemachos is quite capable of bending the truth if discretion so demands. Here we find him saying the outright opposite of his truth. He praises Eurymachos as the best possible host, but the extravagance of the young orator's encomium betrays his sarcasm. If Telemachos can call Eurymachos the bright son of a dazzling father, a man whom the folk in Ithaka behold as a god (15.519-520), that can scarcely be Telemachos' personal persuasion. Athena had already warned Telemachos at Sparta that Eurymachos was the man most likely to win his mother and carry off his possessions in Telemachos' absence (15.17-19). Zeus well understands the irony in the young orator's words, even if modern scholars do not. Zeus sends his omen, which Theoklymenos turns to Telemachos' favor, his interpretation being an assurance that Eurymachos has not won yet and Telemachos is still master of his house (see 15.531-534). Telemachos then reverses himself and entrusts this wise seer, who has just proved his worth, to his loyal friend Peiraios, whom we expected him to nominate as Theoklymenos' host in the first place. Quick thinking for the young fellow who was once too shy to address Nestor without Athena's encouragement, now to test his fate and his new-found seer in a single deft operation. His camouflage of his motives is worthy of the man whom he had gone forth to imitate.[9]

ARETE AND ODYSSEUS

Leaving Telemachos on the shore at Ithaka to practice there the disguises his travels have taught him, we can turn to observe the father now imitating the son. In Odysseus' journey we see even more clearly the correlation between mental perception and the degree and kind of organization. Odysseus moves from dealing with such obtuse figures as Polyphemos at one pole to the masters of nuance at Scheria at the other pole. It requires little intelligence to outwit Polyphemos; Odysseus needs only minimal cunning, and a grain or two of prudence, to gain the advantage over brutish strength. All it takes, really, is a pun. A single word lays the giant low, if it be the right word. Kirke, almost as savage as Polyphemos, needs a more sophisticated response. Hermes must supply Odysseus with a magical drug and certain rites that will outspell Kirke's spell by a kind of homeopathic magic. Once subdued, she and Odysseus meet as equals — no, never quite as equals, since human compassion is alien to her nature. She must be reminded that Odysseus cannot enjoy her hospitality while his men remain bewitched. When Odysseus wishes to take his leave she sends him down to the underworld, and only after his return thence does she offer help for his journey. The sinister always adheres to her nature, however correctly she plays the hostess for Odysseus.

In Kalypso the sinister has been submerged entirely. Whatever noxious influences may radiate from her name, her location, her ancestry or her superhuman nature are kept under control, though when she grants Odysseus his departure he shudders in fear that she might unloose those influences on him. Instead of being the fairy tale witch like Kirke, Kalypso is entirely humanized, a full person rather than a *Märchen-Mädchen*. Her conversation with Hermes is a civilized one, resonant with the nuances between two persons who understand and sympathize with each other. She is angry, but still hospitable. The subject of their colloquy remains anonymous. Hermes is hesitant and apologetic, and with a tactful gesture refrains from naming the man whom Kalypso must release. She replies, also without naming Odysseus. She raises the problem of a ship and crew, but Hermes does not trouble to address himself to an obstacle so obviously factitious. He only repeats that she must obey Zeus if she would avoid his hard anger (5.85-147). That same day, in her last conversation with Odysseus, Kalypso again reveals her elegant style (5.203ff.). She bids Odysseus *chaire* for his voyage home, if home is what he really wants. She warns him of the woes lying in wait for him between her island and Ithaka, woes he could avoid by staying and choosing immortality with Kalypso rather than mortality with Penelope. It is an attempt at seduction, of course, but so phrased as to permit Odysseus to tender his regrets with the least possible embarrassment for both parties.

Odysseus is as tactful in his reply as Kalypso is in her request (vv. 251ff.). He is well aware, he says, that there can be no comparison between Penelope and Kalypso, a nymph who knows not death nor age. Even so, and despite sufferings still in store, his heart is set on his returning home and beholding the day of his homecoming. The clever little Noman has come a long way from Polyphemos' cave. In that encounter a single word was weapon enough. Here too, on Kalypso's island, Odysseus achieves his goal with words, but there is no trickery

in them. No longer weapons, words are beginning at last, in this
episode, to be the medium for communication between two
persons, for hearing the mind of the other and revealing one's
own. In the Kyklops episode a word severs, alienates, polarizes.
Here words have an integrative function. Even if Odysseus
cannot stay with Kalypso, yet in their final conversation they
have achieved a psychological harmony that can outspell any
physical union. Kalypso prepares Odysseus for his experience in
Scheria, where again his only tools will be words. The kind of
integration of two opposing wills, which we see informing
Odysseus' last conversation with Kalypso, will be repeated, in
greater detail and on a larger canvas, in Scheria. The Scheria
episode is a large-scale amplification of Odysseus' conversation
with Kalypso.

The first soul Odysseus meets in Scheria is Nausikaa, and the
first words he utters reveal the gulf now separating us from
Kyklopean caves, and even from nymphs' rustic grottoes.
Trickery, if trickery is the right word for Odyssean *dolos,* has
now been transformed into charm: αὐτίκα μειλίχιον καὶ
κερδαλέον φάτο μῦθον (6.148), so Homer describes Odysseus'
speech to Nausikaa. It is a speech compounded of honey and
profit. He lays a spell on everyone in Scheria, on Nausikaa first,
then on Arete and Alkinoos, but there is no magic *moly* this
time. He is on his own, master of his own destiny, and the *moly*
must emerge from his personality. The Phaiakians, themselves a
charmed folk, respond to those who have the gift to charm.

The Phaiakians give every sign of intelligence in the organization of their lives. But their monarchs are especially recognized for their intelligence: Alkinoos "knows thoughts from the
gods," which is a Homeric way of talking about extraordinary
perception (θεῶν ἄπο μήδεα εἰδώς, 6.12); Arete has a *noos
esthlos* (7.73). Their daughter is no less endowed. All three
members of the family show their intelligence in their behavior
towards each other.

Nausikaa, whom we see first, invents a false pretext when she
asks her father for the use of the wagon. Athena had put
marriage in her mind during the previous night, but Nausikaa is

wise enought to camouflage her true motives. Later, at the river, she shows her poise by standing her ground before the briny apparition who rises from the sea and then by calmly arranging for all his needs. Her full charm emerges only in her conversation with Odysseus when she discusses the best strategy for his entry into the city and palace. She had already exclaimed to her handmaidens, when she had seen Odysseus bathed and clothed (6.243-245): "Now he seems like a god. . . . Would that such a man might be called my husband . . . and it might please him to remain here." But now as she approaches the city with Odysseus, Nausikaa introduces the subject of marriage in a more coquettish manner. Odysseus should enter the city separately, she says, otherwise some fellow of the baser sort, seeing them together, might say (6.276ff.): "Who is this handsome and distinguished stranger with Nausikaa? Her husband he'll be I suppose. . . . Perhaps a god came down in answer to her prayer and he will possess her all her days. Better for her if she finds her husband from elsewhere, since she scorns all her local suitors, and many fine Phaiakians she has as her suitors too."

Modest she is, but modesty doesn't preclude wit. In a brief speech Nausikaa succeeds in relaying much information about herself through the medium of a fictitious gossip. She finds the stranger like a god, so the pretended gossip reveals; she herself has many of the best men in Scheria as her suitors but she has spurned them and prayed to the gods for someone better. And now a better has appeared, like a god. Alas that such winsome oratory is to no avail. The stranger will not tarry and Nausikaa parts from him the next day with the prayer that he may remember her for the guest-gift she had given him, namely his life.

Alkinoos' intelligence shows itself in intuition and discretion. He understands that marriage lies behind Nausikaa's request for the wagon but he keeps his knowledge to himself. He is well aware of what it must mean when his marriage-minded daughter brings a handsome stranger up from the sea, and accordingly he lets the stranger know of his personal feelings (7.312ff.): "Being such as you are, and with your mind thinking as mine does, would that you could have my daughter and be called my son-in-law. . . . But no Phaiakian will hold you here against your will." An honest declaration but without pressure. The way is open for Odysseus to accept or to decline as he chooses.

The next day brings Alkinoos several more occasions to exercise his diplomacy. He schedules athletics in place of song when he sees the melancholy effect of Demodokos' song on the stranger. Here his tact forbids his mentioning the real reason for the change in activity; he merely explains that the court has had its surfeit of food and song and should go outside (8.98ff.). When an incident occurring during the athletic performances almost devolves into a fracas, and Odysseus retaliates to insults by proving himself superior to the Phaiakians at their own sport, Alkinoos diplomatically reestablishes Phaiakian self-esteem by suggesting a change from athletics to dance. Later, when evening comes on and Demodokos takes up another song, Alkinoos again observes the stranger's discomfiture and again calls a halt to the song that is not pleasing to everyone. This time he explains the reason for this intrusion and calls on Odysseus to identify himself. It is the only occasion when Alkinoos resorts to something close to a peremptory command, but he is justified in so doing since he and Arete have already tried several times unsuccessfully to elicit Odysseus' identity. Arete had asked Odysseus point-blank the previous evening but Alkinoos had proceeded more indirectly, hinting once that the stranger might be a god (7.199ff.) and once calling Odysseus "this stranger — I do not know who he is" (8.28). Since Odysseus has resisted all attempts, direct and indirect, Alkinoos must resort to a more insistent tone.

If Alkinoos' insistence is necessary, it also has the beauty of timing. Everything has been prepared for Odysseus' revelation — he has competed with the young men in athletics, he has won the heart of the princess, he has charmed the citizenry into giving generously from their possessions, and his exploits are in the bardic repertory. Alkinoos, in interrupting the story of the

Wooden Horse to call for Odysseus' name, makes the best-timed interruption in literature.

Arete too shows the same qualities as her husband and daughter. The best example of her perspicacity occurs in the scene in the palace when all the other guests have been dismissed for the night. Only Alkinoos and Arete are left to question Odysseus in private. When they are alone with Odysseus she slyly reveals, by a casual question on Odysseus' attire, that she is quite as shrewd and discreet as he. She recognizes the clothes on Odysseus "which she herself had made with her womenfolk," and she asks Odysseus (7.237-239): "Who are you? Who gave these clothes to you?" Odysseus in answering her second question conveniently omits to answer her first, an omission that Arete overlooks because Alkinoos interrupts to ventilate his paternal annoyance at Nausikaa's deficient sense of hospitality.

Here is an apparent irregularity: Arete asks a question and is, it seems, indifferent to Odysseus' failure to answer it. An irregularity invariably brings out the Analyst in us, to root around for the *Bearbeiter*'s tracks, and sure enough the *Arete-frage*, as German scholarship has named the problem, has had its share of researchers to piece together the theory of multiple authorship which will best explain Arete's silence. The question is misformulated, however, unless the formulation explicitly recognizes the spiritual ambience in Scheria. This is not the giant's cave, where language must be perforce raw and violent. Here language is graceful, its movement an insinuation. Arete is a sensitive interrogator and Odysseus a sensitive respondent. When a mother sees a strange man wearing the very clothes her marriageable daughter took to the river in the morning, her first concern must surely be for her daughter. Arete's question, "Who are you?" is not the regular formula of polite encounter, since on this occasion it really means, "What is your relationship to my daughter?" Arete's concern leaks through the tactful irony of her second question, when she allows Odysseus to know that she has noticed his attire. If a man, attired in someone else's clothes, finds himself face to face with a person who intimates that she is the source of that same attire, such a man, if prudent, will address himself first to explaining how those clothes came into his possession. This is what prudent Odysseus does. Fortunately, his explanation distracts Alkinoos into an excursus on his daughter's manners, and the answer to Arete's first question is conveniently held in abeyance. Odysseus and Arete emerge from their first encounter in a draw. She uses her question to reveal herself as a perceptive woman who will not be easily fooled. He, recognizing a challenge, succeeds in "fooling" her anyway by giving only circumstantial information about himself while still keeping his incognito.[10]

"Nothing is stronger than when, thinking alike in their thoughts, a man and woman hold a house together." Arete and Alkinoos are the poem's second exemplars of that domestic harmony which Odysseus praises as the *summum bonum*. Theirs is a family that thinks in the same way, thinks the same thoughts. Nausikaa need not mention marriage for her father to understand. Arete and Alkinoos see a stranger in their halls dressed in the clothes Nausikaa had taken to the river and they understand what she intended when she gave them to him. Alkinoos sees Odysseus weep, even at the moment when he is concealing his grief, and understands. The family notices details unobserved by others and, whether divulging information or eliciting it, know how to phrase themselves with the right degree of ambiguity so as to conceal as much as they reveal.

Odysseus, to win this family as his allies, must be as adept and perceptive as they; he must become one of them. He must gain their respect by understanding their indirect questions. He must show by *his* style that he recognizes their style.[11] *Charis* fills the air of Scheria. Nausikaa's handmaidens have their beauty from the *Charites* (6.18); when Odysseus defends himself against Euryalos' insults, Alkinoos finds Odysseus' words οὐκ ἀχάριστα (8.236); Odysseus discourses on *charis* in his reply to Euryalos' taunts (8.166ff.). *Charis* is distributed, he says, in varying degrees and kind. One man is a match for the gods in physique but no *charis* crowns his words (vv. 174-175).

Another man is inferior in physique "but god crowns his form with words, and people take pleasure in looking on him. He speaks surely and sweetly and he stands out in the assembly. As he goes through the town they look upon him as a god" (vv. 169-173; cf. Stanford's translation). *Charis* is the *Odyssey*'s word for style and Odysseus in his speech on the diversity of *charis* opts plainly for the *charis* of words as superior to all forms of *charites*. Words garland a man, says Odysseus, and endow him with a beauty that all admire.

Odysseus proclaims speech as the highest form of *charis*. From their speeches to each other and to Odysseus we should deduce that Odysseus' view coincides exactly with that of Alkinoos and his family. But even without their speeches we should find evidence of their concurrence in the high stature they accord to Odysseus for his words. Odysseus, naked as a savage, frames a speech in praise of Nausikaa's beauty and Nausikaa's response is to call him "no mean or witless fellow" (οὔτε κακῷ οὔτ' ἄφρονι φωτὶ ἔοικας, 6.187). When Odysseus assures Alkinoos that he is far from being a god, but instead the most wretched of mortals, the assembled guests praise the stranger and bid Alkinoos accede to his request for aid "since he had spoken *kata moiran*" (7.227). When Odysseus defends Nausikaa for her discretion in leaving him to make his way into the palace alone, Alkinoos praises him for his mind. When Odysseus compliments the Phaiakians on their dance, Alkinoos is so pleased at the stranger's showing himself *pepnumenos* (see 8.388) that he calls for twelve kings to bring gifts from their treasures for the stranger. Earlier, Nausikaa too had called Odysseus a man of understanding, shortly after his first speech to her (οὐκ ἀπίνυσσεν, 6.258). Odysseus' words always prompt a recognition of his intelligence.

Scheria is the showplace of the arts. The Phaiakians are proficient first in manual crafts, in sailing, husbandry, weaving, in the building of artifacts, houses, furniture, and ships. Their arts also include the fine arts — sculpture, ballgames for the girls, dancing and athletic contests for the young men. Scheria is the only place within Homeric geography to have a plastic art that frankly imitates for the pleasure of imitation, as witness the mosaic watchdog given to them by Hephaistos and the palace sconces made in the likeness of torchbearers. Everywhere there is craft, and the *charis* shining from objects which testifies to the craftsmen's success at their creation.

If speech is clearly the highest form of craft in Scheria, and its *charis* the highest form of *charis,* within the category of speech there is one form superior to all others which holds in itself the highest concentration of *charis.* Supreme of the imitative arts is that of the singer. When Odysseus is about to request from Demodokos the song of the Wooden Horse, he sends a gift to the singer and says (8.479-481): "Among all men singers have their share of honor and reverence since the Muse has taught them, and she loves the tribe of bards." He continues by praising Demodokos personally (vv. 487-491): "Far above all mortals I honor you. Either the Muse taught you, or it was Apollo. . . . You sing the tale as if you had been present yourself, or had heard it from someone there." As Odysseus is about to begin his story he leads off with a preamble on the *charis* of poetry (9.5ff.): "There is no accomplishment with greater *charis* than the good will [*euphrosyne*] which possesses everyone within a group, as they sit in order and listen to the singer, while the tables are laden with food and drink, and the wine steward draws wine from the bowl and carries it around."

The banquet and its accompanying song, that is the greatest *charis* for Odysseus. So it is for the Phaiakians who respond to Odysseus, when he substitutes for Demodokos, as if he were the prince of singers. After Odysseus, in the course of his tale, finishes the catalogue of the famous heroines in the underworld, Arete is moved to remark on the storyteller's physical beauty, mirroring his inner beauty (11.336ff.): "How does this man seem to you in physique, in stature, and in his well-balanced *phrenes*?" Alkinoos too compliments the substitute poet, and again the emphasis is on both the mind within and the physical appearance without (11.363ff.): "You are not one of those thievish rogues who fit together lies. On you there is a form from your words [*morphe*; cf. Odysseus himself on the capacity of words to bestow *morphe,* 8.170], and your *phrenes* within are good." Arete calls for those in the hall to reward Odysseus' words with gifts, and Alkinoos repeats her call when Odysseus' tale is done. He asks for gifts from all the assembled company for "it would be hard for a single man to render due *charis* with his present" (13.15). The wealth Odysseus carries with him from Scheria to his home is not gratuitous; it is earned wealth.

Odysseus' words win him first Nausikaa's trust, then asylum in Alkinoos' court. His tact and diplomacy are rewarded by gifts which pour in to mark his increasing favor on the island. When his words take shape as poetry the king and queen of the society are moved to open admiration, which they demonstrate with yet more gifts and the guarantee of a safe passage home. On Kirke's island Odysseus had recourse to a magical drug to reinforce his power. By the time he reaches Scheria stage props like *moly* disappear. Athena counsels Odysseus that he must win over Arete's mind if he would achieve his homecoming (7.75-76): "For if she think kindly thoughts in her *thymos,* then there is hope to see friends and home again." Now on his own (as is Telemachos in Sparta, without Athena/Mentor's presence to encourage him), Odysseus must learn (or prove) that only mind can captivate mind. At Scheria, magic is an energy that emanates from within — Odysseus learns to replace the charm of drugs with the charm of poetry.[12]

Eyeing the stranger as a prospective son-in-law, Alkinoos addresses him as a person "who thinks the very thoughts I myself think" (7.312). When Odysseus documents, in a variety of ways, that his thought waves are in alignment with those emanating from all the individuals at the Scherian court, then he is ready for the ordeal in Ithaka, where all the lessons learned in prior locations will be put to their severest test.

PENELOPE AND ODYSSEUS

Nausikaa — everyone agrees that she is a beautiful child, but there are those who feel something gawky in her role — "she shapes up unused," in the unfortunate words of one critic. What her use should be, for such critics, is marriage, and there have been scholarly attempts to prove that somewhere, in some version of the Odysseus saga, there was in fact such a marriage. What we have left in our poem, so the theory runs, is a truncated version of the Nausikaa saga, rather poorly adapted to a plot in which Odysseus cannot stay on Scheria but must move on to his wife Penelope. Recourse to supposititious variants of a legend is a search for hypothetical external relations, and as such a frank admission of inability to recognize internal relations within the poem. It should be the path of last resort, though in Homeric studies it is a much-laureled path.[13]

Nausikaa is not a vestigial fragment from some other poem who has slipped past every sentry until modern critics have proclaimed her imposture in this poem. Unless we understand her as a variant for someone within the poem we shall continue to misread her presence entirely. If the true marriage of like minds is the *telos* of the poem, then Nausikaa does not so much distract from that *telos* but fulfills it by rehearsing it for us. Whether figures like Alkinoos and Arete belong to the original saga — whatever that chimaera may be — is immaterial since their roles, as those also of Menelaos and Helen, derive from the roles of Odysseus and Penelope within this version of the tale. So too for Nausikaa. She is the stand-in for Telemachos, in the Scherian paradigm of the ideal family, as Helen and Arete are stand-ins for Penelope. Like Telemachos, Nausikaa leaves home on a secret mission. Like him, she undergoes a momentous experience while away from home. Like him, she discovers a bizarre vagrant at the seashore, extends protection to him and escorts him to her palace, where he then becomes the concern of the queen. In all her actions she urges us to look forward to Ithaka for the performance there of which hers is but the shadow.

If there is some confusion in the figure of Nausikaa it is perhaps because she is the fusion of two roles. Courtship is an important theme of the poem, and Nausikaa plays a courtship role as well as that of the young helper who guides the courtier to the queen. If marriage is uppermost in Nausikaa's mind, that is because it is the subject uppermost in Penelope's mind. So it is, too, on Telemachos' mind, and prominent in Helen's mind, and prominent as the background for the festivities in Sparta. When Nausikaa talks of marriage, when she expresses to the vagrant her preference for some man from afar as her husband, when she disdains her importunate local suitors, it is Penelope's voice we are hearing, or rather the voice that will prepare us to hear Penelope's voice when it speaks the same themes.

There may be, perhaps, some awkwardness in Nausikaa from the juxtaposition of two roles in her character. Perhaps it is unduly burdensome for an adolescent girl to play the archetype Woman, with whom the vagrant will rehearse a courtship, and the archetype Child, who calls for a courtship of another sort. And yet we have in Nausikaa one of the most successful portrayals of puberty, whether ancient or modern. Nausikaa is no more incomplete than other characters whom Odysseus meets on his journeys, Kirke or Kalypso. Complete characters exist only on Ithaka, of which characters elsewhere must necessarily be but paradigmatic fragments. Telemachos too is a slightly awkward adolescent, and surely it is time to leave off sighing about Nausikaa's lack of fulfillment and take pleasure in her as his female counterpart.[14]

Athena is a busy goddess in the *Odyssey*, back and forth from Ithaka to Sparta, Ithaka to Scheria, accompanying Telemachos on his voyage, then speeding back to console Penelope at home, then off to Scheria just in time to see Odysseus safely inside the palace there. With the three principals widely separated geographically, Intelligence (or Consciousness) hovers over them, each in turn, guiding their steps, securing their safety in their respective perils, and drawing the strands of their lives ever closer together. While she is thus engaged in the external motions of the plot she is as much occupied in weaving their souls together into a single harmonious fabric. It is Intelligence's task to midwife the inner *homophrosyne* among the members of the family as much as it is to engineer the safe return of the hero's physical being.

With Telemachos' integration into the idealized Spartan community assured, and his father's into the idealized Phaiakian community, Intelligence betakes herself to the disorderly community in Ithaka, where the ideals of harmony observed and rehearsed elsewhere must be realized. There she waits to be the first to greet the hero on his home ground. It is an embarrassing moment for the hero. Embarrassing enough to be discovered stark naked by a princess on the shore in Scheria, but how much more so to be discovered not naked, but in the midst of his spoils. Odysseus bluffs his way through the moment as best he can, and Intelligence laughs. She gives then her famous speech in which she jocularly compliments Odysseus for being cut from the same cloth as she (13.291-302). There is something of a reproach in her words for his failure to recognize in her the goddess who is his Olympian alter ego. Odysseus in his mortality, Athena in her Olympian immortality, they are always of the same mind. Athena could never abandon Odysseus, she says, because he is "discreet, has presence of mind [*anchinoos*], and a superior intelligence [*echephron*]" (13.332).

Odysseus' first encounter on his own island makes it clear that whatever his bond with another person, it is founded on *homophrosyne*. The *homophrosyne* that has made Athena stick by Odysseus through thick and thin is the same that is drawing him back to his family in Ithaka. Athena's speech on the *homophrosyne* that binds her and Odysseus is, thus, our best introduction to the events in Ithaka. What Athena says about the understanding between the two of them is true also of Odysseus' relationships with the faithful members of his household. With each individual Odysseus re-creates the psychological bond that had existed before.

After Athena, Eumaios is the first member of his household whom Odysseus meets, and their behavior together shows the pattern that will be repeated, with appropriate modifications, with subsequent individuals. Odysseus remains incognito and from behind his mask can test Eumaios' sentiments towards both his absent master and his present guest. Eumaios is unstinting in his solicitude for his unknown guest, but that is not enough. Odysseus creates in Eumaios a yet more kindly disposition by telling his entertaining stories. Eumaios affects a gruff peasant skepticism towards the stranger's tales and prophecies, but yet a harmony rises up between the two men which is unmistakable.

At one point the degree of understanding between the two men comes close to that which Athena claimed existed between her and Odysseus. Odysseus, to obtain a warm cloak for himself, tells Eumaios a (false?) tale of his Hermes-like legerdemain in conjuring another man's cloak to his own use on the field at Troy. Eumaios reveals that, like the Phaiakians, he can read between and behind the lines (14.508ff.): "Old man, your fable is flawless. You will not lack for clothing or for anything else." Odysseus gets himself a winter cloak, of course, and Eumaios must go without since he owns but one.[15]

The next day, when Eumaios discusses the stranger with Penelope, we see that his sympathies have advanced far beyond what he might feel for some traveler down on his luck (17.514ff.): "He would lay a spell on your heart with his stories," Eumaios tells Penelope, "as when a man looks upon a singer who sings sensual words from the gods . . . so that man has charmed me as he sat in my house." On the following day Odysseus reveals his identity to Eumaios by showing him his scar, but by that time the work of recognition has already been more than half-completed. The scar is but the last of a series of recognition tokens, a merely external proof of a relationship that Eumaios and Odysseus had already been practicing.

Telemachos and Eurykleia come to their recognition of Odysseus in the same way. Psychological sympathy precedes actual disclosure of identity. The case of Telemachos differs from the others in that Telemachos has no prior knowledge of his father. Telemachos must accept Odysseus' identity on faith, without supporting documents. The *homophrosyne* that comes into existence between father and son must, therefore, develop in the course of their collaboration in the palace, since it has no previous foundation. Even in Telemachos' case, however, the revelation of Odysseus' identity comes only after some psychological preparation. While in Eumaios' hut, Odysseus creates a bond of sympathy between himself and Telemachos in various ways. He shows himself properly deferential towards the young squire, and he ranges himself on Telemachos' side against the suitors, thus lending what moral support his beggarly circumstances permit. There is a bond of host and guest between the young man and the stranger, but the stranger is quick to reinforce that bond before he is revealed as the young man's father.

Eurykleia's recognition is brief, a mere interruption in Penelope's recognition scene, but even in its brevity the scene shows the same psychological pattern. Penelope in calling for Eurykleia to wash the stranger's feet sets the cycle in motion by reflecting on the physical similarity between Odysseus and the stranger (19.358-359). Eurykleia weeps as she remembers her master. Her lament begins as an address to her absent master, but by the end of her speech the reference of her second person pronoun is not her master but the stranger (note $\sigma\acute{e}o$ and $\sigma\epsilon$ in 19.363, and $\sigma\epsilon$ in v. 376). Her mind moves from thoughts of the absent man to the present one and it begins to dwell on the similar circumstances in which both men may be at that moment. She concludes what had begun as a lament, now speaking to the man before her, with the direct equation (vv. 380-381): "I say that no one has come here who so resembles Odysseus as you do in voice, appearance, and in feet." Mental reflections on similar circumstances lead to reflections on similar physique, and but a moment later she sees the scar and recognizes that these are indeed the feet of Odysseus. The scar is external confirmation once again of mental intuition.

All these recognition or revelation scenes are preliminary variations on the theme, which receives its fullest orchestration in the conversation between Odysseus and Penelope. Their scene, the great recognition scene of the poem, incorporates elements from all the prior recognitions: the fictitious tales by which the stranger links himself with Odysseus create a favorable impression on Penelope as they had on Eumaios; the enhanced physical appearance that had been instrumental in Telemachos' recognition plays its part here too, as do the physical similarities between the stranger and Odysseus which had persuaded Eurykleia of the stranger's identity. Even Odysseus' dress plays its role, as it had in Alkinoos' court. Physical tokens — articles of dress, bodily features, the construction of the bed — are the signs marking the subliminal path towards psychological reunion.

The harmony that grows between Penelope and Odysseus has its beginning long before their actual exchange. We can, in fact, pinpoint the very moment of its inception. In the omen-laden atmosphere, to which all the principals are acutely sensitive, there is a single event that marks the point when what might be merely an accidental collocation of signs first declares itself to be a pattern and a direction. Odysseus, making his begging round of the suitors to test their hospitality, comes to Antinoos (Antimind) and requests a portion from him. Antimind's response is to shout "What *daimon* brought this baggage in here?" and to hurl a footstool which hits intelligent Odysseus on the right shoulder (17.414ff.). This outrageous insult throws the palace into an uproar. Even mindless suitors are dismayed at this provocation. Penelope of the extraordinary intelligence, sequestered with her maids, hears the uproar, and from that moment her attention is riveted on the stranger. That loud crash of Antimind's footstool against the vagrant's shoulder is the sound that announces that the symphony has begun. The principals poise their instruments and focus on the score.

Penelope at once searches out the man who travels incognito and suffers the insults of Antimind; through her swineherd she issues her royal summons to the stranger. In the course of talking to Eumaios she mentions the name of Odysseus, and at that sound Telemachos coincidentally bursts forth with the sound that announces his entry into the symphony, a violent sneeze that resounds through the halls (17.541-542). To his welcome chord Penelope responds with a laugh. Ornithoscopists, those among us who are omen-watchers both to our sorrow and to our joy, will not be able to suppress their corresponding mirth at this point where the mournful lady's grieving countenance first transforms into a smile.[16] We have felt the same laugh well up in ourselves as the response of our bodily organism to some sudden vibration of energy that the cosmos directs into our immediate vicinity. We can be in the deepest gloom, but suddenly that cosmic vibration tingles our tissues and cells, realigns our protons and electrons, and we find ourselves laughing, quite to our surprise.

Penelope laughs because Telemachos' sneeze is an omen of the same sort as her laugh is to us. She has just felt some change in the atmosphere in her hall, and has sensed its connection with the stranger's arrival. In her words with Eumaios, Penelope links, quite fortuitously, the stranger's presence with her husband's wished-for return, and Telemachos sneezes, to confirm her intuition about the direction whence the vibration emanates. A certain conjunction of ideas has issued forth from her mind clothed in verbal vocabulary, without deliberate orchestration by her. In Telemachos' sneeze, the external world flashes, in its vocabulary, its sign that Penelope's conjunction is neither fortuitous nor an aberration of her private mind. Here for the first time the idea of Odysseus' return induces in Penelope not, as always before, another outpouring of despair at her beauty lost, but a bubble of pleasure. Penelope is quick to make the best of this adrenaline flow (17.544-550): "Go, call the stranger here before me," she commands her swineherd, "do you not see that my son sneezed at all our words?" In the remainder of her speech Penelope refers to the consequences to the suitors of her husband's return and then promises to give the stranger a cloak and tunic if he tells the truth, thus once again reinforcing that conjunction between her husband's return and the stranger's arrival which had elicited a gargantuan sneeze from Telemachos and a truly extraordinary transformation in the lady of mourning.

But Odysseus is in hiding. Eumaios reports back to the queen that the beggar suggests that he postpone his audience with the queen until after nightfall, when they could have greater privacy. The queen is yet more bemused, amazed now at the stranger's discretion. Echoing Nausikaa's reaction at her first encounter with this same stranger, Penelope comments (17.586): "The stranger is not without wits."[17] Thus ends the first movement of the queen's dance with the beggar.

There is an interlude until nightfall. In the external world, the world of the palace *megaron,* the interlude is occupied with a duel between the two beggars, Odysseus and Iros. Odysseus wins the duel and in doing so establishes his prerogative as the officially recognized court beggar. Immediately following that struggle in which Odysseus asserts his external territory, there is another struggle, parallel to the beggars' duel but on another plane. Now the struggle is played out in an internal area, within Penelope's mind, where too the beggar establishes his territorial rights. While Penelope waits for her audience with the beggar, he jostles about in her mind and demands her attention until, despite all her attempts to exclude him, he has successfully established his prerogatives there as he had around the dining tables below.

Penelope, in that interlude of waiting, receives a very strange signal. She has a curious notion, laid against her *phrenes,* as Homer says, by Athena. Penelope feels a desire "to make an appearance before the suitors, that she might spread wide the spirit of the suitors and win honor more than before in the eyes of husband and son" (18.160-162). This notion is startling on two counts. It is the first time that Penelope has felt something resembling an urge to make herself more attractive to the suitors. But more bewildering still is that she should think that flirting with her suitors should please the husband who is, to the best of her knowledge, far away. *Non bene iunctarum discordia semina rerum.* Ovid's description of chaos might well apply to the mental confusion this idea of Penelope's represents.

The notion is enough to make Penelope laugh again, and ornithoscopists will dutifully note it as her second, and last, laugh in the poem. Penelope transforms the idea radically in order to make it suitable for public exhibition. She eliminates the idea of her husband, and the idea of flirting with her suitors.

In her revised version of Athena's idea, as she delivers it to Eurynome, her desire is "to appear before the suitors, hateful though they be. I would speak a word to my son, which would be to his gain. He should not mix at all with the overbearing suitors who speak fair but hide evil intentions" (18.165-168). Thus is thought censored into propriety, and the oddity of Penelope's desire to associate with the suitors transferred from herself to her son, whom she can conveniently scold for his insensitivity.[18]

When Penelope goes to the hall below she scolds Telemachos, as she had said she would. The cause for her complaint, however, is not his association with the suitors. Not a word has she to say to him of the suitors. Instead, the burden of her remarks is directed to Telemachos' relations with the beggar. Resorting again to flagrant psychological projection, Penelope accuses her son of mental disintegration (vv. 215-225):

"Telemachos, your *phrenes* are no longer firm, nor your perception. When you were still a child, you tended more profitable thoughts. But now when you have reached the measure of manhood . . . your *phrenes* are no longer in harmony [*enaisimoi,* v. 220], nor your perception, such was the deed which occurred in the halls. You allowed the stranger to be thus mistreated."

Now at last the impulse that produced the original notion in Penelope's mind stands fully revealed. Ever since Antinoos' ominous stool hit the beggar's right shoulder Penelope's total preoccupation has been to talk to the beggar personally. When she initiates contact Telemachos sneezes to support her initiative. But the beggar resists her first attempt and she is left alone to ponder further the meaning of that footstool's trajectory. Penelope's mind (she herself calls it her *thymos,* though the poet-narrator calls it Athena) concocts another scheme for attracting the beggar's attention. Unfortunately, the scheme, as initially costumed, is unacceptable since it calls for unmitigated flirtation with the suitors. Penelope censors the scheme to adjust it to social mores, and gives Eurynome a revised version which calls for scolding her son. When she sees her son she clothes the impulse in now a third costume and accuses Telemachos of tolerating insults directed at the stranger. All revisions of the script and all costume changes, instead of concealing the initial impulse, simply bring it into clearer articulation. When Penelope scolds her son we realize that she had no real desire to flirt with her suitors, nor even to reproach Telemachos for associating with them. Penelope's mind is concerned with one person, and one person only.

Penelope makes her appearance before the suitors and seduces them with her beauty, thus carrying out the notion Athena had put in her mind. At the same time, Penelope maintains her own dignity by reprimanding her son. Whatever her effect on her suitors, then, it cannot be attributed to deliberate design on her part. She seems to have happily accommodated Athena's original idea and her own sense of decorum, and accomplishes what Athena intended without losing her own dignity. Odysseus was pleased, says Homer, because Penelope used sweet words to lay a spell on the spirit of the suitors, "but her mind thought on other things" (18.281-283). What those other things are she has disclosed in her reprimand of Telemachos — nothing else but the welfare of the beggar.[19] When Athena first encountered Odysseus on his own shores she had enjoyed witnessing his proficiency in speaking one thing while his mind thought on other things. In such proficiency she had discerned their bond and mutual gift. Now it is Odysseus' turn to witness and Penelope's to practice that art which her husband had already so ably demonstrated for his admiring goddess. The appearance of that weird notion in Penelope's head, that she could win honor from her husband by arousing her suitors' desire, is absurd enough to cause Penelope to laugh. When she executes that notion her husband in turn, who sits in the hall incognito, rejoices at its felicity. By such ring-composition we are reminded of the psychological proximity that Odysseus and Penelope have reached even before they speak to each other. Their courtship is far advanced already, though it has proceeded so far only through intermediaries and by mutual observation at a distance.

Night comes at last. The suitors vacate the hall. Telemachos vacates the hall. Finally the slave-girls too vacate the hall, leaving only Odysseus. Penelope enters. Then begins the scene that the poem has already rehearsed on other stages, the scene we may call, "A Stranger's Incognito Observed." Helen in Sparta had earlier discerned through a young man's incognito the familiar features of his father. She also tells her young visitor of a similar incident that took place years before in Troy, when his father had ventured into the city incognito and she alone had pierced his disguise. In Scheria we saw another rehearsal of the incognito theme as Alkinoos and Arete had observed the stranger's words and acts, and pressed him to reveal his identity. In particular we remember Arete's observation on the stranger's first night in her palace, and her discomforting question on his attire. On the Ithakan shore the incognito theme is rehearsed again when Athena discovers the newly arrived vagabond and reveals to him that she can penetrate his disguises. Helen and Arete are perceptive characters, alert to signs and able to arrange the signs into meaningful structures. How much more perception must we expect in the climactic recognition scene, when the lady observing the incognito is *periphron* Penelope, Penelope of superb intelligence, who is, moreover, the vagabond's own wife.

The repetition of the incognito theme makes it evident that this is a courtship poem, almost from beginning to end. Whatever his other skills, in this poem Odysseus is principally a suitor. It may be some exaggeration to call Odysseus' encounter with Helen in Troy a courtship, but the incident, as Helen tells it, has all the intimacies of a courtship. Helen is the only person in the city to recognize Odysseus beneath his disguise, as Odysseus later is the only Greek within the Wooden Horse to recognize Helen's voice for what it is. The recognition itself is a sign of considerable familiarity. In addition, however, Helen takes Odysseus in, washes him, clothes him, and swears to protect his incognito, behaving much as Kirke will later behave towards him. In return for Helen's hospitality Odysseus reveals to her "the mind of the Achaians" (4.250ff.). When the narrative shifts to Odysseus' return, the strategy of courtship becomes unmistakable in Odysseus' behavior towards Arete, and her daughter Nausikaa. It is courtship too in his encounter with Kirke, and even a variant on the theme of *homophrosyne*, since Odysseus' seduction of Kirke consists in matching her various forms of conquest with their mirror reflections. Kirke, amazed at this man whose mind remains inviolate, realizes that he can be only one person, "Odysseus of many turns."

Wallace Stevens writes in "Notes Towards a Supreme Fiction":

>   the going round
> And round and round, the merely going round,
> Until merely going round is a final good,
> The way wine comes at a table in a wood.
>
> And we enjoy like men, the way a leaf
> Above the table spins its constant spin,
> So that we look at it with pleasure, look
>
> At it spinning its eccentric measure. Perhaps,
> The man-hero is not the exceptional monster,
> But he that of repetition is most master.

This is what Homeric formulas are saying, this is the Homeric world, the going round and round.   And in that world much-turning Odysseus and his wife, weaving by day and raveling by night, are of repetition most master and mistress. When in his turns Odysseus returns to his island home we have become well attuned to his style of courtship, and we shall expect his final courtship, that center from which the man and woman and poem radiate, to differ from previous rehearsals only in a heightened sensibility, which earlier repetitions could only adumbrate.

The courtship Odysseus enacts in Ithaka is the performance of an event several times rehearsed in the poem, and therefore includes and fulfills them. At the same time it is a replay of a scene enacted outside the poem twenty years before, starring the same principals. Is it Documentary Fallacy to conjecture that when her onetime husband returns to her palace Penelope must be assailed by a persistent and anxious sense of déjà vu? Well, yes, Penelope is a person only in the hexameters of this poem. But such a poem of persons revolving back to their roots demands some judicious use of the Fallacy. Only so, by a perhaps fallacious but human response to the awe that a woman must experience on beholding herself moving in a mystery in which she had participated twenty years before, can we enter fully into the complex rhythms of her behavior. Her ambivalent notion to appear before the suitors, and thus to catch the stranger's attention, and the events that lead to that notion, all signify that we are witnessing a mystery raveling itself in Penelope's mind. That incident takes us to the silent depth where the data of sense impressions are shaped into constructs which we call thoughts, and from thoughts transformed into acts. That episode heralds the start of the most solemn moments of the mystery. It is the $εὐφημή$ of sacred ceremonies, the ritual cry for words of good omen only, which is to say for silence, stillness, and disciplined concentration on the epiphany about to take place. Penelope's seduction of the suitors is her distraction of the impious and stupid, while the initiates gather closer to participate in mind's discovery of mind.

It is best to have Penelope's situation in mind. Telemachos has grown to manhood, and his maturity entails her remarriage. Her suitors have discovered her weaving and raveling ruse, and no further avenues for prevarication are open. At this moment, when the pressure for her remarriage is extreme, wild things begin to happen. Telemachos leaves home and returns after safely evading a dire threat on his life. He brings with him a seer who swears solemnly to Penelope that her husband is already sleuthing around somewhere in Ithaka, fostering evil for the suitors (17.155-161). The same day Eumaios brings another visitor to the palace, a vagabond who provokes the vilest abuse from her suitors, while sustaining sufficient self-assurance to request a delay for his interview with the queen. The interview, when· it begins, can be no ordinary interview between two strangers. Penelope's impulse to seduce the suitors is indication enough of the mental radar with which she scans the hall as she begins her interrogation.

The queen begins by asking the vagabond (19.104f): "I will ask you face to face, who are you?" Thus begins their overt courtship. It falls into two distinct scenes, with Eurykleia's recognition and the story of Odysseus' scar coming as the climax of the first scene and the introduction to the second. The first scene is mainly occupied with the question of the stranger's identity. There Penelope attempts to elicit information of the most factual sort, who the stranger is, the circumstances of his friendship with her husband, and his reliability as a witness. In the second scene, which occupies the latter part of Book 19, Penelope's questions attempt to elicit not information but advice, guidance for her own conduct. The attention shifts from the vagabond to the queen.

Omen-watchers will surely notice some significance in Odysseus' refusal to answer Penelope's first direct question. A man who claims old ties of friendship with her husband, who claims, moreover, to have reliable knowledge of her husband's imminent return, this man yet refuses at first to reveal his name. Instead, Odysseus pours forth a honeyed speech on the good reputation, widespread as the very sky, of the lady to whom he is speaking (19.107-122). His encounter with Nausikaa had given him good practice in flattery as a frontal offense in his campaign to preserve his own incognito.

Penelope deprecates the stranger's compliments by talking of the evils with which her *daimon* has pursued her (vv. 124ff). Instead of pressing for the beggar's identity, she then reveals hers. She talks first of her situation: a husband absent and suitors from all the isles plaguing her against her will. She declares that her physical *arete* disappeared when the Argives set out for Troy, and then she reveals that some part at least of her *arete* has remained to her, namely her wit. She talks of her evasive tactics (*dolous,* v. 137) to parry the suitors' demands, describing the scheme of weaving and raveling that her *daimon* breathed into her (vv. 138ff). She describes the suitors' discovery of her stratagem, and of the compulsion now upon her to choose her new husband. "Now I cannot escape marriage nor can I conceive any other strategy" (vv. 157). We are reminded of Nausikaa, who likewise, on first meeting this vagabond, had talked of her importunate suitors and of the compulsion upon her to choose a husband. Thus Penelope's answer to Odysseus' evasion of her first question. She talks of her own forms of evasion, and only then reverts back to the vagabond's evasion.[20]

"Who are you?" she asks the vagabond a second time (vv. 162-163). Odysseus, his ears full of Penelope's little parable on weaving and unweaving as a defensive tactic, proceeds to weave a piece of fabric himself. He now gives his false Cretan credentials, claiming to be the brother of Idomeneus (vv. 172ff.). He relates how Penelope's husband had been driven ashore at Crete on his way to Troy, and how he had entertained her husband there in Crete for twelve days. Penelope dissolves; as the snow thaws on the high mountains and from its waters rivers flow in full spate, so she weeps as she hears her husband sitting beside her (vv. 204-209).[21]

Recovering her composure, Penelope decides to test the Cretan beggar's weaving. She asks him for a fully itemized description of her husband's dress when he landed in Crete (vv. 215-219). If the vagabond's evasion of Penelope's first question arouses some curiosity, his prompt and detailed response to this question should arouse equal curiosity. Pleading first the frailty of memory, the vagabond then demonstrates total recall. He describes in detail her husband's purple cloak — ah, that royal cloak again, significant purple — and the gold brooch used to fasten it (vv. 221ff.). He throws in for good measure a description of the herald who accompanied Odysseus twenty years before, Eurybates of the dark complexion and the woolly hair, whom Odysseus had honored above all the rest of his companions "because he knew things which fit the *phrenes* of Odysseus" (vv. 247-248). Royal *homophrosyne.*

At his reference to minds operating in unison Penelope weeps again. She addresses the vagabond in language that marks clearly his promotion (vv. 253-254): "At first you were someone for

me to pity [*eleeinos*], but now you will be dear and honored
[*philos* and *aidoios*] in my halls." She promises him clothes and
laments that her husband will never return. The vagabond
responds to his promotion by admitting to some knowledge of
her husband's itinerary and his present whereabouts
(vv. 262ff.). He tells of her husband's shipwreck off the island
of Thrinakia, of his being *odysseused* by Zeus and the sun
(v. 275). He mentions Scheria, but then includes a fictitious
addition to the travels: Odysseus is consulting the oracle at
Dodona, says the vagabond, to learn whether he should return
openly or by stealth. The vagabond concludes his volunteered
information by swearing a most solemn oath, with Zeus highest
and supreme of the gods as his witness, that her husband will
return "at this very *lykabas,* when one moon is waning and the
other waxing" (vv. 306-307).

Penelope makes a reply quite as full of double entendres as
his. "If this would but happen," she says, "then would you
know my love [*philotetes,* a word used of friendship but also of
sexual relations], and would receive many gifts from me, such
that a person meeting you would call you blessed"
(vv. 309-311). She laments again that her husband will never
return (vv. 312ff.): "Odysseus will not return to his house, nor
will you receive your escort away, since there are no *sign-givers*
[*semantores,* v. 314], such as Odysseus was, for receiving
respected strangers and sending them on their way." There
being no man in the house to assign the vagabond his escort,
Penelope offers him instead a bed, bath, and clean clothes, and
promises in addition that on the morrow the vagabond will be
assigned a place beside Telemachos at the table. She defends her
overtures of hospitality by saying to the stranger (vv. 325-326):
"How will you learn of me, stranger, whether I surpass all other
women in mind and in excellent strategy of mind, if you eat in
my halls unkempt and ill-clad?" Mind and mental strategies –
noos and *metis* – the two qualities that belong to Odysseus *par
excellence,* and Penelope suggests that the stranger might wish
to observe those very characteristics in her. She recommends in
fact a seat beside Telemachos as offering a better observation

post for that purpose. Can this be anything but seduction? Penelope comes as close to advertising her matrimonial availability as circumstances and her character will admit. Has the queen, then, become the sign-maker in her husband's absence?

Nausikaa had once been concerned about the propriety of being seen with a stranger on the city streets. But propriety is stretched a good deal further in Ithaka. The queen is closeted alone with a beggar late at night. She addresses him as a dear friend after but a short acquaintance; she promises him a seat by Telemachos in the hall; she calls for a bath, bed, and clothes — and all this so that the new-found friend can better observe the quality of Penelope's mind. Penelope is clearly uneasy about the degree of her hospitality and covers her unease by dilating on the lasting value of a good reputation (vv. 325ff.).

Penelope is addressing a man, however, who understands her dilemma. He understands why her concern for her good reputation should induce her to offer the friend of her husband the full resources of her palace, yet why that same concern should make her uneasy about putting up a stranger in the palace in her husband's absence. Odysseus politely declines the bed altogether, and for a bath claims he would be content with a foot bath administered by some trusty old serving woman — "someone who has endured as many things in her *phrenes* as I" (v. 347), again a reference to similarity in experience and temperament, to *homophrosyne* (vv. 336-348).[22]

Odysseus correctly divines Penelope's embarrassment. She reacts to his suggestion with a veritable paean to the stranger's intelligence (vv. 350-351): "Dear guest," she begins, but in her excitement her syntax fails her slightly at this point, "for not yet has any man so intelligent come to my home, more dear than any guests from afar." The thought is clear despite the syntax. She has just called the man who but a short while before was a stranger and a vagabond a dear friend, and embarrassment finds its own path. She must defend herself for calling him thus, and her explanation is that he is more intelligent (*pepnumenos*) than any other visitor. But her confession that he is more intelligent than any other man leads her to confess also that he is dearer (*philion*) than any other guest.[23]

"So intelligent and full of thought is everything you say" (v. 352). Would not this be hyperbole if it were only a bed and bath that Odysseus had declined? When a woman known for her extraordinary mind indulges in a florid compliment on her guest's mind, we can be sure that there is more happening than extending or declining items of refreshment. At the vagabond's demonstration of his intuition Penelope's estimation of him leaps forward, and issues in her premature admission that he is dearer than all previous guests.

The syntax in Penelope's compliments (in vv. 350-351) betrays the hectic state in which she is operating. Had we any doubts remaining as to her state of mind, the rest of her speech would confirm our suspicions. The images of the vagabond and her husband had become inexplicably fused in her mind once before, in that interlude when Penelope had waited to see the beggar. Now she has talked about her husband with the vagabond directly and the two images once again fuse into a single focus. She calls for Eurykleia of extraordinary mind (*periphron* like her mistress, v. 357) to "wash your master's . . . peer" (v. 358). She had almost said "your master's feet," but the censor in her brain intervened and replaced feet with the syntactic equivalent "peer." Penelope attempts, now as before, to cover the confusion into which her mental censorship had led her, as she explains why she had called this man the master's peer (vv. 358-359): "And I suppose Odysseus looks pretty much the same in [respect to] feet, pretty much the same in hands."

Penelope had begun with pity for the beggar. Pity had become sympathy, sympathy had become respect, respect had become love. The stranger had progressed from "stranger," to "dear guest," then to "guest dearer than any other," and Penelope finds herself about to call him Odysseus' double, had not her mental censor headed off that imminent equation.[24]

Clearly, recognition is the only possible next step. Recognition is what we all expect and recognition there is, but it is not Penelope's. For a poet to play tomfoolery on a critic's expectations is an act of courage. Critical brows have furrowed over the substitution of Eurykleia's recognition for Penelope's at this juncture. Few indeed have been the critics who have surrendered themselves to the rhythm of the scene, who have experienced its advances, pauses, and retardations, its points and counterpoints. Instead of feeling gratitude for the aesthetic perfection of this scene, critics have more commonly detected that old *Bearbeiter,* busy as a mole at his usual task of collating one version of the tale with another contradictory version. There are two stories of Odysseus' return, so such critics argue, one in which Penelope recognizes him and collaborates with him, and the other in which the killing of the suitors precedes the recognition. Our version of the tale, it is argued, incorporates both plots.[25]

Since Horace's jocular *dormitat Homerus* it has been the mark of erudition to argue that Homer, the stitcher of our Homeric poems, composed only when wrapped in the soundest slumber. Adherents of this doctrine suppose that Homer, heavy with sleep as usual, stitched together the beginning of version A of the reunion and the end of version B. The beginning of the scene implies, so they claim, another conclusion than the one we possess; and vice versa, our present conclusion implies another beginning than the one Book 19 gives us. It is also the doctrine of this Slumber School of Composition that Homer's listeners, as much given to sleep as he, nodded in the hearing of the tale as he in the telling.

It is each critic's privilege to decide for himself the extent of Homer's creative life which he spent snoring. Critics should feel some slight compunction, however, when attributing heavy slumber to the poet at precisely that point in the poem where the principal theme is wakefulness. The contrast between knowledge and ignorance, intuition and obtuseness, sobriety and drunkenness, self-control and loss of control, and wakefulness and sleep runs through the whole poem from Athena's first epiphany in Book 1, but that contrast becomes the veritable obsession of the last books, and particularly of Books 18 to 23. The suitors, living as always in a mental haze, misconstrue all the significant signs, or overlook them entirely, in the last books. They become progressively more stupified by wine and their own idiocies and progressively less able to control their actions. While they lose their grasp, Odysseus and the faithful grow progressively surer of their actions, more receptive to the signs around them and consequently more in control both of their own minds and of the external environment.

Never has Penelope been more awake than on the night she talks to the Cretan stranger about her husband. Never has Odysseus been more awake than when discussing himself with his once and future wife. If we do not feel that Odysseus and Penelope are awake in every fiber of their being when they meet each other in this scene we have understood nothing of the signs that have been appearing thick and fast, the prophecies, the sneezes, the laughs, the insults hurled, the propitious words, the hidden thoughts, and the censored revisions of those thoughts. The air is electric even in Book 18, thought visibly discharging as electricity, but yet Book 18 is a mere preliminary to Book 19. Wakefulness in Book 19 is as palpable as a fabric; it is, indeed, the fabric of the book. We have some difficulty in recognizing wakefulness in Homer since our mechanistic *Weltanschauung* conceives of the state in a much narrower sense than Homer would define it, and perhaps something quite opposite to what he would call wakefulness. Most modern critics would probably dismiss Homer's wakefulness as superstition.

Penelope and Odysseus, both being awake (or superstitious, depending on the school of criticism one prefers) and straining their five senses in order to derive their common sense, enter into a composition of their joint creation. Odysseus sets up the rhythmic ebb and flow of concealment and revelation. He conceals his identity, then becomes obliquely articulate on his identity by describing Odysseus' clothes and friends of twenty years before. Penelope enters into the rhythm which her senses have picked up. She moves with the tide, she too now denying, now revealing, now obscuring a revelation by an apologetic gesture. The two characters proceed by feints and counterfeints, by compliments and compliments reciprocated, by flirtations that are just beneath the threshold of flirtation, flirtations that may be read as such or construed merely as drawing room politesse. Seduction in earnest and the game of seduction are skillfully interwoven in this dialogue between the humble courtier and his queen. The tide carries them forward and then back, forward once again, always ever closer to recognition. When Odysseus asks for an old woman to wash his feet his words lift Penelope up in a great wave that rolls her to the very border of conscious recognition. "Wash your master's *peer*'s . . . feet," Penelope calls to Eurykleia, all but pronouncing the word whose time has not yet come. "Yes, he had such feet and hands," says the queen, suddenly noticing the signs to which her sly sign-maker was pointing.

At that point the wave crests and breaks, but to our surprise we find not Penelope but Eurykleia left standing on the shore. While Penelope is swept back to sea, Eurykleia follows through on the rhythm of Penelope's wave, lifting from Penelope's very mouth, and completing, the sentence Penelope had half begun. "I have never seen a man so like Odysseus as you in physique, voice and feet. . . . Ah, then you are Odysseus, my child," Eurykleia exclaims a moment later, when she has seen the scar (19.380-381; 475).

The rhythm of Penelope's recognition had brought her almost to the syntactic identification of the stranger and her husband (σοῖο ἄνακτος, v. 358). That syntactic accident leads her to muse directly on the similarity between the two men – they are peers not only in age but in physical appearance (vv. 358-359). Then Eurykleia enters and she continues Penelope's line of thought, almost as if the whole scene had been hers. She continues the reflection on the similarity between the two men, first in their present circumstances and then in their physical appearance. Here again syntax is an uncanny mirror of thought, creating the ambiguities that are both the signs of her mental operation and the tools of that operation.

It is rare for Homeric characters to address each other without the first resorting to a formula naming his listener. The name, once used in the first speech, may be omitted in the subsequent speeches of a dialogue where pronouns will usually suffice. Eurykleia as she enters begins addressing someone simply as "you, my child" (v. 363) and continues to address him with the second person pronoun (σέο, v. 363; σύ, v. 367; τοι, v. 369). Eurykleia should be addressing the man before her, and syntax helps to promote this idea since Eurykleia omits any name, as if she were continuing a conversation she had already begun. But syntax misleads us: Eurykleia is addressing an absent and unnamed man, from whom Zeus has taken his day of return. Though Eurykleia looks at the stranger, and while looking at him says *you,* her mind's eye is looking at another Odysseus. Again, in a stroke or two, Homer delineates a fragment of the subconscious.

After her series of second person pronouns Eurykleia changes in verse 370 to the third person pronoun (κείνῳ) to refer to her absent master. Immediately thereafter she reverts to second person pronouns which she uses for the rest of her speech (σέθεν, v. 372; σε, v. 376; σύ, v. 381). Now, however, her pronouns refer to the man facing her, whom she has likewise left unnamed.

It is a deviation from custom for Eurykleia to begin by addressing an absent man as "you, child." It is a greater deviation when she addresses the present stranger without any indication of a change of subject. Only the small word κείνῳ in verse 370 indicates a change of direction. It is the syntactic unit that permits Eurykleia to make a graceful slide from the absent Odysseus to the present Odysseus. When she addresses the stranger with second person pronouns and omits any name or title, the effect is to make her initial σέο (v. 363) operative through her whole speech, her term of address for both men.

In the final observation of her speech, Eurykleia carries recognition one step further than Penelope. Penelope had supposed a resemblance between her husband and her visitor, but Eurykleia goes beyond supposition to notice a resemblance so uncanny that she exclaims on it and Odysseus is compelled to admit the truth of her perception (vv. 383-385). A moment later the scar on Odysseus' leg confirms her intuition with documentary evidence. It is significant that the scar appears only after Eurykleia's perception had already led her almost to the equation that the scar makes inevitable. It is a perception shown in her observation of the resemblance between the two men, but shown too in her syntax, which weaves the two men together into a single composite with almost no trace of the joining.

Book 19, though it flows with the rhythm of great Ocean itself, yet seems to pound against the critical mind like a wall of surf with a riptide beneath. Critics, whose resistance turns a rhythm into an assault, retaliate on that force by denying its rhythm altogether. They talk of conflation when they should talk of elation. Beneath their criticisms is a supposition that the poem is leading up to the killing of the suitors. But Athena tells Odysseus that the suitors are not the problem at all. There could be fifty ambushing parties lying in wait to kill him, says Athena, and Odysseus could drive off all their herds and flocks unscathed (20.49-51). In your weakness lies your devil's strength.

No, that collection of blundering, mindless, drunken suitors cannot be the problem, nor can such louts constitute any significant part of the poem. The poem is about being in phase: about those who are in phase and those who are not, and about the movement from out of phase into phase. We are all familiar with the theory, though we express it almost always only as a joke about operatic divas, of the capacity of a mere vibration at a certain frequency to shatter glass. It requires no effort to shatter the glass, only the correct vibration, and the breakage will occur effortlessly. So with the death of the suitors. Once Odysseus is in phase, then the suitors will disintegrate. The shooting of those 108 suitors is a convenient *mythos* for illustrating the principle of the potency of a man in phase. The poem is the depiction of how a man finds the cosmic phase and fits himself into its rhythm.

Accustomed to thinking that the goal of Book 19 is, or should be, Penelope's recognition of Odysseus, we become irritated at what strikes us as the rhetorical means used to delay this goal. Some poetic embroidery we are willing to accept in this antique poetry, but since we are interested only in the completion of an event we consider to be the goal, our tolerance for delay and circumambulation is low. We talk of the paratactic style of oral narrative, or an inorganic style, of the stitchwork of *Bearbeiters,* and in other ways express our disapproval of a style that ignores our passion for a quick ending. Few critics can understand that in the rise and fall of the hexameters lies the *mythos* of the poem.

The goal of Book 19 is Penelope's recognition, of course, but it is a mistake to concentrate on that second when recognition is crystallized rather than on the formation of that crystal. The poem is more interested in the process than its final completion. Book 19 is about a man and a woman, yang and yin, who come into phase with each other after twenty years of following their individual rhythms — it is the poem of a man and a woman discovering themselves in each other. When they first meet after their long separation each listens to his own rhythm while trying to pick up the other's. Slowly, in fear and awe, each discovers the other's rhythm weaving in and out of his own, and as they continue talking the two rhythms merge into a single rhythm that encompasses them both. Yin and yang are the two voices of a single composition.

What happens in Book 19 is an epiphany, magical and sacred, but you will search in vain to find discussion of it for most scholars will not have noticed it, their attention being occupied elsewhere, in the quest for the saga or layers of saga, or in watching for the occultation of the suitors.[26] It is easy perhaps for us to overlook an epiphany since such occurrences are no longer part of our materialist lives, and if we think of them at all, it is of deities or archangels. In fact, epiphany is but the Coming-into-phase (phasis, to use the English word as obsolete in the language as the event in our lives). In this poem the

Epiphasis is the Coming-into-phase of Odysseus, the Coming-into-phase of Penelope, and then of their discovering each other's phase.

A fundamental law of epiphanology is that epiphanies come only to those who can see, which is to say only to those who seek. In our poem, Theoklymenos sees the epiphany dawning and describes it in some detail, but the suitors, blind and ignorant of their blindness, treat the seer as their tomfool. Not all characters are as blind as they. Those who hold themselves in readiness for the epiphany, Eumaios, for example, and Eurykleia, recognize it when it happens. Penelope too waits in readiness, and her wait, occupied with her weaving and raveling, is no passive surrender but her preparation for that epiphany. When she enters the hall late one night to converse with a stranger who claims a Cretan origin she actually invokes the epiphany of her husband. Just as Eurykleia creates, in her syntax, a composite of the stranger and her master, which is then paralleled by the composite in the external world, so Penelope, as she questions the stranger about her husband, creates that epiphany she had waited long to see.

It is vouchsafed to few to experience an epiphany on the order of Penelope's. Even the humblest epiphany, however, should enable us to recognize the emotions operating in Book 19 and to flow with the dynamic rhythm they impose on that book. An epiphany is an awesome event. People who undergo the experience are lucky if they survive with merely some bodily discomfort. Saul of Tarsus "was three days without sight, and neither did eat nor drink," when he was vouchsafed his epiphany. The drama is more subtle, perhaps, in Penelope's case, but the experience is certainly as intense as that recorded in the Acts of the Apostles.

A young jazz musician, just learning his craft, starts jamming with more professional musicians. One day, after much travail, the novice discovers that his ears, his breath, and his fingers have become at last obedient to his will. Through their harmonious operation he finds himself playing flawlessly the melody and rhythm he hears from the other musicians. His unwonted and unpredicted — though much prayed and worked for – success in achieving a harmony of soul, mind, and body may well unnerve him. He may become conscious of his achievement, and his consciousness will cause him to stumble and lose the rhythm. The only way back may be for him to lapse into unconsciousness or subconsciousness, to search out in that shadowy realm the secret path to lead him back to the rhythm. To discover the conscious and the subconscious moving in phase with each other is exhilarating, but terrifying too. When it happens, the achievement often generates in compensation some kind of relapse. Since the human organism shrinks, it seems, from knowing its own powers, the pressure to discover a psychological truth is balanced by an equal, perhaps even a greater, pressure to cover what has been discovered. For every *Entdeckung des Geistes* there is an equal *Deckung.* The greater the personal consequences dependent on the discovery, the greater the struggle between the contrary motives of discovering and covering, revealing and concealing, learning and unlearning, admitting and denying.

In the episode describing Penelope's desire to arouse the suitors, we had a clear demonstration of the ability of her mind to apprehend a true and complete picture, and then to reject it. Her mind, one side of it at least, *saw* that by enticing the suitors she would enhance her honor in her husband's eyes. Penelope rejects that true idea categorically, as we have seen. But though she does everything possible to prevent its articulation, it continues to make its presence felt regardless of her censorship. Here again, in her conversation with her guest, Penelope's mind follows the same path. The guest's talk of a footbath brings Penelope's eyes to notice his feet, and at once her mind again makes the identification between the stranger and her husband. At such a peak of consciousness, Penelope lapses as suddenly into unconsciousness, distracted when her mind succeeds in coordinating the multifarious information her senses yield. Her mind is turned aside by Athena, says Homer (v. 479), and as we have learned from the earlier scene with Penelope and Eurynome, Athena hovers close to the threshold between Penelope's conscious and subconscious selves.

Penelope invokes the epiphany, but just at the flashpoint averts her eyes, unable to endure what she must inevitably see next. Queens do not let their eyes linger on strange men's feet. But an epiphany once invoked cannot be arrested. At Penelope's negation Eurykleia materializes to receive the vision the queen's eyes were not yet ready to accept. The old slave can do what the queen cannot: she takes the travel-worn feet, hidden in the shadows, those feet that had thrown the queen's mind into disarray, she touches them, she stares at them, as only a slave may be permitted to do, she lets her hand and eye move from feet to shins, from shins to knees, from knees to thighs. Flash. Flashback into essence.

Wolfman, favorite of the Trickster, taking his grandson from a young slave girl's hands, names his essence Pain. A hunt years later in the dense woods on windy Parnassus, the hounds straining ahead to track down the footprints of their quarry, Wolfman's sons bringing up the rear, but Pain, grown to adolescence, presses ahead, sniffing for footprints with the hounds. A boar, brought to bay in a sunless thicket, hair bristling, eyes darting fire, leaps up and tears the flesh away from Pain's thigh, down to the bone. The young hunter of pain, initiated so abruptly into his essence, kills the quarry with a careful aim at its right shoulder. Wolfman's sons come up and staunch the hero's blood with song. Wolfman and his family signify the hunter's initiation on Parnassus with glorious gifts and send him home. "Yes, I am that Pain matured," the vagrant tells the slave-girl, his wet-nurse, herself now aged and as experienced in pain as the man at whose naming she had assisted. Only the slave and nurse, whose rhythm of life had synchronized with that of her nursling from the moment of his birth, could stand fast to let the electric current the queen and her hunter-guest had generated between them discharge through her.

There is a vigorous discharge of electricity at the moment of Eurykleia's recognition, of that there can be no doubt, for the atmosphere in the great hall is palpably different after the beggar's footbath. Though the beggar and the queen reach considerable intimacy in their conversation before the footbath, they remain still at a distance, a queen still and her guest. In restricting themselves to an objective correlative, Penelope's absent husband, they maintain the correct tone in their relations. But after the footbath their relations enter a new mode. The guest, now bathed, draws himself closer to the fire, which is to say out of the shadows and closer to the queen (see 19.55 for Penelope's position in the hall), and their conversation mirrors their physical proximity.[27] Penelope talks less now of her husband, except as the background influence in her thoughts and decisions. She focuses directly on herself. She treats the stranger as her long-time friend and confidant, with whom she is accustomed to share her most intimate thoughts. She talks freely of her state of mind, she asks for advice in the direction of her personal life, and she invites her guest to collaborate in her plans. The stranger had already talked of himself in their earlier conversation, and continues to do so through their second conversation. But now Penelope replies in kind, so that in their second conversation each is talking of himself, Penelope of her mental state and her remarriage, Odysseus of his return.

The intimate content of Penelope's thought forces on her a style that is now wholly symbolic. Odysseus talks of himself through a veil, by impersonating someone who can claim knowledge of her husband. Now Penelope too speaks through a veil, as if only thus could she disclose the inner recesses of her thought. She reveals her inner turmoil with astonishing candor, but candor shaped into three symbolic *mythoi.*

She begins by projecting her disorder into the paradigmatic myth of the nightingale, daughter of Pandareus, who laments for the son she herself has killed. Penelope confesses first that she cannot sleep since cares cluster around her heart at night. She then uses the myth of the nightingale to explain her own situation, both her circumstances and her emotional attitude (vv. 509ff.). The myth, as she relates it, best expresses the ambiguity of a mother's position. The sweet springtime song of the nightingale is, in fact, a funeral dirge for a son slain, and the singer is the murderer (vv. 518-523). The conflict that informs the myth is Penelope's conflict too, as she herself declares (vv. 524ff.): "So my *thymos* is driven from side to side, torn between remaining by my son and protecting everything, and marrying the best of the Achaians who woo me." She explains the reason for her dilemma (vv. 530ff.). Her son is mature now and presses her to leave the house. Through the myth of the nightingale Penelope tries to adumbrate some of the ambivalences in her own emotions. Like the nightingale, Penelope is distraught to the point of madness — note her word *aphradias* in verse 523.

The nightingale serves Penelope as the introduction to her discussion of her personal problems. She follows that myth with a description of her dream, which she asks her confidant to interpret (vv. 535ff.). In the dream an eagle had swooped down and killed her geese; she had wept at her loss, and the eagle had returned to assure her that he was her husband. Odysseus confirms the interpretation that the dream eagle had already imposed on the dream, but Penelope ostensibly dismisses the topic by resorting to another symbolic structure. She describes the gates of fulfilled and unfulfilled dreams, and claims that her dream probably issued from the source of unfulfilled dreams (vv. 560ff.). Signs are hard to interpret and not all come to fruition, so Penelope recognizes, though her remarks are directed here to one genre of signs in particular.

Her discussion about fulfilled and unfulfilled signs at an end, Penelope abruptly turns to a new topic. She announces that the time for vacillation is over, the very next day will see her separated from the house of Odysseus, for she has decided to choose a new husband (vv. 571ff.). She describes her method for making a choice. She will have a contest, and whoever can shoot with Odysseus' bow through twelve axes aligned in a row will be the man to take her from the house which, as she says, she will remember even in her dreams (v. 581). The contest is another form of symbolic thought, or rather symbolic action. It is an exercise in sympathetic magic. The bow takes us into the mythical world, for it is Odysseus' link with the earlier heroes of Herakles' generation. In addition, the bow is the distinctive personal attribute of the hunter Odysseus; Penelope informs us that shooting the arrow through the axes was the special skill of Odysseus (vv. 573-576). Later the suitors are well aware that they are being called on to compete with Odysseus. In failing in the contest, they frankly acknowledge that they are embarrassed less to lose a good marriage than to be proven inferior to him (v. 21.91-95, 250-255, 325-326). Penelope's proposed contest will be an enactment of a ritual from Odysseus' own life, a paradigmatic act as the digression on the scar is a paradigmatic tale. To institute a contest in which the event and the instrument are both the peculiar property of Odysseus is to elicit Odysseus' epiphany. Penelope has read the signs but she needs some confirmation that her senses are reading true. The contest will be definitive proof, either of her folly or of her intelligence.[28]

The stranger gives Penelope the strongest possible encouragement in this decision by asserting that Odysseus, since he is *polymetis* (the epithet receives emphasis from its unusual position, v. 585), will return before the suitors can string the bow. At this point Penelope, who earlier had pleaded insomnia as grounds for interrogating Odysseus late into the night, pleads fatigue and abruptly retires, leaving the stranger to bivouac wherever he wishes.

The stranger is a stranger no more, but the queen's Privy Councillor, and with her has just plotted the strategy for the suitors' occultation and his own epiphany. Penelope, verging ever closer to recognition, lapses from discursive logic into allusive modes, expressing herself through the opaque style of myth, dream, magical rites, and disjunctive transitions. but her lapse is not a lapse into irrationality. For irrationality we look to the suitors who, having passed the boundaries of sanity, dare to accuse Odysseus of alcoholic befuddlement. They demonstrate their irrationality when they fail to perceive meaning in symbolic language. Theoklymenos sees their destruction approaching in all its lurid glare, but when he describes what is before his eyes they guffaw; to their literal minds his symbolism is an absurdity. In the *Odyssey* the literal mind is a half-mind at best.

In contrast, though Penelope's style is opaque, the course she follows is logical and coherent. In the first part of her conversation with the stranger she tests his knowledge of her husband; in their second conversation she continues to test him, but her tests become more rigorous as they become more intimate. She tests the stranger's attitude by revealing her own inner conflicts with respect to her now mature son. She tests him again by revealing her dream, and when he confirms the interpretation of the dream, she suggests one final test, to take place the next day. To that test too the stranger assents, and when she has gained that assent Penelope retires to her own solitude.

Far from creating any confusion, what Penelope says is perfectly intelligible to Odysseus. The *homophrosyne* between the two has reached a remarkable level of cognizance. After the footbath, in fact, Odysseus and Penelope converse as man and wife, as if recognition and reunion had already taken place. Their language is one of private cryptograms. Penelope speaks of her most personal turmoil in allusive ways, Odysseus understands and responds in kind. The extraordinary result is that the scene comes to an end with both parties having agreed on a plan for disposing of the suitors, although there has still been no recognition and they part without the slightest acknowledgment that an agreement has just been concluded. Through allusions they have played their hands quite plainly. "What would happen," asks Penelope, "if I ended my twenty years' wait tomorrow?" "Do that," says the queen's Privy Councillor, who is also, as councillors usually are, an interpreter of dreams, "do that, and the eagle of your dreams will return tomorrow disguised as an archer." Consensus is reached; the couple separate for the night, knowing their plan in its general outline and indifferent, it would seem, to details.

It is not surprising that modern critics have argued that Penelope recognizes the stranger as her husband during their conversation in Book 19, but chooses to keep her silence as he keeps his. Certainly Odysseus has given more than hints of his identity, for the myths he tells of himself reveal as much as they conceal. The story of the stranger's acquaintance with Penelope's husband may be acceptable, but what of the tokens that testify to the stranger's memory, so miraculously intact twenty years after an allegedly brief encounter with Odysseus? What of the stranger's claims to reliable information on her husband's past, his present, and his future? Our Cretan necromancer drops a broad enough hint when he tells the queen that her husband is consulting an oracle to learn whether he should appear in Ithaka in disguise or openly (19.296-299). He drops almost every pretense at a persona when he vows by the highest god in the pantheon that Penelope's husband will return at the dark of the moon, a vow that is the stranger's reciprocal symbol for Penelope's symbolic statements. The dark of the moon is at hand.

The stranger's store of information, his prophecies, his vow, the style, moreover, in which he couches his information, all tend in one direction — towards revealing the one fact none of them can state. From Odysseus' words alone we might infer that he had signalled that his disguise was to be seen as a disguise. Penelope's reaction to his words would strengthen such an inference. Though she may use some deprecating formulas to register formal skepticism, her attitudes belie her formulas. She depends heavily on the stranger for help; she accepts him even into the inner sanctum of her psyche. It seems as if the queen and the beggar were in on some secret as they exchange cryptic allusions, as they weave together the contest of the bow at the dark of the moon. The spiritual harmony between the two, shown in their understanding of each other's language, makes it hardly credible that no recognition has taken place.[29]

We are told in the most explicit ways, however, that Penelope has not accepted the stranger as her husband until her reference to their marriage bed opens the flood of his emotions. Even after the stranger has killed 108 suitors, Penelope is skeptical. When Eurykleia tells her it was Odysseus who strung the bow and killed the suitors, she accuses Eurykleia of mental disintegration (23.11-14). Penelope's incredulity is consistent with everything in her behavior subsequent to her conversation with the stranger. When she retires from their conversation her mind remains in turmoil: she lies sleepless on her bed, she weeps at the thought of the contest, she muses on suicide. To argue that Penelope recognizes unmistakably her husband during their conversation is to etiolate her subsequent anguish. It would be a most conspicuous fall into the Documentary Fallacy to argue for Penelope as a living woman whose cleverness had outwitted not only her husband but even Homer himself.

If we can even consider disregarding Penelope's vacillation after her conversation with the stranger, it is because of our orientation towards the saga instead of the poem. We fix our attention on the points on the saga's linear scroll, on such events as Penelope's recognition of her husband or the killing of the suitors. Such events are integral to the poem, but the poem lies in the shadows behind those events. You can collect as many events as you wish, arrange them however you choose, and you will not thereby have yourself a poem. This poem, our long-suffering *Odyssey,* leads us into a realm of emotional complexity that is but dimly perceptible in Odysseus' previous encounters in the tale. In this encounter in Ithaka both participants stand at the most critical point in their lives, and are aware of it. What makes this a poem, as distinct from the saga, is that it vibrates with their slightest psychic quiver.

The scene portraying Penelope's strange desire to show herself to her suitors is the crucial introduction to her conversation with Odysseus, for it shows her mind quite clearly split into two parts. Call the parts her conscious and subconscious, or express the polarity, as Ezra Pound says, by "whatever terms of whatever cult or science you prefer" (*The Spirit of Romance,* p. 93). It is immaterial so long as we agree that the two sides exist in her in disharmonious conjunction. While one side is convinced that her husband is dead, the other refuses to accept that conclusion and from the available data draws the opposite inference. In the description of Penelope's attempt to render her bizarre idea safe and commonplace, we see the dynamics of that mental conflict — one side going so far as to confuse the stranger with her husband, the other side vigorously suppressing that absurd equation.

Penelope's two minds continue to coexist, and to operate on each other, through her conversation with the stranger. In their dialogue before the footbath, Penelope's censoring, or rational, side is dominant. Penelope asks the kinds of questions a rationalist would ask and calls for rationalist proofs. She does what common courtesy calls for, when she promises the stranger new clothes and invites him to enjoy a bath and an overnight stay. Even while she acts in this decorous and rational manner, however, her other side is exerting its force. She is embarrassed to hear herself addressing the stranger in terms of such familiarity that decorum calls for some apology from her. While one side of her denies the validity of the stranger's prophecies, we overhear the other side complimenting the stranger on his intelligence. Penelope's appearance before the suitors becomes an event that integrates both sides of her mind, and the footbath episode provides the same kind of resolution. When Penelope suggests a bath, it is the gesture of pure decorum, and yet it is the gesture that leads directly to her perception of the physical similarity between the stranger and her husband. At that point, her intuition, or whatever we call it, bubbles to the surface and would have proclaimed the stranger's identity had not Penelope's mental censor stepped in once again and led Penelope's mind down another trail.

When she emerges from her reveries after Eurykleia has administered the footbath, Penelope is almost totally in the realm of the nonrational or subconscious. She talks of her innermost psychological state, but in the language of the subconscious, through myth and allusion. As the guest responds to her revelations she permits herself to be guided more and more by the subconscious. It may be that tradition had always preserved the contest of the bow in the saga of Odysseus' return, but in this poetic version of the saga the contest is the direct creation of Penelope's subconscious. The contest is, on one hand, Penelope's acknowledgment of the veracity of her intuitions; on the other hand, it is the severest test that Penelope can devise for her intuitions. If she has read the data right, the contest will be her glory; if she has miscalculated, it will be her eternal shame. When Penelope proposes the contest and her guest encourages her, she retires with almost impolite haste, quite at odds with her decorous solicitude earlier in the evening. Now her mind is moving in that realm where decorum is almost too painful.

Penelope in proposing the contest relinquishes herself over to the subconscious. This is not to say that she has recognized the stranger as her husband, for recognition suggests a degree of clarity and consciousness that Penelope does not yet possess. Rather, she surrenders herself to the flow of events, as her subconscious seems to be perceiving them. Whether the stranger is her husband or a man who resembles her husband, whether he is a mortal or a god, Penelope's subconscious tells her that the solution to all such questions can come only through a form of divination, through the test of the bow. In his wanderings, Odysseus had voyaged to the kingdom of the shadows, where he had learned to recognize through the murk the *eidola* of what once were such heroes as Agamemnon and Achilleus. Now it is Penelope's turn to practice necromancy, and to discern in the flickering shadows the features of a man long lost and presumed dead. In the kingdom of shadows rational sureties can seem very hollow.

To surrender to one's subconscious is a fearsome thing. It is not surprising that daylight burns away the intuitions of the night, and Cartesian rationality is once again enthroned. The morning after Penelope's conversation with the stranger finds her confronting the enormity of her decision by weeping and longing for death (20.57-90). Odysseus too is sufficiently distraught to resort to a complex divination, for he needs to draw courage from a nonrational conjunction of omens (20.93-101). The rational rues the decision of the nonrational, but it is now powerless to undo those decisions. Penelope institutes the contest, though the act of opening the storeroom and laying hands on her husband's bow calls forth her most bitter tears, for if she has misjudged she will never again see either bow or storeroom or palace (21.56-79). When the contest is underway, and the vagabond requests his turn at the bow where others have failed, we see again the play of the two sides of Penelope's mind. While one side encourages the foolishness of the beggar's entry in the bride contest, the other side allays the suitors' fears by proclaiming it a piece of nonsense, a little sport at the beggar's expense. His entry, she assures the suitors, will be strictly *hors de combat*. If he should string the bow she will give him a token prize — a set of clothes and bon voyage (21.337-342). At this point the two sides of Penelope's mind have moved from confrontation to cooperation. The one side, the nonrational, supplies the action, in pressing for the vagabond's entry into the contest; it is now the rational side's turn to supply the decorum, by assuring the suitors that the vagabond has sufficient status to deserve a try — and to deserve some token compensation if he should string the bow — but that, in spite of his status, he could in no way be a threat to their success. With her contest of the bow Penelope invokes the epiphany for the second time, but just as it is to be revealed to her she disappears, and once again it deflects on to others. On this occasion Telemachos intervenes to order Penelope from the hall. She retires upstairs and falls into a sleep. Her mind goes elsewhere, as it had done during the stranger's footbath, and in its absence the suitors fall victim to the epiphany her test of the bow has created.

The hunter strings the bow and kills the suitors in their sunless thicket, all in accordance with the plan laid out by Penelope's subconscious. Still she is fearful, and how not, when she discovers events in the external world flowing in the channels laid out by her own psyche? We can sympathize with Penelope's paranoia when she hears of the outcome of the contest. Her first impulse is to accuse her maid Eurykleia of irrationality; she then imagines that someone, man or god, has impersonated her husband to torment her (23.11-24). Success in divination is a greater torment than no divination at all. Penelope goes downstairs to look on the apparition who has just killed her suitors. Telemachos reproaches her for her stony heart, but she replies that if this apparition be indeed Odysseus, he and she will recognize each other through signs "hidden from others" (23.110). Odysseus smiles at the mention of their private language. He had smiled before when Penelope had courted the suitors and tricked them into giving her gifts; he smiles now that she will turn her courtly strategies on him and trick him into surrendering his mask. "Allow your mother to make her tests of me," he says to his son. Telemachos, who by his journey abroad in search of his father, and by his arranging of the axes for the contest, had manfully played his part to bring about this moment of recognition, is about to leave the stage. As he leaves he replies to his father (vv. 124-126): "They say that yours is the best mind among men, and there is no man of mortal kind who could rival you." Telemachos then walks off, so missing the opportunity to see the best mind among men give way to the best mind among women.

When Odysseus and Penelope are alone for the second time, and Odysseus freshly bathed, for the second time, Odysseus begins to speak. He doffs the mask of courtier and dons the mask of husband, as he scolds Penelope for an iron heart such as no wife heretofore has displayed. He then calls for the maid to spread his bed (vv. 166-172). Penelope deftly weaves a reply which imitates his speech in both language and structure, addressing him as *daemonic* as he had called her *daemonic*. [30] In her speech she tests the mask of husband with which he now confronts her, and by her test, which is itself another form of divination, she discovers, behind the mask of husband, her lover. "Ah woman, a pain in the soul is this word you have spoken," is the heart's response from her lover when she feigns that their bed has been brought out from its secret place. He proceeds to describe that secret place, the chamber he built around an olive tree, within the chamber the bed he made to grow from the olive tree, and on the bed an identifying mark, secret enclosing secret enclosing secret (vv. 183-201).

"Such is the sign I set forth for you," so Odysseus concludes his description of the temple he had built to house his love, that one construction among his many constructions to be signed with his own personal seal. Penelope's test prevails because she alone knows that nerve in Odysseus which would, when touched, cry aloud its pain. Odysseus reacts to her test as if the ground had given way and he were once more lost in the surging sea. In greatest agitation he insists that he personally had anchored to the earth that chamber in which he would hide his secret self, and describes at length the solid construction of that anchor.

Penelope had twice invoked the epiphany but fled from its manifestation. This third occasion she is ready; she stands her ground to witness and receive it. She aims her arrow at the region of Odysseus' psyche where rational and nonrational meet, and he reacts with a mixture of both. With anger, that some rival has tampered with his wedding bed, but through the anger shines forth his love of the object manufactured by his rational self. For with Athena's olive as the anchor he had built for himself, from stone, gold, silver, and ivory, a green shade as his refuge from the abyss.

We have reached the *telos,* the goal of the poem, as Aristarchos noted. Odysseus, laying aside all masks, bares his true mind, proud in its creations and vulnerable at the same time. As he surrenders his mask, so does Penelope. It is hardly man and woman, or man and wife, facing each other now, but mind looking into mind, and seeing there the reflection of itself. And if Odysseus and Penelope stand free of their masks of ambiguity, so too does Homer. Odysseus reveals himself through his pride in the skill of his own hand and mind to fashion a small and personal bulwark against the chaos. In his revelation is the poet's revelation, for the poet has, with humor, tenderness, wit, and solemnity, led us into that sacred precinct whence his cosmogony and all his art. Andrew Marvell centuries later called it

> The Mind, that Ocean where each Kind
> Does straight its own resemblance find.

V

Archery at the Dark
of the Moon

> To discover an order as of
> A season, to discover summer and know it,
> To discover winter and know it well, to find,
> Not to impose, not to have reasoned at all,
> Out of nothing to have come on major weather,
>
> It is possible, possible, possible. It must
> Be possible.
>
> —Wallace Stevens, "Notes Towards a Supreme Fiction"

Odysseus, aroused back to his senses by his restless comrades, begs Kirke to grant him passage home. She tells him he must first travel the road to the house of Hades and dread Persephone, to consult the *psyche* of Teiresias. At that his heart breaks, for it "no longer wished to live and look upon the light of the sun" (10.498). Odysseus travels to that realm of *zophos* where the sun's rays never penetrate, and there Teiresias prophesies a safe homecoming for him if he will but reverence the sun. Odysseus returns from the darkness to Kirke's island, "where are the house of Dawn, and dancing floors, and the risings of the sun" (12.3-4). He continues on his journey, past Sirens, the Clashing Rocks, Skylla and Charybdis, until he reaches the sacred island where the sun pastures his sacred days and nights. There Odysseus' comrades perform their sacrilege on the inviolable property of the sun and are hurled from the light of the sun forever. Odysseus alone is saved from the storm by finding, "with the rising sun" (12.429), a cave above Charybdis. There he clings to an olive tree through the livelong day like a bat, until the time when a hungry judge goes home for his dinner, when Charybdis vomits up the mast of his ship. Jumping aboard his mast he is carried out to sea for nine days, and on the tenth night he finds refuge with the nymph Kalypso, who hides him away from the sight of man and god for seven years.

"When the year came round in the circling of the seasons [*eniauton*] which the gods, in their spinning, had marked as the time of his return . . ." So begins the poem with a simple, almost formulaic, temporal notation, which gains in significance when we realize that the circling seasons bring around simultaneously Telemachos' maturity, Penelope's remarriage, and the return of the man absent for twenty years, lost at sea and presumed dead for ten years. We are not put *in medias res,* when the poem opens, but *in ultimas res.*

If Odysseus is to return to the light of the sun, it is now or never. But Athena, the divine architect of the poem, is not perturbed by any sense of urgency. To the contrary, she delights in dancing around the urgency. She introduces Odysseus' name quite casually into the conversation on Olympos when Zeus is musing on the fate of that evil suitor Aegisthus. She contrives to have Hermes sent to start Odysseus on his way, while she goes to Ithaka to create further complications. At the time when the pressures on Penelope are the most severe, she leads Telemachos to undertake a voyage across the sea. Odysseus is justifiably angry to hear that Athena has sent his son away at such a time (13.417-419); it seems a gratuitous cruelty for Athena to dispatch the boy into perils at sea, while leaving his mother and his property at the mercy of villains. But an eleventh-hour crisis holds no threat for Athena. It merely enhances her orchestration of time and persons. While events move swiftly to their culmination, she darts in and out, back and forth, now as a dream, now as a bird, now as a young man, a young girl, a wise old man, busy but ever insouciant, full of pleasure in her weaving of individual times into the cosmic time.

Odysseus starts out from Kalypso's island to look once more upon the sun, to regain his time. He steers his ship from Ogygia by the stars, by the Great Bear, the Pleiades, and "late-setting Boötes" (5.272-3). As we have seen in chapter 3, the stars give Odysseus his spatial orientation, which he has lacked since arriving years before at Kirke's island where he could not distinguish *zophos* from *eos*, east from west, darkness from light. But the stars give him also a temporal notation. From Hesiod, as from many other sources, we learn what the constellation of the Pleiades meant for agricultural and seafaring Greeks. If the sun was one hand on their chronometer, the Pleiades were the other.[1] For both farmer and sailor the Pleiades by their risings and settings announced the times for both beginning and closing the essential activities of the year. For the sailor, the rising of the Pleiades signified the start of the sailing season in the spring and their setting the end of the sailing season just before winter. Odysseus sails from Kalypso's island when the Pleiades are visible during the night; this would put his journey very late in the sailing season, just about as the season is to close. The year is far advanced.

Since Homer is wont to give his spatial or temporal notations by two coordinates, we are pleased to find him making the time of the journey precise by balancing the Pleiades with "late-setting Boötes." The expression "late-setting Boötes" has prompted various interpretations, none persuasive. It has been argued that Boötes is "late-setting" because it sets after more southerly constellations that rise simultaneously with it. This is unsatisfactory, because the only star that could bear this relation to Boötes is Spica in Virgo, a constellation not named in Homer. Furthermore, the Pleiades and half a dozen other constellations are close to the declination of Arcturus in Boötes, and could just as well be called "late-setting" as Boötes. Arcturus and the Pleiades, differing some twelve hours in right ascension at the present time, are balanced like a pair of scales in the sky. As Boötes sets, the Pleiades rise. To say "setting Boötes" is the reverse of saying "the rising Pleiades." In their complementary balance, surely, lies the clue to Homer's epithet for Boötes. Odysseus cannot watch both Boötes and the Pleiades simultaneously, or not for very long, since the visibility of one implies the invisibility of the other. Odysseus must watch Boötes as it sets at dusk, while the Pleiades are rising, and he would continue to steer his way through the night by the "late-rising"

Pleiades, until Boötes returns to take up his post in the early hours of the morning when the Pleiades sink below the horizon. "Late-setting" would mean, by this interpretation, the evening, or acronycal setting.

From the reference to Boötes and the Pleiades we can place Odysseus' journey from Kalypso's island between the evening rising of the Pleiades and their morning setting, in that period which in 432 B.C. would fall between 19 September and 8 November on the Julian calendar.[2] From Hesiod we learn that the morning setting of the Pleiades (8 November in 432 B.C.) marks the end of the sailing season; at their setting, winter storms break out and it is time to beach the ships for winter (*WD* 619ff.). Hesiod pinpoints the onset of winter as the coincidence of the falling of the Pleiades and the rising of the winds – as the Pleiades plunge into the misty sea the blasts "of all the winds" arise (*WD* 619-622):

εὖτ᾽ ἂν Πληιάδες σθένος ὄβριμον Ὠαρίωνος
φεύγουσαι πίπτωσιν ἐς ἠεροειδέα πόντον,
δὴ τότε παντοίων ἀνέμων θυίουσιν ἀῆται
καὶ τότε μηκέτι νῆας ἔχειν ἐνὶ οἴνοπι πόντῳ.

Several centuries later an epigram commemorating a death at sea echoes Hesiod's warning (Theocr. *epigr.* [XXV] Gow):[3]

᾽Άνθρωπε, ζωῆς. περιφείδεο μηδὲ παρ᾽ ὥρην
ναυτίλος ἴσθι· καὶ ὡς οὐ πολὺς ἀνδρὶ βίος.
δείλαιε Κλεόνικε, σὺ δ᾽ εἰς λιπαρὴν Θάσον ἐλθεῖν
ἠπείγευ Κοίλης ἔμπορος ἐκ Συρίης,
ἔμπορος, ὦ Κλεόνικε· δύσω δ᾽ ὑπὸ Πλειάδος αὐτήν
ποντοπορῶν αὐτῇ Πλειάδι συγκατέδυς.

The twenty-five days in which Odysseus builds his ship and completes his journey to Scheria are the last sailing month of the year. For seventeen days he crosses the open sea, enjoying calm and a favoring wind, but suddenly, on the eighteenth day of his voyage, a violent storm arises which shatters his ship and lashes him mercilessly for two full days. Odysseus becomes, in Homer's simile, a thistle tossed across the plain by gusts of the autumnal north wind (ὀπωρινὸς βορέης φορέησιν ἀκάνθας, 5.328). Poseidon's savage storm can be none other than

Hesiod's first winter storm. There are close parallels between Hesiod's and Homer's descriptions. In Homer, Poseidon rouses the storm thus (5.292-296):

> πάσας δ᾽ ὀρόθυνεν ἀέλλας
> παντοίων ἀνέμων, σὺν δὲ νεφέεσσι κάλυψεν
> γαῖαν ὁμοῦ καὶ πόντον· ὀρώρει δ᾽ οὐρανόθεν νύξ.
> σὺν δ᾽ εὖρός τε νότος τ᾽ ἔπεσον ζέφυρός τε δυσαὴς
> καὶ βορέης αἰθρηγενέτης μέγα κῦμα κυλίνδων.

That the storm is a joined battle of all the winds Homer continues to emphasize throughout the passage (cf. 304-5, 317), most notably in verses 330 to 332, where Notos and Boreas alternate with Euros and Zephyros in hurling Odysseus' ship back and forth. When the ship is nothing but flotsam, scattered like chaff in the wind (vv. 368-369), the winds subside except for the violent north wind which continues to bluster for another two days until it brings Odysseus in sight of Scheria. The *Odyssey*'s battle "of all the winds," following hard on the reference to the autumnal sky, is poetic amplification of what is a brief almanac date in Hesiod. It corresponds also with the dissolution of the covenant of the winds, which is the mythopoeic way the old Norse work *Konnungs Skuggsjá* describes the beginning of winter (see my chap. 3).[4]

Odysseus reaches Scheria at the very close of the sailing season. He was, in fact, caught in the dreaded first storm of winter. Had he dallied longer on Ogygia he would have had to wait out the winter and Penelope would have remarried. The Phaiakians' extraordinary sailing skill now assumes a new significance. Their supernatural power might seem superfluous when Odysseus has already eluded every kind of peril by his own wits, but Homer's maritime audience would have enjoyed the coincidence that the storm that closed the paths of the sea for the year should have cast Odysseus among a people whose skills were happily not subject to the season. The Phaiakians secure Odysseus' passage across the treacherous winter sea because the weather has now made human navigation suicidal.

From this point several references confirm the meteorological evidence. When the storm casts Odysseus ashore on Scheria he is in a quandary whether to expose himself to the night frost near the river or to find himself a warmer spot in the woods, and thus chance an attack from wild animals (5.466-473). Choosing the latter course, he beds down beneath a dense heap of leaves, autumn's debris, "sufficient to protect two or three men in the winter season, even if winter should be unusually severe" (5.483-5). Later in Ithaka, during the first night of Odysseus' stay in Eumaios' hut, a rain storm blows all night and Odysseus invents a story of how he had tricked a soldier out of his cloak one winter's night in Troy. Eumaios understands the hint; he moves Odysseus' bed close to the fire, spreads sheepskins on it, and throws over Odysseus his own specially thick cloak, designed for protection against harsh winter storms (14.457-522). Eumaios himself spends the night out on the ground near the pigs; for protection against the cold he takes another thick cloak and a goat's fleece, and finds himself a snug shelter against the north wind (14.529-533). In Odysseus' palace the servants heap logs on the fire to give both light and warmth (19.63-64). The nights are long, says Eumaios; there is time enough for both story-telling and sleep (15.392ff.).[5]

In Ithaka, the chronology begins to narrow down from seasons to days. Odysseus twice swears a solemn oath, once to Eumaios and later to Penelope, by Zeus and by the hearth of Odysseus which has given him asylum that "Odysseus will return at this very *lykabas,* when one moon is waning and the other waxing" (14.160-162; 19.305-307):

ἦ μέν τοι τάδε πάντα τελείεται ὡς ἀγορεύω.
τοῦδ' αὐτοῦ λυκάβαντος ἐλεύσεται ἐνθάδ' Ὀδυσσεὺς,
τοῦ μὲν φθίνοντος μηνός, τοῦ δ' ἱσταμένοιο.

In later Greek *lykabas* signified "year," but its etymology is uncertain and scholars divide on whether to take it as year, season, month, or day in the Homeric passages.[6] It is surely not a synonym for *etos* or *eniautos,* the customary and general words in Homer for year (or season), but something more precise since the reference to the moon's cycle seems epexegetic. Also, it would be contrary to the poem's progressive concern for exact chronology that Odysseus make at this point safely vague predictions about an event sometime within the twelvemonth. The solemnity of Odysseus' oath suggests that he is not hiding behind comfortable generality but staking his life on a very precise and, therefore, daring prediction. *Lykabas* must surely be either "this particular month" or, even better, the dark of the moon, a meaning that could accommodate either the etymologies linking *lykabas* with *lyk-* (light) or those linking it with *lykos* (wolf). Maas, for example, understands *lykabas* as winter, the season "when wolves run," but his etymology might just as well apply to the dark of the moon, that period almost universally considered of sinister aspect. Whether *lykabas* be year or month, however, makes little difference in the circumstances, for the year has practically run its course: "this year" and "this month" are, at this point in the poem, synonymous.

During the conversation between Odysseus and Penelope in Book 19, Odysseus swears that Penelope's husband will be home at the dark of the moon. A few moments later Penelope proposes to hold a contest for her remarriage on the morrow. The stranger immediately assures her that "Odysseus, wily man that he is, will be home before the suitors stretch the bowstring and wing an arrow through the iron" (19.586-587). Thus does he confirm what events in the next books will reveal, that Penelope's morrow and the stranger's dark of the moon are one and the same. Behind their veiled language the two exchange concrete and precise information as to what will happen and when. Penelope would grasp at once the import of the stranger's talk of the dark of the moon, for preparations were about to begin for the feast of Apollo which, as the scholiast remarked, must be the feast of Apollo Noumenios, Apollo of the New Moon. Odysseus' first night in Ithaka is a "moon-obscured night" (*nyx skotomenios*), which brings a vile storm of rain and wind.[7] It could be argued that all night storms obscure the moon, but in Homer storms obscure the sky. This is the only storm in Homer in which the disappearance of the moon is emphasized. It was not the storm that hid the moon, but the dark of the moon that brought the storm.

On the following day Eurykleia busies herself and her staff with the preparations for the lunar feast; the suitors gather in their usual way. Ktesippos demonstrates the suitors' ignorance of both marksmanship and sacral moments by aiming an oxhoof at Odysseus' head and hitting the wall instead. Before Penelope can produce the bow to give him his second chance at Apollonian skills, Theoklymenos has a harrowing vision of death. Heraklitos Rheter interpreted Theoklymenos' vision, which occurs, as he notes, on the day "which the Athenian youths call ἔνην τε καὶ νέαν," as a description of a solar eclipse that can occur only at the time of the new moon.[8] Modern critics, their lives no longer regulated by the lunar calendar, might reject such an interpretation as an anachronism for Homer, but for a people whose livelihood was dependent on the cycles of sun and moon, who, moreover, sanctified every new moon with religious ceremony, the connection between new moon and solar eclipse must have been apparent from a very early time. Theoklymenos' vision remains a vision and not a literal eclipse; the *Odyssey* is not an almanac, but it incorporates almanac data into its dramatic exposition. The suitors laugh at Theoklymenos' wild fantasy, but Homer's audience, knowing their calendar, would have understood what Theoklymenos meant when he said on the eve of the new moon: "Your heads are shrouded in night, the walls run red with blood, the sun has perished from the sky, and a murky gloom has settled over everything" (20.351-357). Theoklymenos' prophetic vision is one more announcement of the exact moment of the denouement, an announcement of the most emphatic sort, for it describes that calamitous and awe-inspiring event that can happen in that moment of equilibrium between one moon and the next.

Wilamowitz, who understood *lykabas* as the day that in the Athenian calendar was called ἔνη τε καὶ νέα, interprets Odysseus' oath to mean "*heute kommt Odysseus,*" but goes further to suggest that it is a particular new moon, the new moon that begins the new year.[9] Although there is no explicit statement to this effect in the poem, the air suddenly becomes alive with intimations of spring. Penelope, recounting her grief to Odysseus, likens herself to the nightingale which sings its beautiful song in early spring, perched amid the thick foliage on the trees (19.519-520):

καλὸν ἀείδῃσιν ἔαρος νέον ἱσταμένοιο,
δενδρέων ἐν πετάλοισι καθεζομένη πυκινοῖσιν.

Shortly before Penelope's conversation with Odysseus, he had replied to Eurymachos' insults by suggesting that the two men compete in field work "in the spring season when the days are long" (18.367). At the moment of vengeance the tokens of spring become unequivocal. The bowstring in Odysseus' hand "sang out fair like a swallow's note" (21.411). In the midst of the fray, Athena taunts the suitors in Mentor's shape and then darts up to the rafters in the form of a swallow (22.240). Moments later the suitors are routed in panic like a herd of cattle goaded by the gadfly "in the season of spring when the days are long" (22.299-301). Autumnal and winter pictures which had accompanied Odysseus' journey from Scheria to Ithaka — the windblown chaff, night frosts, fallen leaves, bitter storms — give way, on the day of vengeance, to the sounds and sights of nightingales, swallows, farmers breaking the soil or cutting grass, and pasturing cattle.

The association of swallows with spring is almost universal wherever the swallow is known. In extant Greek literature swallows appear infrequently, but in most cases they come as harbingers of spring.[10] Aeschylus, it is true, likens barbarian tongues to the twittering of swallows (*Ag.* 1050, fr. 450) and Eustathius inclines towards this association in his discussion of the Odyssean passage (see his Commentary, 1914-20ff.). But if the sound of the bowstring is barbarous, it is barbarous only to the suitors, who turn pale with fear at the note. For Odysseus and his family it is a beautiful omen, *kalon* as Homer calls it. The sound of the bow and Athena's metamorphosis into a swallow that perches beneath the rafters can mean nothing else but the arrival of spring.

Tradition has preserved from antiquity a certain type of popular song which celebrates the annual return of the swallow. In the Rhodian song *Chelidonismos,* as recorded by Athenaeus (VIII.360b), and in the Samian *Eiresione,* attributed to Homer's authorship in the *Vita homeri herodotea* (chap. 33), children impersonate swallows and make a tour of houses, standing at the doors to demand entrance and promising prosperity on the house in return for gifts and threats if no gifts are forthcoming. "The swallow has come bringing lovely seasons and lovely years," the Rhodian song begins, and concludes after a set of promises and threats, "open up, open up the door to the swallow. We are not old men, but children." The Samian song, according to the *Vita,* was one that Homer, accompanied by the local children, used to sing at the doors of the most prosperous houses when he wintered one year in Samos. The occasion of the song was exactly the occasion of the swallow's song in the *Odyssey,* the new-moon festival in honor of Apollo. The song wishes prosperity on the house, and concludes, "I come, I come yearly as the swallow who perches with bare and nimble feet in the forecourt. Give something if you will; but if not, we will not stay. We did not come here to remain with you."[11]

Sir James Frazer, in an article citing examples from Greek literature as well as from contemporary folklore, offered further clarification of the Rhodian swallow song by showing that the swallow is often welcomed into houses since it is a good omen for the swallow to make his nest in the rafters.[12] In both the Rhodian and Samian versions the children imitate the behavior of swallows: if invited into the house and given gifts they will assure prosperity; if rejected they will work harm and pass on to a more hospitable house. They impersonate, it is obvious, the harbingers of spring.

The pseudo-Herodotean *Vita,* in reality less *vita* than hagiograph, attempts, as do the other *Vitae,* to make Homer an honorary citizen of as many cities as possible, particularly those that claimed to be his birthplace. In the *Vita,* Homer is a wandering minstrel who goes from one city to another, accepting work where he finds it and rewarding his hosts with song in proportion to their hospitality. Superficially he has become a mendicant poet, but in reality a hero figure whose prowess lies in his gift for song. Like other hero figures he suffers misfortune, performs exploits, though these are in song, and undergoes periods of servitude. For weapons he has his incantations, with which he blesses or curses according to the treatment he receives — his arrival at a city brings either prosperity or calamity. Many of the songs and epigrams in the *Vita* are undoubtedly local products which tradition attributed to Homer, but the structure of the *Vita* is clearly an extrapolation from the *Odyssey.* Mentor, Mentes, and Phemius, for example, the *Vita* transforms into the helpful friends and teachers of Homer whom he gratefully immortalized in his poem. By a method familiar to all students of literary criticism, the *Vita* has read the *Odyssey* as cryptic autobiography of the poet. There are no wandering bards in the *Odyssey* but there is a wandering hero who pays high compliments to bards, and in fact entertains his hosts with song in return for their hospitality. In the *Vita,* bard and wandering hero merge into a single figure. It is the poet who travels, both from financial necessity and from a desire to explore the world, who arrives at a house or city and appeals for the rights of hospitality and for outright gifts. The *Vita* owes its most apparent debt to the Phaiakian episode of the *Odyssey* and to the last part of the poem when Odysseus arrives at his palace in Ithaka, that is, to those episodes where the emphasis is on Odysseus as an indigent guest, who entertains the company with tales in return for clothes and supplies. In his own house he plays the mendicant, praying for the good health of those who treat him kindly and threatening those who mistreat him with the vengeance of heaven. The owners of the house receive him kindly; Penelope, in fact, after one evening's conversation with him, treats him as next of kin.[13]

The connection of the Samian *Eiresione* with Homer's name is not coincidental. The song itself probably has no connection with Homer but it lends itself readily to inclusion in a Homeric hagiography. Homer sang the song, says the *Vita,* at the new-moon festivals for Apollo during a winter in Samos. But the swallow song, celebrating the arrival of the swallow, would be apt at only one new-moon festival of winter, namely, the new moon marking the end of winter and the beginning of spring.

The *Odyssey* is, in fact, our earliest *Chelidonismos*, in an amplified and dramatized version. Celebrations of the annual arrival of the swallow seem to have been a custom widely practiced in Greece and no audience could fail to notice the *Odyssey*'s use of the popular tradition. The arrival of the hero, who is both beggar and itinerant "poet," signals the end of disintegration and the beginning of reconstruction. The itinerant in disguise, like the children disguised as swallows, makes his rounds to test each man's hospitality and dispenses rewards accordingly. He is even barefoot and shabby, as the children seem to be in the Samian *Eiresione*. He arrives in winter and takes his vengeance at the feast of the new moon in honor of Apollo. At the moment of vengeance his bow sounds the swallow's note, the first note of spring, and Athena, the miracle worker, perches in the rafters in a swallow's disguise, a good omen for a prosperous new year. Athena is the first swallow of the season.[14]

Northrop Frye has reminded us that comedy has its roots in the celebration of spring's victory over winter, the New Year's conquest of the Old.[15] So it is in the *Odyssey*, our earliest comedy. Odysseus, put back into time, sails on his last voyage in the autumnal season, becoming one with the season, chaff blown by the autumnal wind. He survives the first storm of winter, arrives at Scheria when there is frost on the ground, and buries himself beneath the year's fallen leaves. It is dead of winter when he arrives in Ithaka to warm himself at Eumaios' humble fire. He proceeds to his palace and there vows vengeance at the dark of the moon. There Theoklymenos sees a solar eclipse on the day of the Old and the New — instant of transition between waning and waxing, ending and beginning, point of equilibrium pregnant with potential for either good or bad. The suitors mock his talk of darkness, for had not

Eurymachos already joked that there was light enough in the hall (18.353-355): "Not without god comes this man into the house of Odysseus, for most bright is the light shining from his head, since there is not a hair on it." Odysseus has become the only light there is in the house.[16]

Penelope institutes her contest on that day of contraries. Odysseus' bow sounds the swallow's note and his arrow, *hora* made visible, threads the twelve axes with the same deadly accuracy as nimble Odysseus threads the calendar. The gods' destined plan comes to fruition with not a moment to spare. Accurate in timing as in marksmanship, Odysseus, with a prayer to Apollo — god of both timing and marksmanship — fulfills his vow and the gods' plan on the last day of the appointed year, in the last hours of the last day. A swallow darts in among the rafters; the suitors, personification of waste and dissolution, are routed like cattle stung by the gadfly in the long days of spring. Winter in Ithaka is at an end. As we expect in comedy, the rout of winter calls for a feast. "Now is the hour come to set a banquet for the Achaians in the light, and then to turn to song and the lyre, which are the glory of the feast" — so Odysseus triumphantly calls out to his son (21.428-429). The feast begins. The bard takes up his lyre, the halls resound with the noise of the lyre and the feet of men and women dancing, and passersby exclaim: "Ah, then someone has married the long-courted queen" (23.143-149).

Once every twenty-nine days or so the moon moves into conjunction with the sun, when it is veiled from our sight. It then travels on its orbit slowly out from the sun until full moon, when it stands in opposition and greets the sun from afar. As it continues its orbit it wanes and approaches the sun until it surrenders once again to the sun's embrace. The monthly dance of sun and moon is repeated on a vaster scale by sun and stars. Constellation after constellation disappears behind the sun and then moves outward in its orbit. Conjunction and opposition in a ceaseless cycle is the visible pattern of order in the universe.

Such are the ceremonies in the heavens on which Homer's courtly hexameters rest, the phases of sun and moon moving in quiet harmony, the phases of sun and star crossing paths once every year, the phases of the winds merging with the phases of the stars, the swallow by day, the nightingale by night heralding to farmer and sailor the completion of one phase and the start of another. Set in the midst of this dance of all creation is man, than whom, as Odysseus says, "earth nourishes nothing more frail" (18.130). At the mercy of those beings that live at their ease in courtly disport, man is swept from prosperity to poverty, from joy to despair, from life to death — "such is the *noos* of men on the soil" (18.136). Sun, moon, and stars move in their majestic circuits, while beneath them man is wracked by storm, war, disease, and age.

But Odysseus chooses for himself the lot of man. He returns home "to accept in silence the gifts of the gods, whatever they might give him" (18.142). His acceptance of mortal fortune is the opposite of passive resignation; it is a ceaseless effort to build with hand and mind a world that the gods may — no will — sooner or later destroy. Odysseus builds a world of objects around him — houses, furniture, ships, arms — and builds too a world of people attuned to his mind. And his mind, despite what he says through his beggar's mask, is not fixed on his belly. His is the mind that has seen a nymph who can change men into other species, and another who can offer him immortality. It has looked upon the property of the sun and the property of Hades. It has looked into its own birth and death, and into the realms in between. When Odysseus returns to his obscure little island to create *homophrosyne* there, he has already begun to recreate *homophrosyne* between his mind and the heavenly paradigms. Thus he enters into a courtship, which he had performed many years before, in phase now with the courtship of sun and moon.[17] The courtship on earth coincides precisely with the courtship in heaven. Such is the *Odyssey*'s definition of *hora,* the right season, and its definition too of mind, a definition vaster than that bequeathed to us by our tradition of the individual body housing an isolated soul, man set in an adversary position towards the universe.[18]

Penelope alleges that the burial shroud she weaves is for her father-in-law. We are not fooled. It is for Odysseus, not Laertes. In weaving and unraveling the shroud Penelope lays her husband in his grave by day and raises him, Lazarus-like, from the dead by night. She too performs her daily ceremony of opposition and conjunction, accepting her husband's death and from his death creating his life anew, in a ceaseless process of waxing and waning.[19] What is her weaving but the rhythm of the life of the man who moves between the realms of Hades and Helios, now disappearing from the light, now coming into being once more? And in her weaving is the paradigm too of Homer's poetics. For man, build as he will his own microcosm, must as inevitably leave the splendor of the sun, and his microcosm must disintegrate with him. Only in the weaving and unweaving of Homer's formulas into hexameters can Odysseus hope for anything beyond a momentary affirmation of his frail existence. The singer is like the gods in speech, and there is no purpose of greater grace than when banqueters sit to listen to their singer — so Odysseus says to the Phaiakian artists. Of the gifts the gods give, the greatest in the *Odyssey* is song.

Notes

NOTES TO CHAPTER I

1. Denys Page, *History and the Homeric Iliad* (Berkeley, Los Angeles, 1959), p. 222 (referred to as *HHI*).

2. Milman Parry, "Homer and Homeric Style," in *The Collected Papers of Milman Parry* (Oxford, 1971), p. 269. Since Milman Parry's French theses are not widely available, all citations of his works are from the edition of his collected works published by his son Adam Parry. I have adopted the practice of putting the title of M. Parry's original work in quotation marks, whether it was a journal article or an independent publication. Page references are to *Collected Papers.*

3. F. M. Combellack, "Milman Parry and Homeric Artistry," *CompLit* 11(1959):197. Parry had also attacked Ruskin on the same point in "Traditional Epithet," *Collected Papers,* p. 125, although the Homeric phrase "life-giving earth" is a unique expression.

4. Page, *HHI,* p. 228, echoing Parry's assumption. For some reason, obscure to me, the extinct hexameters, in which the devotees of the formula believe as in an article of faith, would be expected to reveal a quite different ratio of repetitions to unique expressions from that in our extant hexameters. The discovery of those extinct hexameters would yield, so we are to assume, a harvest of "traditional" formulas but be barren of nontraditional formulas. Recourse to lost hexameters is merely attending on the *deus ex machina.* If, with some 27,000 extant hexameters and 9000 words, the formulaic system is still vastly incomplete, as any hard-line formulaic theorist will readily admit, how many thousand words and hexameters in addition should we call for to complete the system? Can we be so confident that there were a hundred other Homers, a thousand, walking the Aegean strands? In some distant day will they lament that of so many hundred Shakespeares who were undoubtedly our Will's coevals, the work of only one survived?

5. Page, *HHI,* pp. 301-303, athetizes Phoenix' speech in the Embassy scene in *Iliad* 9, since it implies a concept of moral responsibility that is alien to the *Iliad.* Any choice of words, of course, implies a concept of moral responsibility in a poet. We can understand why Page, with his views of the primitive Greek, would welcome Parry's formula theory so heartily, since it seems to eliminate choice from Europe's early poetry, whether moral or aesthetic.

6. A. B. Lord, *The Singer of Tales* (Cambridge, Mass. 1960), p. 66. Referred to as *ST*.

7. For Eumaios' behavior in this scene, and the pattern of his evasion in relation to other similar evasions in the *Odyssey,* see my article, "Name Magic in the *Odyssey,*" *CalifStudClassPhil* 5(1972):1-19.

8. Page, *HHI,* p. 234. Parry's assumption that the formulaic system must be the work of generations of oral poets led him to think of the frequently repeated epithets as part of the traditional bardic repertoire. This opened the way for D. H. F. Gray to use frequency of occurrence as the criterion for the age of epithets in her "Homeric Epithets for Things," *CQ* 41(1947):109-121. In her analysis of the words for *sea,* Miss Gray divides the often-repeated phrases and the unique or seldom-repeated phrases into "traditional" and "individual," at first simply for convenience (p. 109). But after tabulating the phrases she concludes (p. 110) "the overwhelming predominance of phrases derived from an epic tradition is obvious," though her tables have proved only a predominance of repeated over unique phrases. Page followed in her steps with extravagant results. That there exists a correlation between frequency and antiquity of epithet is a fallacy so striking that it is hard to credit a sober historian's acceptance of it. If Homer had invented but a dozen new formulas, one, or all, of them might have been a frequently repeated formula; one of them might have been as common as *Telemachos pepnumenos.* Should we suppose that the memory of the bard preserves, by frequent repetition, only those formulas created in remote antiquity, while promptly forgetting any that his own Muse might lead him to invent? What poetic theory is this? Page's concept of a traditional formula is not based on frequency alone, but on the presence in the formula of some object long forgotten, or of some obsolete grammatical construction. In this respect he again follows Miss Gray, who saw that her criterion for "traditional" would not apply equally well to the words for *shield.* Realizing the absurdity of applying his arguments for the Mycenean origin of Ajax to all Homeric nouns uniformly, Page retracts his argument (at p. 267, n. 19) and admits that the Mycenean formulas are few in number and that a substantial number of Homeric formulas are the creation of the Ionian poets. For a criticism of Page's argument for Mycenean formulas, see G. S. Kirk, "Objective Dating Criteria in Homer," *MH* 17(1960):189-205. Sterling Dow, in his review in *AJP* 83(1962):90-97, is dubious about much of Page's book, but concedes, somewhat hesitantly, that chapter 6 is "where the author is most at home. . . . At least in it he is more nearly safe from historians."

9. Parry, "Traditional Epithet," *Collected Papers,* p. 13.

10. T. G. Rosenmeyer, "The Formula in Early Greek Poetry," *Arion* 4(1965):295-311, divides Parry's followers into the "hard Parryites," who adhere to Parry's original definition of formula, and "soft Parryites," who

would extend the definition to include single words or simply rhythmic patterns. For examples of the hard Parryites, see J. B. Hainsworth, "Structure and Content in Epic Formulae." *CQ* 58(1964):155-164, and his *Flexibility of the Homeric Formula* (Oxford, 1968); A. Hoekstra, *Homeric Modifications of Formulaic Prototypes* (Amsterdam, 1965); W. W. Minton, "The Fallacy of the Structural Formula," *TAPA* 96(1965):241-253. For soft Parryites, see J. A. Notopoulos, "The Homeric Hymns as Oral Poetry," *AJP* 83(1962):355ff.; J. A. Russo, "A Closer Look at Homeric Formulas," *TAPA* 94(1963):235-247, and his "The Structural Formula in Homeric Verse," *YClS* 20(1966):219-240. C. M. Bowra, "The Comparative Study of Homer," *AJA* 54(1950):186, takes repeated lines and repeated themes as formulas, a view with which A. B. Lord disagrees in his "Composition by Theme in Homer and South-slavic Epos," *TAPA* 82(1951):71-80. Lord, *ST,* pp. 142ff., accepts Parry's definition, though he includes single words as formulas (e.g., *oulomenen,* at *Il.* 1.2), and lays as much stress on proximities that he calls "formulaic" as on identical verbal repetitions. M. Nagler, "Towards a Generative View of the Oral Formula," *TAPA* 98(1967):269-311, perceiving the impasse produced by the lack of consensus on basic definitions, argues for the formula as a mental template in the mind of the poet, of which each uttered phrase is but one allomorph. Nagler thus analyzes oral poetry with the techniques of structural linguistics; this may well be the necessary direction if Homer is oral, and his hexameters but a specialized form of the spoken word. For a discussion of the lines along which the study of the formula has proceeded since Milman Parry, see Adam Parry's introduction to his *Collected Papers,* pp. xliff. Adam Parry writes, p. xxxiii, note 1, that the definition of formula "is a question of nomenclature, and therefore of limited interest," but surely definitions are important when the formula has been made the essential feature of Homeric language and style.

11. Hoekstra, *Modifications,* pp. 10-11.

12. Miss Gray's study of the words for *sea,* "Homeric Epithets for Things," is one of the few along these lines. Her study, like Parry's, ignores context, and therefore her statistics on frequency of formula occurrence are misleading since many of the formulas for *sea* occur in repeated whole lines. Even a cursory glance through the concordance reveals the formulaic systems for common nouns is extremely deficient by comparison with the name-epithet systems. To plead lost hexameters here will not help us. The formulaic "families" that Nagler discusses in his "Generative View" remind us of the variety of formulaic systems in Homer, each working, it seems, according to its own logic.

13. Parry, "Traditional Epithet," *Collected Papers* p. 149.

14. Parry, "Traditional Epithet," p. 165. See his lengthy discussion of the problem in his "The Meaning of the Epithet in Epic Poetry," *Collected Papers,* pp. 118-172.

15. M. W. M. Pope, "The Parry-Lord Theory of Homeric Composition," *Acta Classica* 6(1963):1-21. See also Lord, *ST,* p. 53, who uses the formulaic thrift in individual Yugoslav singers as "an important argument for the unity of the Homeric poems." On p. 63 he shows how one singer's style will be recognizable from the many repetitions of a particular formula that occurs only rarely in another singer's repertoire.

16. In "Cor Huso," *Collected Papers,* pp. 444-445, which gives instructive hints as to the direction of Parry's thought at the time of his death, Parry confronts the problem directly. He concludes that either "the *Iliad* and the *Odyssey* in their entirety, perhaps with some small exception, as well as some of the Homeric *Hymns,* are all the work of a single singer" — an assumption quite at odds with his theory of oral composition which forbids the question of individual style — "or else . . . there existed for the Greek heroic songs a fixity of phrasing which is utterly unknown in the Southslavic." If we accept the latter alternative, Parry posits "a closed professional association" to account for the uniformity of the system, or else he supposes that "the rigour of the hexameter as a verse form might have imposed a highly rigorous conservatism of phraseology." It must seem to many thoughtful readers that Parry near the end of his life was approaching conclusions almost the very opposite of those he formulated in his first French thesis.

17. This is the assumption throughout Page, *HHI,* chap. 6. Page's Ionians neither know the meaning of many of their formulas, nor care, being content to sing of obsolete objects in obsolete syntax. For but one among many passages in Parry which helped to canonize this assumption, see his "Traditional Epithet," *Collected Papers,* p. 137, where the curious may also read that Parry characterizes our most unique Homer as "an author who has no individual style." Likewise in the same passage readers will find Parry's view of Homer's ancient audiences which, we are asked to believe, cared as little for the quality of an epithet as did their poet. "Homer's listeners demanded epithets and paid them no attention." The orthodox argument against the heretic fallacy of poetic invention in Homer Page puts succinctly at *HHI,* p. 233: "What he [sc. the Ionian poet] knows, and what he would describe if he could, is very different from what his formular vocabulary compels him to describe; and he has not yet attempted, or has failed in the attempt, to create new formulas to describe new objects." Page attempts no resolution between this belief and its apparent antithesis, expressed at p. 267, n. 19, that a good number of the formulas are of late origin. What new experiences were those late originators attempting to describe? Implicit in Parry's theory of Homeric poetics is the belief that Homeric imagination is diachronic, the net returns from centuries of hexameter creation, and that Homer is both the culmination of the tradition and its weakest member.

18. Marcel Jousse, *Le Style oral rythmique et mnémotechnique chez les verbo-moteurs. Archives de philosophie,* vol. 3, cah. 4 (Paris, 1925):1-240. Adam Parry, *Collected Papers,* p. xxiii, calls attention to the influence of Jousse on Milman Parry's thought. On p. 115ff. Jousee asserts that all the mnemonic techniques of rhythm and repetitions are purely functional in an oral society but later, with the advent of literacy, become valued as a source of aesthetic pleasure. The absence of aesthetics in utterances of an oral age, or of utility in *poésie* of our desperate age, is a fallacy so patent that one stands astounded at its influence in Homeric studies.

19. Jousee, *Le style oral,* pp. 127-128; see also p. 131.

20. Jousee, *Le style oral,* p. 115, writes in reference to a culture that becomes literate: "La sensation de plaisir que le rythme cause à l'organisme a peu à peu remplacé et même fait oublier, dans notre poésie écrite, l'utilisation primitivement mnemonique des Schèmes rythmiques du Style oral, de même que le caractère esthétique de nos *ornements* sacerdotaux nous voile les qualités pratiques des *habits* romains dont ils sont dérivés par lente et insensible évolution." That one sentence has been the bedrock of Homeric criticism in this country for an entire generation.

21. Lord, *ST,* p. 43, asserts that it is the singer's facility in creating new phrases "rather than his memory of relatively fixed formulas that marks him as a skillful singer in performance." See also his "Homer's Originality: Oral Dictated Texts," *TAPA* 84(1953):126-129.

22. Lord, "Homer's Originality," p. 129.

23. Lord, "Homer as Oral Poet," *HSCP* 72(1967):45-46, appeals for an approach to oral poetics that will recognize that "all the elements in traditional poetry have depth, and our task is to plumb their sometimes hidden recesses; for there will meaning be found." On the other hand, he warns us against the pathetic fallacy of imputing intentional beauty to Homeric epithets (see *ST,* p. 66).

24. Parry, "Winged Words," *Collected Papers,* pp. 414-418, criticizes Calhoun for arguing that Homer uses the formula "winged words" for its meaning rather than its metrical usefulness. The equation, oral composition equals improvisation, is deeply imbedded in Parry's studies as in most subsequent formulaic studies, as Hoekstra notes in *Modifications,* p. 18. It is the essential base for Parry's argument that epithets have only metrical value, for if we do not insist on improvisation we need insist no more on metrical convenience as the supreme arbiter of vocabulary in this kind of poetry. Hoekstra, *Modifications,* pp. 18-19, argues for some degree of memorization and recitations, as does Pope in "The Parry-Lord Theory." Parry himself, "Epic Technique," *Collected Papers,* p. 134, comes close to admitting memorization to account for repetitions of whole passages. Mark W. Edwards, "Some Features of Homeric Craftsmanship," *TAPA*

97(1966):115-179, argues against extemporaneous composition and for verbatim repetion. Edwards writes, p. 178: "This implies, of course, that our poems were not composed extempore; I imagine that no one would think they were, but sometimes a rather loose application of the term 'oral poet' can give that impression." The arguments, however, for utilitarian formulas are based on the premise of extemporaneous delivery. Fore-thought and conscious reworking of lines, these belong to literary *poésie*, but there is no room for them in the Oral Theory of Homeric Composition. J. A. Notopoulos, "Homer, Hesiod and the Achaean Heritage of Oral Poetry," *Hesperia* 29(1960):178, states the orthodox position: "The touchstone of the oral style is the formula, whose convenience in oral improvisation was first pointed out by Meillet and thoroughly illustrated by Parry."

25. Lord, *ST*, pp.58-59, compares two versions of a song sung by *Zogić*, the first in 1934 and the second in 1951. For one run of eight lines the later version is a verbatim repetition of the earlier version. We might suggest here that the singer had seventeen years to think on the formulas of those lines; that he retains them unchanged over the years suggests that they may satisfy the singer's personal aesthetics as much as his convenience. Douglas Young, "Never Blotted a Line?" *Arion* 6(1967):279-324, argues that illiteracy does not preclude a fixed, i.e., memorized text, and his example of the Scots poet, Duncan Macintyre, who composed poems in his head but did not deliver them extemporane-ously, may suggest a better analogy for Homer. Those interested in the words of a modern poet on the subject of poetic composition without pen and paper might consult p. 64 in Vladimir Nabokov's *Pale Fire* (New York, 1962). In "Cor Huso," *Collected Papers*, p. 460, Parry mentions, without further discussion, that several singers knew some songs only part way through, since they had never heard them to the end. These do not sound like singers ready to improvise at a moment's notice.

26. See Lord, *ST*, p. 100 and n. 3.

27. See Lord, *ST*, p. 124ff. Lord stresses the extraordinary difficulty of transcribing a text from dictation, but does little more than recognize the difficulty for the Homeric texts.

28. Parry paid no attention to transmission. Lord, "Homer's Origi-nality," believes that the Homeric Poems are oral poems dictated by the poet to a literate scribe. In recent years the problem of transmission has engaged more serious attention. C. M. Bowra, *Heroic Poetry* (London, 1952), pp. 240-241, believes Homer to be both an oral poet and a literate man, but with this catholicism Lord, in "Homer's Originality," strongly disagrees. G. S. Kirk, "Homer and Modern Oral Poetry," *CQ* 10(1960):270-281, would attenuate the miracle of transmission by inserting an interval of 100 years between the composition and the

transcription, though this is but to say that Homer was the last of those who memorized the original oral poem. Adam Parry, "Have We Homer's *Iliad?*" *YCIS* 20(1966):177-216, believes that the *Iliad* must be composed and written by Homer. He is, I believe, the only scholar to recognize the thoroughgoing romanticism in current theories of the transmission, which posit two geniuses, one the oral poet and the other the scribe — "a genius in his own way, but one who had no oral style to lose" (p. 183).

29. Lord, "Homer as Oral Poet," rightly objects to the spate of articles on the Parry-Lord theory based on suppositions without further statistical analysis of the Homeric texts.

30. Parry, "Traditional Epithet," *Collected Papers,* pp. 29ff.

31. W. Whallon, *Formula, Character and Context* (Washington, D.C., 1969), p. 69, wonders whether *polymetis* announces the eloquence of the speech that follows. In the name-epithet formulas that introduce speakers in Homer, only Odysseus and his family have epithets connoting intelligence. We could not argue, then, that the epithets for other characters call attention to some feature of the ensuing speech. Yet there is an aptness that when Achilleus speaks he is remembered less for his eloquence than for being a sprinter. Oscar Kretzschmar, *Beiträge zur Charakteristik des homerischen Odysseus* (Leipzig, 1903), discusses the character of Odysseus as revealed in his epithets. At pp. 6-13 he discusses the use of *polymetis* in the *Odyssey,* an epithet he considers to be almost always germane to its context.

32. Parry touches on the problem only briefly in "Traditional Epithet," *Collected Papers,* p. 144. He nowhere argues that formulaic thrift demands that all names metrically equivalent should have identical epithets, but when Ὀδυσσεύς, Ἀχιλλεύς, Ἀπόλλων, and Ἀθήνη, all metrically equivalent, do not share epithet systems, we conclude that before metrical convenience comes into play the context (here the name) first exercises its control in permitting certain epithets and barring others.

33. Penelope uses the epithet *thymoleonta* of her husband twice in Book 4 (vv. 724, 814), and then her lion-hearted husband emerges from his leafy lair on Phaiakian soil as a mountain lion proud in his strength (6.130). Thus once again does the poet demonstrate what C. H. Whitman observed of the lion images surrounding Achilleus in the *Iliad.* "In Homer's scheme," writes C. H. Whitman in *Homer and the Heroic Tradition* (Cambridge, Mass., 1958), p. 115, "instead of wearing themselves out, the formulae keep gaining symbolic weight, like rolling snowballs."

34. For parallels in other characters' speeches, see my article, "Name Magic."

35. Nagler, "A Generative View," p. 281, suggests, in view of the contradictory definitions of *formula,* that we avoid the word in favor of some term like a *family* of phrases. The kind of phrases Nagler analyzes on

p. 277 fit well into his "families," but they are very different from the usual name-epithet formula that seems not to belong to any family, being simply one of the most frequent devices for the poet to say "X spoke."

36. Imagine, good friend, a Homer who invents, to pleasure his fellow wayfarers on bitter winter nights, an epithet for his gods, as felicitous in its spondees as in its metaphysic: ῥεῖα ζώοντες, *Existing with Ease.* Whence comes our arrogance to challenge such eschatology in hexameters defined? Are we of the Muses' grace so anointed as to pretend to but one hexameter woven of such formulas? Should we suppose those *Existences Easy* could as well be manifest through our formula *God?* Let him who dares pluck a single epithet from that peerless fabric.

37. Martin Nilsson, *Primitive Time Reckoning* (Lund, 1920). See also the extraordinarily vivid names for the twelve moons of the year in native American languages in *Shaking the Pumpkin,* ed. Jerome Rothenberg (New York: Doubleday, 1972), pp. 297-300. These calendars will draw us closer to the orbit of Homeric language than any talk of metrical fillers and formulaic economies.

38. F. M. Combellack, "Some Formulary Illogicalities in Homer," *TAPA* 96(1965):41-56, treats us to an elegant review of some such nods, as when olives, quite appropriate within the conventional orchard "theme," find themselves less appropriately placed over Tantalos' head. Sometimes in Homer barking dogs are mute, loud-voiced heralds are quiet, swift steeds move slowly, but there are hardly sufficient examples to warrant belief in a somnambulist poet.

39. Whallon, *Formula,* ch. 2.

40. Whallon, *Formula,* pp. 49ff.

41. Hainsworth, *Flexibility,* passim.

42. Lord, "Homer as Oral Poet," pp. 34-46, argues that Anne Amory Parry's discussion of the Gates of Horns and of Ivory is an example of subjective criticism. His warning, p. 35, that in traditional oral poetry "associations are traditional and not *ad hoc* phenomena," is well taken, but his stricture does not invalidate Anne Parry's analysis on principle. Whatever the traditional associations of horn, in the *Odyssey* it is certifiably associated with Odysseus (his eyes and his bow). If, as Lord is willing to grant, the bow is associated with Odysseus in the tradition, then why not horn too, the substance from which the bow was made?

43. Page, *HHI,* p. 227. Page gleans his figures from Miss Gray's article, "Homeric Epithets for Things." It requires, I confess, almost an act of faith to harmonize Miss Gray's data with Parry's theory. What, for example, does *thalassa* have to tell us of oral composition, or of epithets ornamental versus particularized, when the word occurs 119 times in all but yet on only 18 occasions in all of Homer does it enter the hexameters in the company of an epithet? What *system* of formulas have we here?

Miss Gray's article has many such mysteries for the confirmed formulary theorist.

44. Page, *HHI*, p. 229.

45. Charles P. Segal, "Andromache's Anagnorisis: Formulaic Artistry in the *Iliad* 22.437-476," *HSCP* 75(1971):33-57, argues for a style in which "the freer melodies" of the nonformulaic are played off against the formulaic, but he too believes, p. 34, that the "*non-connotative, non-expressive* noun + epithet formula and similar kinds of formula are essential elements in Homer's style" (italics mine). Adam Parry, "The Language of Achilles," *TAPA* 87(1956):1-7, argues that Achilleus expresses his disillusionment in *Iliad* 9 in formulaic language, but through a misuse of that language. It is an interesting thesis which unfortunately Parry did not investigate as exhaustively as we should have liked. Seth Benardete, "Achilles and the *Iliad*," *Hermes* 91(1963):1-16, argues for the importance of certain epithets in the *Iliad*, *megathymoi*, for example, which Achilleus uses of the Greeks (1.122ff.), though otherwise only the Trojans are *megathymoi*. The posthumously published monograph by Anne Amory Parry, *Blameless Aegisthus* (Amsterdam, 1973) is an exhaustive attempt to prove that one single epithet, *amumon,* is no mere ornament in Homer.

46. Mark W. Edwards, "Some Stylistic Notes on *Iliad* XVIII," *AJP* 89(1968):274. Here Edwards' concern is with runover adjectives, which he has treated at greater length in his earlier paper, "Features of Homeric Craftsmanship," pp. 139-140. His view is that runover adjectives may convey intentional poetic effect but that *ambrosie* at *Iliad,* 18.268 is an example of a meaningless adjective. Here he disagrees with Parry, who had considered a runover epithet always particularized.

47. To treat *ambrosial* as anything less than a majestic concept in Homer, wherever it occurs, is to deprive ourselves. Jaan Puhvel, "Greek ANAΞ," *Zeitschr. f. vergleich. Sprachforschung,* n.s. 73(1956):210, discusses the etymology of *ambrosios* as "containing or dispensing vital force." The etymology would explain the epithet's connection with night, the character of which in the *Iliad* is precisely to renew the vital force.

48. Aristarchos initiated a long history of scholarly quibbles on the epithet in φαεινὴν ἀμφὶ σελήνην. He decided that since a full moon would obscure the stars, the moon in this simile must be the new moon, hence φαεινήν here must be generic (ornamental), not particularized. It should hardly be necessary to state that φαεινήν is not necessarily a measurement of candlepower. A full moon is bright, but so is a half moon and, some might say, so too is a new moon. To note that a full moon obscures some stars, as indeed it does, is the kind of irrelevancy that dogs Homeric criticism. Adam Parry, "The Language of Achilles," pp. 1-3, remarks that though the simile occurs when the Greek fortunes are at their lowest point

it presents a picture that "fills the heart with gladness." Parry concludes that the nature of the formulaic language does not permit the poet "to present the particular dramatic significance of the fires in question. Instead, he [sc. Homer] presents the constant qualities of all such fires." Wrong. Lessing's brief on the importance of perspective in Homer (Helen seen by the Trojan elders at the city wall) has been all but ignored in the study of Homeric poetics. The simile here is neither generic nor ornamental; it refers specifically and precisely to the events of that particular evening on the Trojan plain. The reason that it fills the heart with gladness is that it situates us within the Trojan camp, and gives us Trojan emotions. We now, as Trojans, rejoice to see city and plain lit up like a bright moon surrounded by stars. Milman Parry, "Traditional Epithet," *Collected Papers,* p. 121, also discusses this passage with others where Aristarchos discovered an ornamental epithet. Why anyone (to cite another example) should read ἐρατεινά as ornamental in Skamander's thunderous shout to Achilleus (*Il.* 21.218), "My lovely streams are plugged with corpses," is beyond comprehension, but such is our Alexandrian heritage. These are typical of the treasures that the search for the generic epithet has mined.

49. There has been dispute as to the relevance of the moon in the simile. But the emphasis in Hektor's speech at 8.497-540 is on the necessity for the Trojans to light up both city and plain as brilliantly as possible to prevent the Greeks' making a getaway during the night, or gaining an entrance unobserved into the city (see vv. 517-522 for the strategy within the city). The city must surely be included in the simile, as Hermann Fränkel, *Die homerische Gleichnisse* (Göttingen, 1921), p. 34, concluded, and if so the presence of the moon in the simile needs no special pleading.

50. See F. M. Combellack in "Milman Parry and Homeric Artistry."

51. For some discussion of the etymology of *pepnumenos* see R. B. Onians, *The Origins of European Thought* (Cambridge, 1951). Onians argues against translating the word as "nimble" or "vigorous" (as if derived from ποιπνύew), but prefers to derive it, with Ameis-Hentze, from πνέω and would connect the word with ideas of consciousness. Such a meaning certainly seems to fit the usage of the word in the *Odyssey,* especially when used of Teiresias who alone, of all the beings in the afterworld, retains his mind *pepnumenos.* Poulydamas, the Trojan seer, who is *pepnumenos* (at *Il.* 18.249), is also a person who sees "before and behind." *Pepnumenos* used thus of Teiresias and Poulydamas suggests a meaning something like "filled with the spirit."

52. Mark W. Edwards, "Features of Homeric Craftsmanship," p. 164, discusses briefly the usage of *pepnumenos* in Homer, especially in the *Odyssey.* He notes an interesting stylistic feature when he remarks that the

epithet is never used of any of the suitors "(many of whom have names metrically similar to that of Telemachus) except by the crafty lips of the young man himself (*Od.* 18.65)." While *pepnumenos,* in reference to Telemachos, has all the practical connotations of diplomacy, acute observation before and behind, and common sense, there is a particular significance in the use of the epithet connoting breath applied to the young man whose intelligence we observe newly born.

NOTES TO CHAPTER II

1. Bruno Snell's book, *Die Entdeckung des Geistes,* is translated by T. G. Rosenmeyer as *The Discovery of the Mind* (Oxford, 1953), but *Spirit* or *Soul* might perhaps better translate Snell's *Geist.* All citations are to the English translation, referred to as *Discovery.* Claude Lévi-Strauss, *La Pensée Sauvage,* translated as *The Savage Mind* (Chicago, 1966), chap. 1, gives a brief but good critique of the limitations in Snell's method of delineating intellectual sophistication. I am much in debt to such scholars as Ernst Cassirer, Susanne Langer, and Lévi-Strauss for their efforts to show that we can comprehend cultures, our own no less than alien ones, only through their symbolic structures, for which words are but a partial revelation.

2. Snell, *Discovery,* p. 4.

3. Snell's illustration of the difference between the primitive and modern minds is misleading. A Geometric figure and a child's drawing are not really comparable representations. The one is a sophisticated stylization from a sophisticated age, the other the product of an infant intelligence first seeing its world and first attempting to transpose that world on to the page with grossly clumsy tools, fingers and crayons. For more cogent persuasion we should prefer to see children's drawings from the eighth century *B.C.* compared with children's drawings from the twentieth century *A.D.,* or a sophisticated artist from antiquity set against his modern peer — say, Exekias and Picasso. That we can weigh Geometric art in the balance with a child's fumbling, and find Geometric art intellectually lighter, is a measure of our unbounded enthusiasm for modern man's intellectual attainments.

4. The question of abstract concepts in Homer, and of his awareness of human individuality, has continued to engage the attention of scholars, particularly in Germany. See Joachim Böhme, *Die Seele und das Ich im homerischen Epos* (Leipzig & Berlin, 1929); Walter Marg, *Der Charakter in der Sprache der frühgriechischen Dichtung,* 2nd ed. (Darmstadt, 1967); Hermann Fränkel's review of Marg in *AJP* 60(1939):475-479, and his *Dichtung und Philosophie des frühen Griechentums,* 2nd ed. (München, 1962), pp. 83ff.; Albin Lesky, "Göttliche und menschliche Motivation im homerischen Epos," *Sitzb. Akad. Heidelb. Phil.-hist. Kl.* (Heidelberg, 1961). Marg and Lesky would agree that there are no words to express a person's individuality, but would still claim that Homer's characters are drawn as individuals. H. Gundert continues the discussion in his review of Fränkel's book in *Gnomon* 27(1955):465-483. Hans Schwabl, "Zur Selbständigkeit des Menschen bei Homer," *Wiener Studien* 67(1954):46-64, concerns himself mainly with the relationship of gods and men in Homer, but criticizes Snell for his negative approach to Homeric psychology.

5. It is a common assumption that the "naive" narrative style of Homer gives us but a colorful series of events, where each moment is treated only for its own sake. We see the force of this assumption in, for example, Erich Auerbach's *Mimesis,* trans. W. Trask (Princeton, 1953), chap. 1, where he argues that the scar episode in *Odyssey* 19 is just such a narrative bead strung on the paratactic chain of the poem. The affinity between such views of Homer's paratactic style and Snell's view of Homeric concepts is clear to see. Parataxis is fundamental also to the oral theory of composition. See B. A. van Gronigen, "Eléments inorganiques dans la composition de l'Iliade et de l'Odyssée," *RevÊtHom* 5(1935):3-24; and J. A. Notopoulos, "Parataxis in Homer," *TAPA* 80(1969):1-23.

6. Hermann Fränkel, "Die Zeitauffassung in der frühgriechischen Literatur," *Wege und Formen frühgriechischen Denkens,* 2nd ed. (Munchen, 1960), pp. 1-22.

7. The whole *Odyssey* is a revelation in hexameters of the moral, physical, social, and cosmic dimensions of *hora.* In chaps. 3 and 4 I attempt to sketch the topographical and psychological outlines of *hora,* and in chap. 5 to relate those to the elements that determine the cosmic *hora.* Hora is the motivating impulse of the poem.

8. Fränkel, "Zeitauffassung," pp. 1-2. Fränkel's discussion of time in Homer is excellent, but his omission of the word *hora* from consideration leads him to emphasize unduly the role of *chronos.* When he concludes, p. 13, "Am frühesten Anfang den wir erreichen können, war die Zeit erstens immer nur Dauer (noch nicht Punkt)," it is exclusively *chronos* about which he speaks, not *hora.* Hora is, however, a more common word in the *Odyssey* than *chronos* (according to Dunbar's concordance), and is one of the significant keys of the poem.

9. One of the errors in the study of Homeric thought that has been long allowed to stand unchallenged is the confusion between poetry and analytic philosophy. Many post-Renaissance poems, analyzed as intellectual historians insist on analyzing Homer, would probably reveal their creators to be as "primitive" as Homer.

10. See, for one example, Emile Durkheim and Marcel Mauss, *Primitive Classification,* trans. R. Needham (Chicago, 1963).

11. G. E. R. Lloyd, *Polarity and Analogy: Two Types of Argumentation* (Cambridge, 1966), pp. 43ff. Lloyd concludes, p. 47, that we cannot talk "of any developed or systematic Table of Opposites in Homer or Hesiod." The opposites are, I believe, more systematic than Lloyd would allow, although the system can only be tentatively deduced.

12. Robert Hertz, "La prééminence de la main droite: etude sur la polarité religièuse," *Revue philosophique* 68(1909):553-580, translated in R. and C. Needham, *Death and the Right Hand* (Glencoe, Ill., 1960). Hertz, reflecting the orientation of the French sociological school, argues

that it is religious and social modes of thought that maintain such polarities as left and right. I would argue the reverse, that physiological asymmetries are the stuff of religious thought.

13. F. M. Cornford, *From Religion to Philosophy* (London, 1912), pp. 59ff., adopts the view that the principle of contrariety that early Greek thought finds in nature derives from social organization. J. Burnet, *Early Greek Philosophy*, 4th ed. (London, 1930), pp. 8-9, on one hand believes that the natural cycle of growth and decay gives rise to the doctrine of opposites, yet on the other hand states that the process of alternation in nature was "described in terms borrowed from human society; for in early days the regularity and constancy of human life was far more clearly realized than the uniformity of nature." The voice here is of a man for whom the concept of human institutions conjures up such durable edifices as the University, the Church, Monarchy, or Parliament. In a simple agrarian society the unpredictability of human existence would provide, surely, a striking contrast to the tireless cycle of sun and moon, the Pleiades, the tides, and Earth's annual rebirth. Homer's words on the frailty of humankind hardly tally with Burnet's "regularity and constancy of human life." Should we not rather argue that man's self-imposed polarities are his heroic attempt to align himself with the symmetries of the cosmos? The belief that polarities in social organization precede physiological polarities (as the left and the right) reflects also a modern prejudice against deriving metaphysics from biology. We prefer instead to insist that man's true nature is visible in his social mind which constructs schools, churches, and cities. Modern delinquents, who remain partial to biological metaphysics, take some pleasure in knowing that twentieth-century physics is beginning to believe that the biological asymmetry of left and right has its counterpart in low-grade interactions on our planet.

14. It is perhaps some support for Durkheim's polarity between the sacred and the profane that whereas Eos is personified as a goddess, her counterpart, *zophos*, is not personified at all. In general, both in Homer and in Hesiod, personification, so vividly applied to the Olympians, has made little progress with the chthonic deities. Ge, Hades, and most of the Titans are personifications more in name than in fact. But then humans too, once they become shadows and pass beneath the *zophos*, are more names than persons. Personification disintegrates within the *zophos*.

15. Strabo (1.2.28; 9.2.12) identified πρὸς ἠῶ τε ἠέλιόν τε as the south and ζόφος as north. There is one reference in Homer specifically to north and south, given in terms of the winds: the cave on the shore at Ithaka at *Ody*. 13.110-111 has one entrance facing Boreas, the other facing Notos. For the most complete discussion of the temporal and spatial fields represented by Homer's πρὸς ἠῶ τε ἠέλιόν τε and ζόφος, see Joseph Cuillandre, *La droite et la gauche dans les poèmes homériques* (Paris, 1944).

16. Cuillandre, *La droite et la gauche*, esp. pp. 195ff. Cuillandre's argument follows Strabo's identification. See his p. 203, n. 1 for the agreement of other modern scholars.

17. The Greek orientation is exactly paralleled by Latin and the Romance languages. The sun gives the three directions, as in the French *Levant, Couchant,* and *Midi,* and the north is variously described in Latin – *Septentrio, Aquilo, Boreas.* The variety of terms for north suggests the difficulty of definition for that zone unvisited by the sun. In English as late as the seventeenth century, according to the Oxford English Dictionary, *midday* was in use as a word for the south. That may support Cuillandre's view that for Homer the sun must define the south as it does the east and the west. For the equation, midday equals south, in Greek, see LSJ, s.v. μεσημερίος, II.

18. Apart from cultural prejudice, difficulties stem from our uncertainty as to the normal direction of orientation in Homer, and as to the extent of the horizon included in such terms as *eos* and *zophos.* The only passage in Homer that suggests an orientation is *Ody.* 13.241, ἠδ᾽ ὅσσοι μετόπισθε ποτὶ ζόφον ἠερόεντα, which Cuillandre, *La droite et la gauche,* pp. 215-220, uses as evidence for an eastern orientation. Linguistic evidence seems to corroborate the Odyssean passage. The Indo-European etymology for north as the left seems beyond dispute. See C. R. Buck, *Dictionary of Selected Synonyms in the Principal Indo-European Languages* (Chicago, 1949), pp. 870ff., on the words for our compass directions; also Jaan Puhvel's review of J. W. Poultney's *Bronze Tables of Iguvium,* in *Romance Philology* 15(1962), esp. p. 444 and n.3. See also the brief article by F. B. Jevons, "Indo-European Modes of Orientation," *CR* 10(1896):22-23. Linguistics inclines us to accept *Ody.* 13.241 as expressing a general, not a particular truth. The problem is compounded, however, when we introduce the idea of motion into directional terms. Jevons argues that a bird of good omen flies clockwise as he circumnavigates the Homeric Greek (πρὸς ἠῶ equals "sunwise" in the days when the sun was the clock). Cuillandre, *La droite et la gauche,* p. 215, agrees, arguing from Hektor's reference to the direction of birds of omen at *Il.* 12-238-240. Aristotle, *de Caelo* 2.2.285b, says that stars move ἐπὶ τὰ δεξιά, which sounds as if he means clockwise. A. F. Braunlich, " 'To the Right' in Homer and Attic Greek," *AJP* 57(1936):245-260, argues that Aristotle means counterclockwise. She cites other examples from Attic to substantiate this view. She claims that ἐπὶ δεξιά as counterclockwise movement originated in the social circle (where food and drink is passed to the right) and was later transferred to the movements in the sky. The passage at *Il.* 12.239-240 she takes for proof that ἐπὶ δεξιά meant counterclockwise for Homer, but the passage, despite its simplicity, resists dogmatic interpretation.

19. See W. B. Stanford's edition of the *Odyssey* at 10.2.

20. Vergil's description of Aeolus and his slave winds at *Aen.* 1.51-63 makes for an interesting comparison. However truly the passage, with its hobgoblin terrors of bridles, chains, and dungeons, represents the *Geist* of Vergil's imperious *Princeps*, it falls far short of the *Odyssey*'s acuity in observing the structure of ethereal phenomena. If we were to rank the two poets, on the basis of such passages, according to their proximity to the modern scientific point of view in their understanding of the winds, there could be no doubt as to who would place first.

21. On this point see Wesley D. Smith, "Physiology in Homer," *TAPA* 97(1966):547-556.

22. Böhme, *Die Seele*, argues against the theory that the words for mental activity must originally have referred to purely physical organs. See particularly his discussion of νοεῖν, pp. 24-27, where he distinguished ἰδεῖν as the term for the outer experience, i.e., perception through the eyes, and νοεῖν as the term for inner experience. The two expressions could not, he believes, have been synonymous. Alfons Nehring, "Homer's Description of Syncopes," *CP* 42(1947):106-121, believes that *thymos* is never anything but bodily energy. Even where scholars avoid terminology suggesting physical organs, however, their discussions are still oriented along the axis of modern concepts of physiology.

23. At *Ody.* 4.369 the stomach is the organ affected by hunger, but in many passages the *thymos* first commands, or chooses, to eat and is subsequently satisfied by the food. See *Il.* 1.468; 4.263; *Ody.* 7.228, passim. At *Il.* 9.705 the satisfaction of food and drink resides in the *etor.* For examples of putting the word into the *thymos*, see *Il.* 15.566; 23.313; *Ody.* 1.361 (= 21.355); 12.217; 12.266 (where the meaning is to recall a previously spoken word rather than to hear it when first uttered). For the synthesizing process of the *thymos*, see *Ody.* 15.27 and 318 (where the *thymos* is omitted). For the relation of *thymos* and sight see *Ody.* 5.76 (= 7.134); 15.132; 24.90. Compare the connection of the *noos* with eyes, ears, and feet in Theoklymenos' words at *Ody.* 20.365-6, where again a mental organ seems to function as both the recipient of sensory data and as their integrator. See Böhme, *Die Seele*, pp. 30ff., for fuller documentation and a discussion of the *thymos* as the mental adjunct to physiological processes; see his pp. 70-71 for the variety of actions of which the *thymos* is capable. P. Th. Justesen, *Les principes psychologiques d'Homère* (Copenhagen, 1928), is one scholar who has perceived that the *thymos* is fully rendered as a person in Homer. He writes, p. 27, that the *thymos* "est aussi le Moi de l'homme, ou, plus exactement dit, l'un des ses Moi." Though Homer nowhere expressly describes the *thymos* as a homunculus, we are reminded of what James Frazer has to say on "The Soul as Mannikin" in *The Golden Bough* (New York, 1935), 3:26-30.

24. I cannot pretend to judge Homer's medical knowledge, but Charles Daremberg, *La mèdecine dans Homère* (Paris, 1865) concluded that Homer's knowledge rivalled that evidenced in the Hippocratic corpus.

25. That *thymos* and *noos* represent our basic dichotomy between emotion and intellect, as Snell argues, is almost universally accepted among modern scholars. D. J. Furley, "The Early History of the Concept of Soul," *Bull. Univ. London Instit. Class. Studies* 3(1956):1-18, recognizes that the terms for mental operations are assimilated to each other. He would define *noos* as the recipient of mental images, but prolonged thought, he argues, takes place in the *thymos* or *phren*. Kurt von Fritz, "Nóoς and Noeῦν in the Homeric Poems," *CP* 38(1943):79-93, argues against Böhme's view that the *noos* is "rein intellektuell." Von Fritz shows that emotion, often of a violent sort, is more frequently associated with the *noos* than Böhme would admit. In this impasse comparison with external communities, both human and divine, may prevent our demanding polar extremes. If Odysseus and Achilleus are both good speakers and good warriors, should we insist that *thymos* and *noos* cannot perform each other's functions? Should we suppose a rigidity within the physiological community quite at variance with the versatility in social communities?

26. Böhme, *Die Seele,* pp. 89ff., expressly disagrees with the view that the various terms for the mind imply the concept of a unified individual. The terms, for him, merely express varying experiences: "Der homerische Mensche kennt also nicht 'die' Lebenseele, sondern eine Vielheit von Lebenseelen oder funktionellen Seelen, die den verschiedenen Erscheinungsformen des seelischer Lebens entsprechen" (p. 91). Fränkel, *Dichtung,* p. 84, believes that amid the diversity of experiences Homeric man "fühlte sich nicht als eine gespaltene Zweiheit, sondern als ein einheitliches Selbst." See also Victor Larock, "Les premières conceptions psychologiques des Grecs," *Revue Belge de Philologie et d'Histoire* 9(1930):377-406, for much the same conclusion.

27. Fränkel, *Dichtung,* p. 85, has a good analysis of this passage as illustrating Homer's concept of a functioning organism. He aptly terms the Homeric man "ein Kraftfeld . . . dessen Linien in Raum und Zeit hinausziehn ohne Grenze und Schranke" (p. 88).

28. Wesley Smith, "Physiology," pp. 553ff., discusses such description as illustrative of the Homeric way of seeing the human organism as integrated in health and disintegrating with death, old age, sickness, inebriation, or shock. My discussions with Professor Smith on Homeric physiology and psychology have been most beneficial for me, and I take this appropriate moment to express my appreciation for his insights.

29. E. L. Harrison, "Notes on Homeric Psychology," *Phoenix* 14(1960):64, argues that *soma* means simply the body: "the presence or absence of life is irrelevant to the word's meaning." Compare H. Herter in

Charites für E. Langlotz (Berlin, 1957), pp. 206-217. If Harrison is correct, it is still almost exclusively the lifeless body that Homer sees as *soma,* i.e., the human physique bereft of all that gives it definition as a living being. Fränkel, *Dichtung,* p. 84, talks of the living human as a whole which becomes separated into parts (*soma* and *psyche*) only after death.

30. According to the Dunbar and Prendergast concordances: σκιερόν x1 (*Ody.*), σκιερῷ x1 (*Il.*); σκιόντα x11 (*Ody.*), x4 (*Il.*); σκιῇ x1, σκιαί x1 (*Ody.* 11.207; 10.495). For the verb: σκιόωντο x7 (*Ody.*), σκιάσῃ x1 (*il.*).

31. H. Fränkel, *Die homerischen Gleichnisse* (Göttingen, 1921). Michael Coffey, "The Homeric Simile," *AJP* 78(1957):113-132, continues the analysis of similes along Fränkel's lines.

32. Fränkel, *Gleichnisse,* understood that the similes are Homer's method for expressing complex and invisible relations through visual images. See also Kurt Riezler, "Das homerische Gleichnis und der Anfang der griechischen Philosophie," *Antike* 12(1936):253-271; and G. E. R. Lloyd, *Polarity,* pp. 187-192, who discusses the way in which similes make manifest psychological states or physiological processes. Snell, *Discovery,* pp. 200-204, also discusses the similes as an intellectual mode of thought.

33. Günther Jachmann, *Der homerische Schiffskatalog und die Ilias* (Köln & Opladen, 1958), pp. 267-338. My quote is from p. 269. Jachmann's case for a single, simple *Vergleichspunkt* in the triple simile at *Il.* 18.392-401, where sound is translated into movement, will persuade only those already convinced of Homer's monocular vision. D. J. N. Lee, *The Similes of the Iliad Compared* (Sydney, 1964), follows Jachmann's approach with approval. See also G. P. Shipp, *Studies in the Language of Homer* (Cambridge, 1953) and C. M. Bowra, *Tradition and design in the Iliad* (Oxford, 1930), p. 117, who inclines to the same view but without Jachmann's rigidity.

34. Claude Lévi-Strauss, *Structural Anthropology,* trans. C. Jacobson and B. G. Schoepf (New York, 1963), pp. 181ff. The whole of his chapter 10, "The Effectiveness of Symbols," is a good refutation of Jachmann's thesis that symbolic thought is alien to the "primitive" mind.

35. Lloyd, *Polarity,* p. 181, gives a good discussion of the use of homeopathic magic in the prayers offered at *Il.* 3.298ff., where the pouring of wine is a symbolic enactment of the fate the Greeks wish on their enemies. Odysseus' solicitation of the double omens, however, is a far more elaborate example of homeopathic magic since his mimesis of the desired result extends to detailed correspondence.

36. Felix Jacoby, "Die Geistige Physiognomie der Odyssee," *Antike* 9(1933):159-194, while mostly a very general discussion, has some remarks at pp. 175-178 on Penelope's description of the gates of dreams as indicating a movement towards Ionian scientific research.

37. *Il.* 19.77, which describes Agamemnon as seated during his speech of reconciliation, was athetized in antiquity, doubtless because it seemed to contradict Agamemnon's reference to a standing speaker in v. 79. I, for one, would be sorry to lose the line since it harmonizes so well with the self-pitying and paranoid character of Agamemnon as shown through the poem, and particularly here in his speech of flagrant self-exculpation. For a criticism of the passage see Page, *HHI*, pp. 313-314. Page's interpretation of Agamemnon's ἑσταότος in v. 79, as "*when a man is standing up as I am*," insists on a referent which the Greek may perhaps imply, but nevertheless omits.

38. Claude Lévi-Strauss, quoted in *The Guardian*, January 7, 1974.

NOTES TO CHAPTER IV

1. The Analytic approach has been to write off all, or a large part, of the Telemachy as a later, unwarranted, and awkwardly attached preface to the original *Odyssey*. For the views of Kirchhoff and subsequent scholars who have followed his approach, see Denys Page, *The Homeric Odyssey* (Oxford, 1955), pp. 73ff. (referred to as *HO*). More sympathetic approaches are in Friedrich Klingner, "Über die vier ersten Bücher der Odyssee," *Akad. d. Wissensch. z. Leipzig, Phil.-hist. Kl.* 96(1944):1-55; and in Uvo Hölscher, *Untersuchungen zur Form der Odyssee, Hermes* Einzelschriften 6 (Berlin, 1939). English scholarship of this century has generally voted to accept the Telemachy within the poem's orbit. See W. J. Woodhouse, *The Composition of the Homeric Odyssey* (Oxford, 1930), pp. 208-214; Howard Clarke, *The Art of the Odyssey* (Prentice-Hall, 1967), pp. 30-44; and the briefer study by G. M. Calhoun, "Télémaque et le plan de l' Odyssée," *RÉG* 47(1934):153-163. Édouard Delebecque is another warrior on Telemachos' behalf, in his *Télémaque et la structure de l' Odyssée* (Aix-en-Provence, 1958). There are good observations in G. P. Rose, "The Quest of Telemachus," *TAPA* 98(1967):391-398.

Much of the Analytic criticism is, at bottom, a desire to get on with the subplot of Odysseus' vengeance and an impatience with the slowly unfolding main plot, which is the awakening, after twenty years of numbed isolation, of a husband, a wife, and a child. The Telemachy has much to say about the awakening of all three figures, though its primary emphasis is on Odysseus and Telemachos. The myths of Odysseus, as they are pieced together in the Telemachy, are the forms of incantation that will resurrect both voyagers, father and son. So misunderstood is the basic function of the Telemachy that even some of the correspondences between it and the rest of the poem are deposited as evidence of the Telemachy's inauthenticity, as if the whole poem were not one vast and joyful paean to correspondence. G. S. Kirk, *The Songs of Homer* (Cambridge, 1962), pp. 228ff. (referred to as *SH*), shuns the *Bearbeiter* theory of composition but accepts many of the structural anomalies alleged against the poem by Analysts. Kirk ascribes the Telemachy to the poet Homer, but finds little to satisfy him in it (p. 359): "Certainly Telemachus learns little of his father, and apart from the *subsidiary* [my italics] theme of his education and development the so-called Telemachy contributes little to the main plot of the poem." Ah, there it is again, that spurious main plot of the poem.

2. It disturbs some critics that Helen could recognize Telemachos when he was but a baby at the beginning of the war. J. A. Scott, "Helen's Recognition of Telemachus in the Odyssey," *CJ* 25(1930):383-385,

defends the passage, noting that her recognition of Telemachus is true to the Odyssean portrait of her as a clever and perceptive woman, able to discover identity beneath disguises.

3. Klaus Rüter, *Odysseeinterpretationen, Hypomnemata* Heft 19 (Göttingen, 1969), pp. 141ff., has intelligent comments on the psychological parallels between the journies of Telemachos and Odysseus. He is particularly good on the awakening of consciousness in both father and son. For similarities between Telemachos' stay in Sparta and his father's in Scheria, see also Alfred Heubeck, *Der Odyssee-Dichter und die Ilias* (Erlangen, 1954), p. 56.

4. *Ody.* 3.373ff.

5. *Ody.* 3.122-123.

6. *Ody.* 4.71-75.

7. The drug *nepenthes* and Helen's ability to transform grief through storytelling is a perfect example of the coordination of microcosm and macrocosm that runs throughout Homer. See Otto Brinkman, "Telemach in Sparta," *Gymnasium* 59(1952):112, for a good discussion of the integration of inner psychology at this point with the external and mythical.

8. Ulrich von Wilamowitz, *Die Heimkehr des Odysseus* (Berlin, 1927), pp. 106, 118, argues that Telemachos evidences no sign of change from the beginning to the end of his journey. "Für sein Wesen ist die Reise erfolglos geblieben" (p. 118). Such a misreading of Telemachos' behavior in Sparta, or in Ithaka after his return from abroad, we must attribute to an age in which education is measured in diplomas, baccalaureates, and doctorates of philosophy. For a defense of Telemachos' maturation see J. A. Scott, "The Journey made by Telemachus and Its Influence on the Action of the *Odyssey, CJ* 13(1917):420-428; C. M. H. Millar and J. W. S. Carmichael, "The Growth of Telemachus," *Greece & Rome,* n.s. 1(1954):58-64; Howard C. Clarke, "Telemachus and the Telemacheia," *AJP* 84(1963):129-145; and W. J. Woodhouse *Composition,* pp. 212ff.

9. Theoklymenos has vexed critics inordinately. Page, among the most articulate of the saga hunters, argues in *HO,* pp. 83-88, for an earlier version of the saga in which Theoklymenos may have been Odysseus himself in disguise. Page admits that his speculation leaves problems unsolved and indeed we must agree, for his suggestion would offer not the least particle of help towards interpreting the dynamics of the interchange between Telemachos and Theoklymenos on the shore of Ithaka in Book 15. Kirk, *SH,* pp. 240-242, writes off Theoklymenos simply as a mistake, concluding, after some attempt to unravel the situation on the shore of Ithaka, that "Theoklymenos cannot have been conceived by the main poet especially for his part in the monumental Odyssey." As for Telemachos' behavior towards Theoklymenos in Book 15, C. H. Whitman,

Homer and the Heroic Tradition (Cambridge, Mass., 1958), p. 341, n. 13, argues that Telemachos performs a kind of divination by eliciting from the gods the opposite of what he hopes to be true. Whitman's interpretation makes good sense of the passage, and finds eminently satisfactory corroboration in the tone of Telemachos' speech. No sympathetic reader of the poem could so miss the sarcasm in Telemachos' speech as to suppose that Telemachos seriously believed what he was saying about Eurymachos. I have discussed the passage further in my "Telemachos Polymechanos," *Calif. Stud. in Classical Antiquity* 2(1969):58-59.

10. Uvo Hölscher, "Das Schweigen der Arete," *Hermes* 88(1960):257-265, takes issue with Schadewaldt's interpretation of Arete's silence, and of her role in the Phaiakian episode. Hölscher argues for the appropriateness of her behavior. Wilhelm Mattes, *Odysseus bei den Phäaken* (Wurzburg, 1958), pp. 123-142, also discusses the problems of Arete's question, Odysseus' answer, and his silence. His is the best defense of the structural and psychological veracity of the scene.

11. Scholars have commented on the importance of the Phaiakians as intermediaries on Odysseus' journey towards the recovery of his humanity. See in particular Charles P. Segal, "The Phaeacians and the Symbolism of Odysseus' Return," *Arion* 1(1962):17-64, for his analysis of Odysseus' role in that ordered and civilized community on Scheria. What Segal and others gloss over is that in the *Odyssey* a large, perhaps the largest, component of humanity is style. We knew from Antenor's vignette in *Iliad* 3.216-224, that Odysseus had style beyond most other men. Here among the Phaiakians we see him relearning and rehearsing the vocabulary of that style in order to court a lady in Ithaka.

12. Hölscher is one scholar to note the texture of Odysseus' humanity. In his "Schweigen," pp. 264-265, he remarks that in Odysseus' last adventure, among the Phaiakians, Odysseus must learn to forego guile and deceit in favor "der Charis des Mannes, der 'das Rechte weiss.' "

13. Woodhouse, *Composition,* pp. 54-65, analyzes the folktale motives visible in the story of Odysseus and Nausikaa. He grants that "many of the old elements actually gain in aesthetic significance" in Homer's adaptation of the anonymous folktale to the story of Odysseus (p. 65). His analysis is perceptive, but since he restricts his vision solely to the Nausikaa episode, he does not consider whether certain elements in that episode may be generated not by an anonymous folktale, but by the story of the marriage of Odysseus and Penelope which occurs later in the poem. For arguments on the aesthetic infelicities of the Nausikaa episode see Gerald Vallillee, "The Nausikaa Episode," *Phoenix* 9(1955):175-179.

14. David E. Belmont, "Telemachos and Nausikaa: A Study of Youth," *CJ* 63(1967):1-9, is good on similarities in the two characters, but he does not venture much beyond noting these similarities.

W. Schadewaldt, "Kleiderdinge: Zur Analyse der Odyssee," *Hermes* 87(1959):13-26, comes closer than most scholars to understanding Nausikaa's role in the poem when he talks of her as created for the purpose of being "die 'Vorbereitung' jenes von Arete wiedererkannten Kleides." I would argue that her *Vorbereitung* role is of larger extension, but agree with Schadewaldt that the figure and role of Nausikaa are generated by the poem itself, not by the saga. Richmond Lattimore, "Nausikaa's Suitors," *Classical Studies Presented to B. E. Perry* (Urbana, Chicago, London, 1969) pp. 88-102, also argues against the view that marriage between Odysseus and Nausikaa was ever intended or contained in any version of the Odysseus tale.

15. Kirk, *SH* p. 360, finds Odysseus' story told to elicit a cloak from Eumaios "one of the poorest digressions in the whole poem." In general, Kirk finds the conversations between Odysseus and Eumaios, Odysseus and Penelope, to be improbable, tedious, and preoccupied with trivialities. Again the prejudice is for getting on with the "story" and against those trivial details by which the man Odysseus and the woman Penelope are shown coming into their existence.

16. It is at points like this that commentators' pursuit of the false plot stands revealed most fully. Penelope's smile is one of the most significant actions in the plot of the *Odyssey,* but of its significance not a word finds its way into learned discourse on the poem.

17. Compare Nausikaa at 6.187, after hearing Odysseus' first speech to her: οὔτε κακῷ οὔτ ἄφρονι φωτὶ ἔοικας.

18. Analysts, to whom the concept of mind in Homer is anathema, have argued that this lovely and miraculous scene at 18.160ff. shows the *Bearbeiter*s at their worst. Page, *HO,* pp. 125-126, judges the scene, which depicts with extraordinary finesse the progress of an idea through the human mind, to be "not organically connected with our *Odyssey.*" Page finds it illogical that Penelope should expect to increase her honor in her husband's eyes by appearing before the suitors. See Kirk, *SH,* p. 246, for much the same criticisms of the scene. Any reader who follows with care in Penelope's steps from 17.414ff., when Antimind hurls the stool at the stranger, must come away with the highest admiration for Homer's organic concept of human thought and deed.

19. Page, *HO,* p. 125, is vexed that Odysseus could rejoice to see his wife enticing gifts from her suitors, "unless the two have already met and concocted the deception between them." All vexation should vanish forthwith when we recall that Odysseus has just heard Penelope castigate their son, sharply and at length, for tolerating the suitors' abuse of the stranger. Homeric scholars seem bent on proving Odysseus, his wife, and his son, to be extraordinarily dull-witted persons.

20. E. Bethe, "Odyssee-Probleme," *Hermes* 63(1928):81-92, would excise 19.133-156 since Penelope has no reason to entrust personal information to the stranger until he has proved himself in the test of his clothes at v. 215. On the contrary, Penelope has received several tokens of the stranger's worth before her interview with him begins. Already at 18.158-225 we see Penelope's mind obsessed by the figure of the stranger who is being mistreated in her halls.

21. At 4.716ff., Penelope, distraught at the news of her son's departure from Ithaka, retires from the public glare of the *megaron* to indulge her grief privately in her own chamber. That she weeps openly before the stranger in Book 19 is an indication of the degree to which she separates him from her suitors. As Odysseus emerges from hiding, so too does Penelope, both emerging concurrently.

22. Here again the Analysts detect the conflation of two conflicting stories. See Wilamowitz, *Homerische Untersuchungen* (Berlin, 1884), pp. 50ff. (referred to as *HU*); his *Heimkehr*, pp. 44ff.; Page, *HO*, pp. 126ff.; and Woodhouse, *Composition*, pp. 73ff. Odysseus can have no motive, writes Page, for calling for an old woman to wash his feet who will be the very person to recognize his scar. If we ascribe Odysseus' behavior here to rhapsodic botchery, then we must also ascribe Penelope's ecstatic effusion on his intelligence at 19.350-51 to the same hexameter factory. But there is no fault in either her intelligence or her husband's. Decorum would dictate that Odysseus should refuse to expose himself to the slave girls who have mocked him to his face. It is as decorous as natural that he should prefer someone whose *homophrosyne* would ensure her discretion, not about the scar, but about the presence of a man in the queen's palace late at night. Only after he has seen to that delicate matter does Odysseus remember that the person who has that degree of *homophrosyne* must necessarily recognize him also.

23. W. Büchner, "Die Niptra in der Odyssee," *RhM* 80(1931):129-136, gives us a good essay on the footwashing scene. At pp 133-134 he comments on Penelope's phrase "dear guest" (19.350) and recognizes Penelope's appreciation of her guest's tact.

24. Paolo Vivante, *The Homeric Imagination* (Bloomington, 1970), pp. 172-76, has excellent observations on the process by which the Cretan stranger becomes progressively transparent to the eyes of others: "Odysseus, on his part, stands transfigured by the impact of attentive looks."

25. For Analysts the footwashing scene, more than any other single scene, is the Great Divide between the two plots they allege have been rudely jostled together in our *Odyssey*. Until that scene we have version A, the original plot, in which Penelope recognizes Odysseus; but then the hexameter factory, so the theory runs, excised Penelope's recognition from that plot and attached to Eurykleia's washing scene another plot,

version B, in which Penelope does not recognize Odysseus until after the death of the suitors. R. Merkelbach, *Untersuchungen zur Odyssee* (München, 1951), p. 6, finds the second half of Book 19 after the scar scene, "so sprunghaft und unklar, dass man diese Fortsetzung nicht dem Dichter der Niptra zutrauen kann." Most Analytic criticism of Book 19, and of Penelope's role in the poem, hinges on the alleged slovenly pasting together of two contrary versions of Penelope's recognition. See Wilamowitz, *HU,* pp. 49-66; Page, *HO,* p. 126; and Kirk, *SH,* pp. 246-47. Fortunately there are treatments of Book 19 that are more sympathetic. See, for example, W. Büchner, "Die Penelopeszenen in der Odysee," *Hermes* 75(1940):129-167; P. W. Harsh, "Penelope and Odysseus in *Odyssey* XIX," *AJP* 71(1950):1-21; Helmut Vester, "Das 19. Buch der Odyssee," *Gymnasium* 75(1968):417-434; and, perhaps the most perceptive of all, Anne Amory, "The Reunion of Odysseus and Penelope," *Essays on the Odyssey,* ed. C. H. Taylor, Jr. (Bloomington, 1963), pp. 100-121. Beate Stockem, "Die Gestalt der Penelope in der Odyssee" (Diss. Köln, 1955), despite the promising title, is a regression to the old-time religion of *Bearbeiters.*

26. One scholar to recognize the epiphany is Paolo Vivante, in his *The Homeric Imagination,* p. 175.

27. Kirk, *SH,* p. 247, finds Penelope's insistence that the stranger should take his turn with the bow at 21.312ff. "poorly motivated . . . if she really thought him a humble stranger." If she ever thought thus of the stranger, certainly she has ceased to do so at 19.253. Her conversation with him after the footwashing scene is not such as a queen would hold with one of her serfs. The man for whom she demands the right of participation in the contest is far from *Outis* in her eyes.

28. One of the most egregious faults in Book 19, as alleged by the Analysts, is Penelope's decision to hold the Contest of the Bow. Merkelbach, *Untersuchungen,* p. 5; Kirk, *SH,* pp. 246-247; Page, *HO,* pp. 123-124; and Woodhouse, *Composition,* pp. 80-91; all are severely critical of Penelope for what they variously term her "collapse," or her "surrender," just at the moment when the stranger's information gives her reason to hold herself in patience. "The fault in the construction is very great and very obvious" declares Page, *HO,* p. 124. On the contrary, there is no fault either in the construction of the scene or in Penelope's behavior. Penelope announces to the stranger that she will hold the contest on the very day he had already vowed that her husband would return. Far from being evidence of psychic collapse, her act is the declaration of her belief in the stranger's solemn vow. Analytic misunderstandings have been well, if not exhaustively, answered in Anne Amory's "Reunion." She understands that Penelope's mention of the contest and the contest itself are forms of divination by which Penelope tests her intuitions. I would add

that Penelope uses the contest not only to test the stranger's prophecy of light appearing at the dark of the moon, but also to guarantee it, to bind fate by her own spell. Otto Seel, "Variante und Konvergenz in der Odyssee," *Studi in Onore di U. E. Paoli* (Firenze, 1956), pp. 643-657, gives a brief but excellent defense of Penelope's contest. He is one of the few scholars to recognize that coincidence is one of the main devices for structuring the plot of the *Odyssey.*

29. The strongest exposition of the thesis that Penelope recognizes Odysseus but merely affects ignorance is in Harsh, "Penelope and Odysseus." His arguments have been rejected out of hand by Analysts and generally have been as little pleasing to Unitarians. The fullest attempt to counter his position is in Anne Amory's "Reunion." For further discussion of Penelope's recognition see also Vester, "Das 19. Buch."

30. Odysseus' speech at 23.166-172 and Penelope's reply at vv. 174-180 are virtually the obverse and reverse of the same coin. At times the structure of their sentences runs parallel; at other times one is the reverse image of the other. Where Odysseus uses superlatives Penelope uses negatives, and she uses superlatives when he turns to negatives. There is rhetorical *homophrosyne* to an extraordinary degree in the few verses of these two speeches that precipitate the final recognition of husband and wife.

What does *daemonic* mean here? Let Diotima, Socrates' daemonic teacher, offer her gloss on the passage. The daemon is the hermeneutic bridge between men and gods; through the daemonic proceeds all divination, rituals, and incantations. Only through the meditation of the daemonic is dialectic possible between gods and men, between mortality and immortality. The man wise in such dialectic is daemonic; the man wise in any other kind of craft, whether of head or hand, may be a craftsman, but will never be daemonic. So Diotima explains the word to Socrates on his quest for Eros (Plato *Symp.* 202e-203a). Such a definition applies precisely to the family of the *Odyssey,* which enjoys hereditary connections with Hermes Psychopompos, which learns through pain the craft of synchronizing, through observation and practice of daemonic signs, their mortal rhythms with the rhythms of the gods. Odysseus and Penelope at the end of their quest for Eros recognize in each other the reflection of their own mantic skills, both makers of signs and fulfillments of signs, wise in the art of making bridges and therapeutic incantations. Discovering in the other the hermeneutic guide to their immortality, they exclaim, as their lives synchronize at last, "daemonic Odysseus," "daemonic Penelope."

NOTES TO CHAPTER V

1. For the importance of the Pleiades in the measurement and regulation of the year among agricultural peoples, see M. P. Nilsson, *Primitive Time Reckoning* (Lund, 1920), pp. 274-276, and *RE,* s.v. "Pleiaden," Bd. XXI.2.2486-2523. See also Athen. XI.489ff. for his discussion of the importance generally of the Pleiades, and specifically for their place in Hesiod and Homer. For the time of Odysseus' sea journey from Ogygia see, for example, the edition of Ameis-Hentze-Cauer at *Ody.* 5.272ff. The prevailing modern school of thought finds Homeric astronomy, like other Homeric *Realien,* naive and primitive. So argues Agnes M. Clerke, *Familiar Studies in Homer* (London, 1892), pp. 30-57. She believes that Odysseus' star guide in *Odyssey* 5, besides being proof of primitivism, is borrowed almost thoughtlessly from the constellation passage on the shield of Achilleus in the *Iliad.* Her view is echoed more recently in Grace H. Macurdy, "Rainbow, Sky, and Stars in the *Iliad* and the *Odyssey:* A Chorizontic Argument," *CQ* 8(1914):212-215, who goes further to argue for a signal lack of sensibility to the phenomena of the heavens in the *Odyssey.* It should not be necessary to linger over such views, when a scholar like Wilamowitz has demonstrated finer sensibilities, were it not that on such contempt for context cunning theories of multiple authorship have been erected.

2. See *RE,* s.v. "Fixsterne," for risings and settings in 432 B.C. There would be some adjustment in dating to conform to the time of the *Odyssey*'s composition, but the minor adjustment need not concern us here.

3. This epigram is in Gow's two-volume edition of Theocritus (Cambridge, 1965).

4. In confirmation of the time of Odysseus' voyage, the scholiast at *Odyssey* 5.171 says that Odysseus hesitates to accept Kalypso's offer of a passage home because he fears the dangers of the season. The same autumnal storm lashes earth in the simile at *Iliad* 16.384ff. On the connection between the autumnal storm in the *Odyssey* and that in Hesiod, see Cuillandre, *La droite et la gauche,* p. 176.

5. See J. van Leeuwen's edition at *Odyssey* 5.467ff. for a fuller citation of references to wintry weather conditions in the *Odyssey.* That the *Odyssey* unravels in winters was well known and understood by scholars of an earlier generation — of such varying temperaments as Gilbert Murray and Wilamowitz, for example — and receives due recognition in older editions (Ameis-Hentze-Cauer, van Leeuwen). Both the fact and its significance have generally been ignored in more modern interpretations of the poem.

6. See Stanford's note at 14.161 for some discussion of the possible interpretations. Manu Leumann, *Homerische Wörter* (Basel, 1950), p. 212, is probably the best source for the etymology and meaning of *lykabas*. Understanding correctly that a vague temporal notation would be inappropriate at 19.306, he interprets *lykabas* as meaning the day of the new moon, the *Noumenia*. C. J. Ruijgh, on the other hand, is opposed to such precision. In *L' Elémént Achéen dans la langue epique* (Assen, 1957), p. 147, he argues that Odysseus is trying to keep Penelope in suspense, hence *lykabas* must mean "year" (Arcadian for *eniautos*). This, however, is a misreading of the rhythm of the poem, which manifests itself in progressive temporal precision. Furthermore, although Odysseus may adopt fictional semblances of the truth in his conversation with Penelope in Book 19, there is no suggestion that either he or Penelope attempts to mislead the other when the discussion turns to the time of her husband's return or the manner of his vengeance. When Odysseus claims that her husband will return at the new moon Penelope shows her lucidity by deciding to hold the marriage contest at the very next new moon. Odysseus' prophecy at 19.306-307 gives as exact a moment as it is possible to give before the discovery of modern chronometry. If one proposed etymology for *lykabas* were acceptable − as from *λυκ ("light") and βαίνω, giving, in Stanford's words, "a going of light" − then we should have in the word a fine explication of the lunar reference in the previous line: *lykabas*, "the dark of the moon." For further discussion of *lykabas* see F. Focke, *Die Odyssee* (Stuttgart, 1943), pp. 320ff.; R. Merkelbach, *Untersuchungen zur Odyssee. Zetemata* 2 (München, 1951), p. 3; Page, *HO*, pp. 134-135 (n. 28); Wilamowitz, *HU*, pp. 54ff.

7. *Odyssey* 14.457. The night is not only moon-obscured but vile, such a night as never was elsewhere in Homer. Richmond Lattimore, *The Odyssey of Homer* (New York, 1965), translates v. 457: "A bad night came on, the dark of the moon."

8. Heraklitos *Alleg. hom.* chap. 75. See Felix Buffière, *Les mythes d'Homère* (Paris, 1956), pp. 226ff. A. Shewan, "Two Ancient Eclipses," *CW* 21(1928):196-198, not only accepts Theoklymenos' vision as a description of a solar eclipse, but proceeds to date it to 1178 B.C.

9. Wilamowitz, *Heimkehr,* p. 43, and *Der Glaube der Hellenen* (Berlin, 1931), vol. 2, p. 29.

10. In *Poetae Melici Graeci,* ed. D. Page (Oxford, 1962), references to swallows in Stesich. 211, Simon. 597, Carm. pop. 848, are all tokens of spring.

11. Though only two examples of the swallow's song of spring have survived, it was a type of song of wide dispersion and practice. See *Vitae Homeri et Hesiodi,* ed. U. von Wilamowitz-Moellendorff (Berlin, 1929), for parallels. See also Plut. *Thes.* 22; schol. Arist. *Equites* 720.

12. James G. Frazer, "Swallows in the House," *CR* 5(1891):1-3, a short but invaluable article for folk customs and ceremonies that elucidate the pattern of the *Odyssey*.

13. E. Meyer, "Homerische Parerga," *Hermes* 27(1892):359-380, is one scholar to see the importance of the connection between the *Odyssey* and the *Vita herodotea*. See particularly his pp. 376-377, where he argues that the *Vita* 33 indicates that Apollo's feast in the *Odyssey* falls on the *Noumenia*. On Apollo's new moon feast in the *Odyssey* see also George Thomson, "The Greek Calendar," *JHS* 63(1943):52-65, especially p. 57, n. 40, and Einar Gjerstad, "Lunar Months of Hesiod and Homer,"*Opuscula Atheniensa* I. *Acta Instit. Athen. Regni Sueciae,* series 4 (Lund, 1953), pp. 187-194.

14. Franz Dirlmeier, *Die Vogelgestalt homerische Götter* (Heidelberg, 1967), p. 28, takes Athena's swallow shape here as her very self, "das heisst in ihrer eigentlichen Gestalt." Athena is very much the orchestral conductor, virtually the personification of Season in the *Odyssey,* and the choice of the swallow to embody her epiphany is most apt. At the same time however, it is a misinterpretation of Homeric theology to insist that the Olympians are content to be defined by any of the ephemeral contours of their various epiphanies. Athena is indeed Spring at the peripety of the poem, and for that reason simply adopts a visible and significant manifestation of that truth.

15. Northrop Frye, *The Anatomy of Criticism* (Princeton, 1957), pp. 163ff., 182-183. Readers of Frye's pages on the mythos of comedy can find much of value for a structural understanding of the *Odyssey*. That the *Odyssey* conforms to the comic mode was recognized in antiquity. See Hermogenes, *Peri Heur.* 177-178, for a brief comparison of Homer with Menander, and Eustathius 1745.30.

16. Light and fire imagery play insistently around Odysseus as the poem approaches its peripety. Howard Clarke, *The Art of the Odyssey* (Prentice-Hall, 1967), pp. 73-75, notes such instances as Odysseus' adopted name *Aithon* ("Blazes") at 19.183, and the comparison of Odysseus to the bright sun in the simile at 22.384-389. We have here, however, not merely imagery or metaphor, but something so entirely physical as to be almost beyond the reach of our metaphysics. Odysseus, descending into his death with winter's decline of the sun, and emerging into life anew with the sun's spring ascent, so aligns the microwaves of his organism with the macrowaves of the sun that, when once in phase with the cosmos, he becomes the focus that gathers the sun's rays and directs them in one piercing beam on to the little island of Ithaka, to shed there its light, its warmth, and its restorative powers. Odysseus' brilliant bald pate at 18.354-355 is the focal lens for the sun's fierce intensity. Through that lens, in Odysseus' answer to Eurymachos' foolish jest, we glimpse the

first signs of the change in the season (v. 367): ὥρη ἐν εἰαρινῇ, ὅτε τ᾽ ἤματα μακρὰ πέλονται. And just prior to Eurymachos' merry observation on the focal powers of the stranger's gleaming pate, Odysseus gathers to himself the formulas that are the property of the sun (18.343-344):

αὐτὰρ ὁ πὰρ λαμπτῆρσι φαείνων αἰθομένοισιν

ἑστήκειν ἐς πάντας ὁρώμενος.

Hidden in αἰθομένοισιν is the cognomen *Aithon* behind which Odysseus will masquerade shortly in his conversation with Penelope. Hidden in λαμπτῆρσι φαείνων are the two daughters of Helios, Lampetie and Phaethousa, whose duty it is to report mortal transgressions against the cosmic light. Hidden too in φαείνων is Helios himself, who had earlier threatened to abandon mortals and gods and shine for the corpses instead (φαείνω, 12.383) if the sacrilege on his powers were not avenged, and whom Zeus had entreated to shed his light still (φαείνε, v. 385) on gods and earthbound mortals. Finally, in Odysseus' posture of silent but brilliant scrutiny of all the folk in his palace (v. 384), we glimpse a frail mortal no longer in conflict with his ancient enemy, but incarnating now Helios ὃς πάντ᾽ ἐφορᾷ καὶ πάντ᾽ ἐπακούει (11.109; 12.323; cf. the same formula in Agamemnon's prayer at *Il.* 3.277, where it occurs immediately after a strangely emphatic reference to Odysseus *polymetis* in v. 268). Such physics, since Descartes' invention of the mind, seems accessible to us only as metaphor.

17. The conjunction of sun and moon is a particularly propitious time for marriage. See Roscher's *Ausführl. Lexicon der griech. und Röm. Mythologie* (Leipzig, 1894-1897) vol. 2, pp. 3159ff., s.v. "Mondgöttin," for a discussion of the association of marriages with the new moon. See also Margarete Bieber, "Eros and Dionysos on Kerch Vases," *Hesperia,* suppl. 8(1949):31-38, on new-moon marriages. Particularly interesting is her mention of marriages consummated at the dark of the moon between the months Gamelion and Anthesterion, i.e., exactly between the last day of winter and the first day of spring, as in our *Odyssey.* When Odysseus and Penelope retire to their secret bed in the darkness at the conjunction of sun and moon, this is the point, to quote Northrop Frye (*Anatomy of Criticism,* p. 203), "at which the undisplaced apocalyptic world and the cyclical world of nature come into alignment, and which we propose to call the point of epiphany." Frye talks of that point first as a physical site, but then adds that it can be a "place of sexual fulfillment, where there is no apocalyptic vision but simply a sense of arriving at the summit of experience in nature" (p. 205). An excellent summary of the *telos* of the *Odyssey.*

18. The significance of the calendrical indicators in the *Odyssey* was clear enough to such scholars as Wilamowitz, or Gilbert Murray who, in *The Rise of the Greek Epic*, 4th ed. (Oxford, 1934), pp. 210-212, connects Odysseus' return in the nineteenth year with the cycle of Meton's *Eikosieteris*, which was a coordination of solar and lunar cycles. Solar and lunar symbolism has since fallen into deep disrepute, partly because the hunt for traces of primitive nature religion became merely pell-mell confusion. We can see the rather uncritical solar methodology at work in E. Meyer's "Der Ursprung des Odysseusmythos," *Hermes* 30(1895):241-288, or in Carl Fries, *Studien zur Odyssee: Das Zagmukfest auf Scheria. Mitteilungen der vorderasiatischen Gesellschaft* (Leipzig, 1910). Fries isolates the Phaiakian episode and argues for it as preserving a New Year's celebration. Émile Mireaux, *Les poèmes homériques* (Paris, 1948), vol. 1, pp. 232-238, also argues that the Phaiakian episode represents the ritual of agricultural fertility celebrated at the beginning of spring. Gabriel Germain, *Genèse de l'Odyssée* (Paris, 1954), pp. 306ff., though sensitive to ritual patterns in the poem, perceives the awkwardness of the indiscriminate attempt to explain every event or gesture in a poetic narrative as embodying a cryptic ritual. In addition to Germain's reservations, I would add that it does the poem an injustice to isolate one incident as a ritual merely embedded in an otherwise mundane narrative. Fries, "Homerische Beitrage," *RhM* 81(1932):25-29, discovers solar mythology among the Phaiakians, lunar mythology in Kalypso, but yet considers the later books of the poem as social and political narrative unconnected with the earlier solar and lunar revelations. Solar mythology is, to my mind, even more explicit in Books 17ff. than in the episodes of the Apologos.

Excesses, or deficiencies, of the solar school, however, are no reason to abandon belief in the rituals that are indubitably shadowed forth in literary modes. One reason for discrediting the solar school was its insistence on pinning the label of faded deity on heroes with solar affinities. The *Divine Comedy* overflows with solar, lunar, and astral symbolism, but no one argues that the helpless little mortal who travels through that poem under Dante's name is really Helios in disguise. H. F. Dunbar, *Symbolism in Mediaeval Thought* (London, 1961), chaps. 3 and 4, gives a good account of the prevalence of solar symbolism in the Middle Ages, and particularly in the tales of heroic quests. It is precisely the heroes' mortal status that accounts for the solar affinities in their tales. Sun, moon, and stars define man's place in the universe, and he learns to orient his soul as well as his corporal being by them. So too for the *Odyssey*. Odysseus is no faded deity, but quite the opposite, one of the frailest of frail mortals, as he is quick to inform the Phaiakians and his son Telemachos. J. van Leeuwen, "Homerica," *Mnemosyne*, n.s. 39(1911):15, in discussing the solar symbolism of the *Odyssey* reminds us that "celebratus fuit *heros mortalis, Troiae victor,* non *deus* procul ab hominibus degens." The *Odyssey* is the poem of the travail of a pitiable, and even cowardly, wight who discovers his heroic self by learning to integrate his personal rhythm with the rhythms of the cosmos. So well does he take his bearings from the sun that he becomes, in the end, its conductor on earth. Northrop Frye's observations (*Anatomy of Criticism,* pp. 187-188) on the connection between heroes and cyclical imagery drawn from nature are apposite here.

19. Ludwig Radermacher, "Die Erzählungen der Odyssee," *Sitzungs-berichte d. Kaiserl. Akad. d. Wissenschaften in Wien, Phil.-hist. K1.* 178(1915):32ff., considers briefly Penelope as a lunar figure, and her weaving and unraveling as the pattern of the waxing and waning moon. It is an attractive suggestion. We cannot help feeling some lunar affinity in her weaving, and in the schedule of Odysseus' journey from Ogygia to Ithaka, so precisely fitted between one new moon and the next. Whatever lunar associations Penelope enjoys, however, they seem subliminal in contrast to her husband's extraverted solar light. But then the moon radiates a subtler light.

Bibliography

Amory, Anne (Parry). "The Reunion of Odysseus and Penelope." In *Essays on the Odyssey,* edited by C. H. Taylor, Jr., pp. 100-121. Bloomington, 1963.

Auerbach, Erich. *Mimesis.* Translated by W. Trask. Princeton, 1953.

Austin, Norman. "Name Magic in the *Odyssey." Calif. Stud. Classical Antiquity* 5(1972):1-19.

————. "Telemachos Polymechanos." *Calif. Stud. Classical Antiquity* 2(1969):45-63.

Aymard, André. "Hierarchie du travail et autarcie individuelle dans la Grèce archaique." *Rev. d'histoire et da la philosophie,* fasc. 33. 1943.

————. "L'Idée de travail dans la Grèce archaique." *Journal de psychologie* 41(1948):29-45.

Belmont, David E., "Telemachos and Nausikaa: A Study of Youth." *CJ* 63(1967):1-9.

Benardete, Seth. "Achilles and the *Iliad." Hermes* 91(1963):1-16.

Bethe, E. "Odysee-Probleme." *Hermes* 63(1928):81-92.

Bieber, Margarete. "Eros and Dionysos on Kerch Vases," *Hesperia,* suppl. 8(1949):31-38.

Böhme, Joachim. *Die Seele und das Ich im homerischen Epos.* Leipzig and Berlin, 1929.

Bowra, C. M. *Heroic Poetry.* London, 1952.

————. "The Comparative Study of Homer." *AJA* 54(1950):184-192.

————. *Tradition and Design in the Iliad.* Oxford, 1930.

Braunlich, A. F. " 'To the Right' in Homer and Attic Greek." *AJP* 57(1936):245-260.

Brinkman, Otto. "Telemach in Sparta." *Gymnasium* 59(1952):97-115.

Buchholz, E. *Die homerischen Realien.* 2 vols. Leipzig, 1871.

Büchner, W. "Die Niptra in der Odyssee." *RhM* 80(1931):129-136.

————. "Die Penelopeszenen in der Odyssee." *Hermes* 75(1940):129-167.

Buck, C. R. *Dictionary of Selected Synonyms in the Principal Indo-European Languages.* Chicago, 1949.

Buffière, Felix. *Les mythes d'Homère.* Paris, 1956.

Burnet, John. *Early Greek Philosophy.* 4th ed. London, 1930.
Calhoun, G. M. "Télémaque et le plan de l'Odyssée." *RÉG* 47(1934):153-163.
Clarke, Howard C. *The Art of the Odyssey.* Prentice-Hall, 1967.
————. "Telemachus and the Telemacheia." *AJP* 84(1963):129-145.
Clerke, Agnes M. *Familiar Studies in Homer.* London, 1892.
Coffey, Michael. "The Homeric Simile." *AJP* 78(1957):113-132.
Combellack, F. M. "Milman Parry and Homeric Artistry." *Comparative Literature* 11(1959):197.
————. "Some Formulary Illogicalities in Homer." *TAPA* 96(1965):41-56.
Cornford, F. M. *From Religion to Philosophy.* London, 1912.
Cuillandre, Joseph. *La droite et la gauche dans les poèmes homériques.* Paris, 1944.
Daremberg, Charles. *La médecine dans Homère.* Paris, 1865.
Delebecque, Edouard. *Télémaque et la structure de l'Odyssée.* Aix-en-Provence, 1958.
Diller, H. "Der vorphilosophische Gebrauch von κόσμος und κόσμεῖν." In *Festschr. B. Snell,* München, 1956. pp. 47-60.
Dirlmeier, Franz. *Die Vogelgestalt homerische Götter.* Heidelberg, 1967.
Dow, Sterling. Rev. of *History and the Homeric Iliad,* by Denys Page. *AJP* 83(1962):90-97.
Dunbar, Henry. *A Complete Concordance to the Odyssey of Homer.* Rev. ed. Hildesheim, 1962.
Dunbar, H. F. *Symbolism in Medieval Thought.* London, 1961.
Durkheim, Emile, and Marcel Mauss. *Primitive Classification.* Translated by R. Needham. Chicago, 1963.
Ebeling, H. *Lexicon Homericum.* 2 vols. Leipzig, 1885.
Edwards, Mark W. "Some Features of Homeric Craftsmanship." *TAPA* 97(1966):115-179.
————. "Some Stylistic Notes on *Iliad* XVIII." *AJP* 89(1968):257-283.
De Farcy, H. "Homère et la campagne." *Les études classiques* 4(1935):626-635.
Focke, F. *Die Odyssee.* Stuttgart, 1943.
Fraisse, Paul. *The Psychology of Time.* Translated by J. Leith. New York, 1963.
Fränkel, Hermann. *Dichtung und Philosophie des frühen Griechentums.* 2nd ed. München, 1962.
————. "Griechische Wörter." *Glotta* 14(1925):1-13.
————. *Die homerischen Gleichnisse.* Göttingen, 1921.
————. "Die Zeitauffassung in der frühgriechischen Literatur." In *Wege und Formen frühgriechischen Denkens.* 2nd ed., pp. 1-22. München, 1960.

Frazer, James G. *The Golden Bough.* New York, 1935.

————. "Swallows in the House." *CR* 5(1891):1-3.

Fries, Carl. "Homerische Beiträge." *RhM* 81(1932):25-29.

————. *Studien zur Odyssee: Das Zagmukfest auf Scheria. Mitteilungen der vorderasiatischen Gesellschaft,* Heft 2/4. Leipzig, 1910.

Fritz, Kurt von. "Nόος and Noεῖν in the Homeric Poems." *CP* 38(1943):79-93.

Frye, Northrop. *The Anatomy of Criticism.* Princeton, 1957.

Fuld, E. "Quelques remarques sur les sciences naturelles et médicales dans Homère." *Rev. études homériques* 2(1932):10-17.

Furley, D. J. "The Early History of the Concept of Soul." *Bull. Univ. London Instit. Classical Studies* 3(1956):1-18.

Gehring, Augustus. *Index Homericus.* Leipzig, 1891.

Germain, Gabriel. *La Genèse de l'Odyssée.* Paris, 1954.

Gjerstad, Einar. "Lunar Months of Hesiod and Homer." *Opusc. Atheniensa* I. *Acta Instit. Athen. Regni Sueciae.* Series 4, pp. 187-194. Lund, 1953.

Gray, D. H. F. "Homeric Epithets for Things." *CQ* 41(1947):109-121.

Groningen, B. A. van. "Éléments inorganiques dans la composition de l'Iliade et de l'Odyssée." *Rev. études homériques* 5(1935):3-24.

Hainsworth, J. B. *Flexibility of the Homeric Formula.* Oxford, 1968.

————. "Structure and Content in Epic Formulae" *CQ* 58(1964):155-164.

Harrison, E. L. "Notes on Homeric Psychology." *Phoenix* 14(1960):63-80.

Harsh, Philip W. "Penelope and Odysseus in *Odyssey* XIX." *AJP* 71(1950):1-21.

Helbig, W. *Das homerische Epos aus den Denkmälern erläutert.* Leipzig, 1887.

Hennig, R. "Kulturgeschichte, Naturkunde und Homerlektüre." *Rev. études homériques* 2(1932):18-27.

Hertz, Robert. "La prééminence de la main droite: Étude sur la polarité religieuse." *Rev. philosophique* 68(1909):553-580. Also translated in R. and C. Needham, *Death and the Right Hand.* Glencoe, Ill., 1960.

Heubeck, Alfred. *Der Odyssee-Dichter und die Ilias.* Erlangen, 1954.

Hoekstra, A. *Homeric Modifications of Formulaic Prototypes.* Amsterdam, 1965.

Hölscher, Uvo. "Das Schweigen der Arete." *Hermes* 88(1960):257-265.

————. *Untersuchungen zur Form der Odyssee. Hermes Einzelschriften* no. 6. Berlin, 1939.

Jachmann, Günther. *Der homerische Schiffskatalog und die Ilias.* Köln & Opladen, 1958.

Jacoby, Felix. "Die geistige Physiognomie der Odyssee." *Antike* 9(1933):159-194.

Jevons, F. B. "Indo-European Modes of Orientation." *CR* 10(1896):22-23.

Jousse, Marcel. *Le style oral rythmique et mnémotechnique chez les verbo-moteurs. Archives de philosophie*, vol. III, cah. IV. Paris, 1925.

Justesen, P. Th. *Les principes psychologiques d'Homère.* Copenhagen, 1928.

Kirk, G. S. "Homer and Modern Oral Poetry." *CQ*, n.s. 10(1960):270-281.

————. *Myth: Its Meaning and Functions in Ancient and Other Cultures.* Cambridge, Berkeley, Los Angeles, 1970.

————. "Objective Dating Criteria in Homer." *MH* 17(1960):189-205.

————. *The Songs of Homer.* Cambridge, 1962.

Klingner, Friedrich. *Über die vier ersten Bücher der Odyssee. Akad. d. Wissensch. z. Leipzig, Phil.-hist. Kl.* 96(1944):1-55.

Kretzschmar, Oscar. *Beiträge zur Charakteristik des homerischen Odysseus.* Leipzig, 1903.

Larock, Victor. "Les premières conceptions psychologiques des Grecs." *Rev. Belge de philologie et d'histoire* 9(1930):377-406.

Larson, L. M., trans. *Speculum Regale (The King's Mirror).* New York and London, 1917.

Lattimore, Richmond. "Nausikaa's Suitors." In *Class. Stud. Presented to B. E. Perry,* pp. 88-102. Urbana, Chicago, London, 1969.

Lee, D. J. N. *The Similes of the Iliad Compared.* Sydney, 1964.

Van Leeuwen, J. "Homerica." *Mnemosyne*, n.s. 39(1911):13-50

Lesky, Albin. *Göttliche und menschliche Motivation im homerischen Epos. Sitz. Akad. Heidelberg., Phil.-hist. Kl.* Heidelberg, 1961.

Leumann, Manu. *Homerische Wörter.* Basel, 1950.

Lévi-Strauss, Claude. *Structural Anthropology.* Translated by C. Jacobson and B. G. Schoepf. New York, 1963.

————. *La Pensée Sauvage.* Translated as *The Savage Mind.* Chicago, 1966.

Lloyd, G. E. R. *Polarity and Analogy: Two Types of Argumentation in Early Greek Thought.* Cambridge, 1966.

Lord, Albert B. "Composition by Theme in Homer and Southslavic Epos." *TAPA* 82(1951):71-80.

————. "Homer as Oral Poet." *HSCP* 72(1967):1-46.

————. *The Singer of Tales.* Cambridge, Mass., 1960.

Macurdy, Grace H. "Rainbow, Sky, and Stars in the *Iliad* and the *Odyssey:* A Chorizontic Argument." *CQ* 8(1914):212-215.

Marg, Walter. *Der Charakter in der Sprache der frühgriechischen Dichtung.* 2nd ed. Darmstadt, 1967.

Mattes, Wilhelm. *Odysseus bei den Phäaken.* Wurzburg, 1958.

Merkelbach, Reinhold. *Untersuchungen zur Odyssee. Zetemata* 2. München, 1951.

Meyer, E. "Homerische Parerga." *Hermes* 27(1892):363-380.

————. "Der Ursprung des Odysseusmythos." *Hermes* 30(1895):241-288.

Millar, C. M. H., and J. W. S. Carmichael. "The Growth of Telemachus." *Greece and Rome*, n.s. 1(1954):58-64.

Minton, W. W. "The Fallacy of the Structural Formula." *TAPA* 96(1965):241-253.

Mireaux, Émile. *Les poèmes homériques.* Paris, 1948.

Mugler, Charles. *Les origines de la science grecque chez Homère.* Paris, 1963.

Murray, Gilbert. *The Rise of the Greek Epic.* 4th ed. Oxford, 1934.

Nagler, Michael, "Towards a Generative View of the Oral Formula." *TAPA* 98(1967):269-311.

Nilsson, Martin. *Primitive Time Reckoning.* Lund, 1920.

Notopoulos, J. A. "Homer, Hesiod and the Achaean Heritage of Oral Poetry." *Hesperia* 29(1960):177-197.

————. "The Homeric Hymns as Oral Poetry: A Study of the Post-Homeric Oral Tradition." *AJP* 83(1962):337-368.

————. "Parataxis in Homer." *TAPA* 80(1949):1-23.

O'Neill, Eugene G., Jr. "The Localization of Metrical Word-types in the Greek Hexameter: Homer, Hesiod, and the Alexandrians." *YClS* 8(1942):103-178.

Onians, R. B. *The Origins of European Thought.* Cambridge, 1951.

Page, Denys. *History and the Homeric Iliad.* Berkeley & Los Angeles, 1959.

————. *The Homeric Odyssey.* Oxford, 1955.

Parry, Adam. "Have We Homer's *Iliad?*" *YClS* 20(1966):177-216.

————. "The Language of Achilles." *TAPA* 87(1956):1-7.

Parry, Adam, ed. *The Making of Homeric Verse: The Collected Papers of Milman Parry.* Oxford, 1971.

Parry, Anne Amory. *Blameless Aegisthus: A Study of AMYMΩN and other Epithets in Homer.* Amsterdam, 1973.

Parry, Milman. *The Making of Homeric Verse: The Collected Papers of Milman Parry.* Edited by Adam Parry. Oxford, 1971.

Pope, M. W. M. "The Parry-Lord Theory of Homeric Composition." *Acta Classica* 6(1963):1-21.

Pound, Ezra. *The Spirit of Romance.* London and New York, 1910.

Puhvel, Jaan. "Greek ΑΝΑΞ," *Zeitschr. f. vergleich. Sprachforschung,* n.s. 73(1956):202-222.

Radermacher, Ludwig. "Die Erzählungen der Odyssee." *Sitzungsberichte d. Kaiserl. Akad. d. Wissensch. in Wien, Phil.-hist. Kl.* 178(1915):3-59.

Riezler, Kurt. "Das homerische Gleichnis und der Anfang der Philosophie." *Antike* 12(1936):253-271.

Rose, Gilbert P. "The Quest of Telemachus." *TAPA* 98(1967):391-398.

Rosenmeyer, Thomas G. "The Formula in Early Greek Poetry." *Arion* 4(1965):295-311.

Rothenberg, Jerome, ed. *Shaking the Pumpkin: Traditional Poetry of the Indian North Americans.* New York, 1972.

Ruijgh, C. J. *L'Élément Achéen dans la langue épique.* Assen, 1957.

Rüter, Klaus. *Odysseeinterpretationen. Hypomnemata,* Heft 19. Göttingen, 1969.

Russo, J. A. "A Closer Look at Homeric Formulas." *TAPA* 94(1963):235-247.

————. "The Structural Formula in Homeric Verse." *YClS* 20(1966):219-240.

Schadewaldt, W. "Kleiderdinge: Zur Analyse der Odyssee." *Hermes* 87(1959):13-26.

————. *Von Homer's Welt und Werk.* Stuttgart, 1944.

Schwabl, Hans. "Zur Selbständigkeit des Menschen bei Homer." *Wiener Studien* 67(1954):46-64.

Scott, John A. "Helen's Recognition of Telemachus in the *Odyssey.*" *CJ* 25(1929-30):383-385.

————. "The Journey Made by Telemachus and Its Influence on the Action of the *Odyssey.*" *CJ* 13(1917-18):420-428.

Seel, Otto. "Variante und Konvergenz in der Odyssee." In *Studi in Onore di U. E. Paoli,* pp. 643-657. Firenze, 1956.

Segal, Charles P. "Andromache's *Anagnorisis:* Formulaic Artistry in *Iliad* 22.437-476." *HSCP* 75(1971):33-57.

————. "The Phaeacians and the Symbolism of Odysseus' Return." *Arion* 1 no. 4 (1962):17-64.

Shewan, A. "Two Ancient Eclipses." *CW* 21(1928):196-200.

Shipp, G. P. *Studies in the Language of Homer.* Cambridge, 1953.

Smith, Wesley D. "Physiology in Homer." *TAPA* 97(1966):547-556.

Snell, Bruno. *Die Entdeckung des Geistes.* Translated as *Discovery of the Mind* by T. G. Rosenmeyer. Oxford, 1953.

Stockem, Beate. *Die Gestalt der Penelope in der Odyssee.* Diss. Köln, 1955.

Taylor, Charles H., Jr. "The Obstacles to Odysseus' Return: Identity and Consciousness in the *Odyssey.*" *Yale Review* 50(1961):569-580.

Thomson, George. "The Greek Calendar." *JHS* 63(1943):53-65.

Vallillee, Gerald. "The Nausikaa Episode." *Phoenix* 9(1955):175-179.

Vernant, Jean-Pierre. "Travail et nature dans la Grèce ancienne." *Journal de psychologie* 52(1955):18-33.

Vester, Helmut. "Das 19 Buch der Odyssee." *Gymnasium* 75(1968):417-434.

Vivante, Paolo. *The Homeric Imagination.* Bloomington, 1970.

Whallon, William. *Formula, Character and Context.* Washington, D.C., 1969.

Whitman, Cedric H. *Homer and the Heroic Tradition*. Cambridge, Mass., 1958.

Wilamowitz-Moellendorff, Ulrich von. *Der Glaube der Hellenen*. Berlin, 1931.

————. *Die Heimkehr des Odysseus*. Berlin, 1927.

————. *Homerische Untersuchungen*. Berlin, 1884.

Woodhouse, W. J. *The Composition of the Homeric Odyssey*. Oxford, 1930.

Young, Douglas. "Never Blotted a Line?" *Arion* 6(1967):279-324.

Index

294   Index

kairos, 87-88
Kalypso, 32, 44, 52, 94, 104, 138-140,
    142-143, 157, 169, 172-173,
    192-193, 239-240; character and
    landscape compared, 149-152, 154
Kastor, 68
Key to Odysseus' store-room, 73-74
Kikonians, 101
Kimmerians, 93-94
King's Mirror, 135-136, 243
Kirk, G. S., 174-175
Kirke, 27, 32, 40, 52, 94, 97, 105, 136,
    138-140, 143, 157, 173, 183, 191,
    239; character and landscape com-
    pared, 98, 152-153
Ktesippos, 47, 51, 246
Kyklopes, 143, 162; *see also* Poly-
    phemos

Laertes, 31, 42, 45, 48, 51, 102-105,
    164, 253
Laistrygonians, 143
Lakedaimon, 94
Lamont, Julie, 182
Lampetie, 134
Language, Homeric, 6, 65-66, 180, 193,
    198, 200; anatomical vocabulary,
    106-114; *see also* Spatial orientation;
    Time
Leiokritos, 31, 47
Lemnos, 69
Lévi-Strauss, Claude, 117, 173-174,
    177-178
Lloyd, G. E. R., 90
Lord, A. B., 12, 17, 19, 21-24, 69
Lotos-eaters, 138
Lucian, 68
lykabas, 216, 244-246
Lykaon, 69, 86

Marvell, Andrew, 238
Medon, 60, 75
Mekistiades, 111
Melanthios, 47, 51, 165
Melantho, 165
Meleager, 125
Melville, Herman, 142
Menelaos, 42, 44, 48, 52, 60, 72, 75-76,
    78, 135, 169, 183-184, 186-187,
    189-190
menos, 106, 111-112, 114
Mentes, 249
Mentor, 45, 249
Meriones, 75

Milton, John, 176
Mind, 7, 82-83, 179, 193, 200, 209, 211,
    215, 218, 222, 226, 233, 237, 238;
    of Odysseus, 195, 198-199, 203, 208;
    of Penelope, 207, 210, 213, 216;
    polarity in, 233-234, 236
moly, 193, 200
Moon, 216, 232, 244, 246, 248,
    250-251, 262 n. 48
Mykenai, 94
Muglar, C., 175

Natural phenomena in the *Odyssey,*
    133-139
Nausikaa, 162, 181, 193-194, 198,
    200-202, 215, 217
nepenthes, 127-128, 188
Nestor, 42-43, 52, 60-61, 65, 72, 74-75,
    121, 125, 183, 186, 188, 191
Night, epithets for, 71-73
Nightingale, 228-229, 247
Niobe, 125
noos, 82-83, 85, 106, 108-109, 113-114,
    193, 216, 252
nostoi, 183

Ocean, 68, 72, 86, 90, 94
Odysseus, 7-8, 15-16, 23, 38-39, 60, 65,
    68-69, 71-72, 76-77, 79, 93-94, 97,
    99, 101-105, 109-111, 122-123,
    127-128, 142, 151-153, 168-171,
    185, 204-205, 208, 239-242,
    244-247, 249-253; among Phaiakians,
    154, 159, 161-162, 181, 189, 192,
    194, 196, 197, 198; character, 98;
    conversation with Penelope, 211-238;
    epithet formulas for, 26-36, 40-53;
    his Apologos, 7, 131-141; his name,
    12-13, 227, 240; his scar, 214, 221,
    223; solicits omen, 119-121
Omens, 96, 118-121, 129, 191, 206,
    208, 215, 250; *see also* Signs
O'Neill, Eugene Jr., 25
Oral Poetry, 11, 21; transmission of,
    22-23; *see also* Epithets; Formulas
Orestes, 138
Oukalegon, 75
Ouranos, 91

Page, Denys, 4, 11-13, 18, 70
Paradigmatic structures, 7, 124-126,
    228-230
Parataxis, 6, 8, 84
Paris, 124-125, 189